DAVE HASLAM has written for *Time*, the *London Review of Books*, the *Observer* and *Les Inrockuptibles*. His first book, *Manchester, England*, was the *Sunday Times* Pop Music Book of the Year and was shortlisted for the Ericsson Prize. His second, *Adventures on the Wheels of Steel*, documented the history of superstar DJs, drawing on travels round Britain meeting clubbers, DJs and promoters. He was a resident DJ at the Hacienda in Manchester in the late 1980s, and at clubs like Cream in Liverpool. His DJ-ing career has more recently taken him to gigs round the world, including Ibiza, Chicago, Paris, Berlin, Detroit and Reykjavik. The first record he ever bought was 'Telegram Sam' by T-Rex, in 1972, from Woolworths.

Visit www.AuthorTracker.co.uk for exclusive information on your favourite HarperCollins authors.

By the same author

Manchester, England:
The Story of the Pop Cult City

Adventures on the Wheels of Steel:
The Rise of the Superstar DJs

DAVE HASLAM

Young Hearts Run Free

The Real Story of the 1970s

HARPER PERENNIAL
London, New York, Toronto and Sydney

Harper Perennial
An imprint of HarperCollins*Publishers*
77–85 Fulham Palace Road
Hammersmith, London W6 8JB

www.harperperennial.co.uk

This edition published by Harper Perennial 2007
1

First published in Great Britain by Fourth Estate 2005 under the title *Not Abba*

A catalogue record for this book is available from the British Library

ISBN-13 978-0-00-714640-6
ISBN-10 0-00-714640-X

Set in Meridien by Rowland Phototypesetting Ltd, Bury St Edmunds, Suffolk

Printed and bound in Great Britain by Clays Ltd, St Ives plc

To Catherine (born 1972)

CONTENTS

INTRO

'Boogie Wonderland' (1979)

The Seventies are frequent fodder for nostalgia TV, and the image of the decade is dominated by a selection of the most anodyne, obvious symbols: the Bee Gees, flares, platform shoes and Abba. In recent years the portrayal of the decade as a parade of disastrous fashion set in a mindless boogie wonderland has been relentless. We've allowed misrepresentation to become fact. We've allowed the Abbafication of the Seventies to create a powerful but partial version of the history of the decade, a version which omits the tribalism and violence on the streets, IRA bombs, PLO hi-jackings, overt racism, football hooliganism, Linda Lovelace, *Mean Streets* and *Apocalypse Now*; history without the rawness and unpredictability and a soundtrack that omits heavy rock, roots reggae, Northern Soul, Ziggy Stardust, Patti Smith and Bob Marley. The chapters that follow will document and explain all this, fighting back against the Abbafication of history, and searching for more, other, ways to represent the Seventies.

This isn't a work of nostalgia for many reasons, most obviously because nostalgia waves a golden wand over the past, whereas we'll be witnessing cold, complicated reality. One of the key characteristics of the Seventies generation is the knowledge that we missed out on the Sixties. Growing up in the Seventies you were aware of this: that the optimistic, idealistic Sixties generation – who'd had a taste of the Cavern and Woodstock – had had it all.

Nostalgia is a weapon wielded by old people to deny young people their dreams. It closes doors. The Seventies generation has forever been the victim of the nostalgia of others. We arrived too late, the generation before us told us then, and have been telling us ever since. So while it's clear that the Seventies were violent and dark, and a lunatic decade for fashion, generally the odds were stacked against us from the start; they were stacked as high as a pair of platform shoes. Optimism was not in our vocabulary.

Over the last few decades, the music and the politics of the Sixties have been documented heavily, thoroughly, in a way the Seventies have yet to merit. We have in our minds some sense of what it's like to have been a child of the Sixties, and we're also aware of the difference between us and Thatcher's children, those whose formative years were the 1980s.

Away from the shallow waters of pop TV, the Seventies generation is still trying to work out what was going on, aware that we grew up between two more clearly defined, watershed decades. In *The Rotters' Club*, a novel by Jonathan Coe, he creates a persuasive version of the decade while admitting 'the ungodly strangeness of it, the weird things that were happening all the time'.

In America, one of the most gifted of the generation caught between the Woodstock festival and the inauguration of Ronald Reagan is Spike Lee. His film *Summer of Sam*, about a serial killer who stalked New York in 1977, has a scene that stands as a neat illustration of the disjunction between the boogie wonderland and the ungodly strangeness of the era. We witness the killing of two victims; as bullets puncture the bodies in the front seat of the car, the dashboard is splattered with blood. The scene is played out to the sound of 'Fernando' by Abba. The carefree harmonies of the song are a stark contrast to the discord and destruction of the murders.

I could think of nowhere better to begin my mission than Flares, a chain of bars with a 1970s theme in various locations around Britain. Branches can be found in Hull, Bradford, Glasgow and, my chosen destination, Wolverhampton. The publicity for one of the branches explains their music policy – 'Every night is disco night' – and goes on to say that the bars are popular with a wide section of the public looking for light-hearted fun. Apparently, they've just opened a Flares in Cleethorpes. The marketing material for the club is adamant: 'Flares is as close as you'll get to the original 70s experience.'

Back in the 1970s there were no themed bars in town centres. There were pubs, lots of pubs, all with traditional names like the Royal Oak, the Red Lion, and the Prince of Wales; Firkins were few and far between. Local bands would play in rooms above pubs, while bigger bands played at the local theatre, cinema or art college. Most high streets had a discotheque. You'd see people drunk or off their heads, but there were no alcopops; wine was pink, champagne was foreign. Even in the mid-1970s, yoghurt and pizza were exotic delicacies. Supermarkets were yet to deliver knockout blows to independent high street shops, but some global names were beginning to dominate: Coca-Cola and Pepsi were fighting a brand war. There was a sense that we were on the threshold of some new technological era: Germany's greatest group of the 1970s, Kraftwerk, appeared on *Tomorrow's World* to explain the digital revolution, and Texas pocket calculators began to invade classrooms, but no-one had seen a laptop or a mobile phone.

In 1975 none of Atomic Kitten had yet been born. There were only three TV channels available in most households, and after an evening showing *Dixon of Dock Green* and *The Mike Yarwood Show*, BBC1 shut down at ten past midnight on a Saturday night, marking the end of the day's broadcasting with a rendition of the National Anthem. Since then we've had the advent of multiple channels, a huge jump in house prices, and an alarming increase in traffic on British roads. We've come a long way, but not as far as we were told we would. Millions more of us regularly travel abroad, but we're no nearer those holidays on Mars we were promised by the scientists at NASA during Apollo rocket journeys thirty years ago.

In music, much, but not all, has changed. Many of the recent hitmakers seem as irksome as groups like The Rubettes did nearly thirty years ago, and the *Top of the Pops* stage still seems to be full of novelty acts, over-hyped one-hit wonders, and bands on bandwagons. On the edge, though – now as much as then – there's music that's raw, surprising and uncontrolled.

History can only be a partial truth, but there are always choices to be made. It's my contention that allowing Abba, flares and the Bee Gees to dominate our view of the Seventies is like telling the story of our current era by sidelining Enron, ecstasy, Al Qaeda and inner city gun crime, and serving up Westlife, thongs and *Hollyoaks* instead. It's also my contention that these things matter. The last time I watched more Seventies clutter being scooped up and recycled on TV – space hoppers, afro wigs, Suzi Quatro, Rod Stewart doing 'Da Ya Think I'm Sexy' – I wondered whether I'd been afflicted with some kind of false memory syndrome. Was I the only person whose collection of Seventies records didn't include anything by the Bee Gees?

Abba are given huge prominence in received versions of the Seventies story, yet they clearly fail to represent the violence or strangeness of the decade even half adequately. It's also worth noting that, of course, commercially Abba were successful, but none of their singles are in the top hundred best-selling singles of all time, and they sold many hundreds of thousands fewer LPs than, say, Bob Marley. As fashion icons, all four of the band combined had less influence on how people dressed in that decade or since than the Afro-and-proud Angela Davis, the punk designer Vivienne Westwood, or even the godfather of 2-tone Jerry Dammers. As for influence on music, Abba can probably only lay claim to have influenced one group: Brotherhood of Man (whereas recent music papers are full of bands desperate to declare their love for The Stooges, Joy Division and Blondie). As for their ability to shed light on the worlds of politics and history, Abba's achievements are restricted to their in-depth coverage of what happened at Waterloo (when, you remember, Napoleon did surrender).

One reason why Abbafication is rife is the way stories are told, or where stories are told; our present as well as our past. Life and history are mediated through television. There's a practical but powerful reason why the likes of Abba have a high profile in history, and it's to do with the state of the archive that TV researchers draw upon. Then, as now, the mainstream is obvious and the obvious is mainstream, but life on the margins is rarely acknowledged, let alone well documented. Thus TV researchers are reduced to rooting about in old episodes of *Top of the Pops*, where no appearances by Patti Smith, Led Zeppelin or Cabaret Voltaire are to be found. The reason Curtis Mayfield seldom gets mentioned? Mud stole the limelight.

Of course, the confusion of real life and the mass of details require editing, but the particular blandness of the regular view of the history of the Seventies is perhaps also a result of the way the media likes to keep things as simple as possible, avoiding problems, or questions without answers, or conflicts without resolutions. The bland identity created for the Seventies is perhaps also part of a general tendency to see history as nostalgia, as a comfort blanket, empty of bad news.

The Abbafication process has distorted our view of history; it's not just about the music, it's about how our lives are valued and represented. Abbafication has been so successful that some of us who grew up in the 1970s are likely to have begun to doubt the validity of our own memories. Like some poor soul suffering Alzheimer's, it's as though our society is in danger of losing touch with our past.

I grew up in Birmingham in the West Midlands, my teenage years falling almost exactly in the Seventies, an era, and an area, traumatised by IRA bombs in 1974, at the heart of far-right racism, and disrupted by strikes and stoppages at local car factories like British Leyland. My last memory of visiting Wolverhampton is of getting very lost on my way to see a Rock Against Racism gig headlined by The Au Pairs. All these years later, Flares in Wolverhampton is easier to find.

The venue, overlooking a small traffic island, doesn't open until 8 o'clock in the evening, and, dodging a 529 bus pulling away sharply from the bus station, I make it down there about 10pm on a quiet, warm, spring evening. Every night in this theme bar has its own theme. Tonight (a Tuesday), it's 'Chic'. Thursdays sound interesting: 'Fantom Funk' they're called. Studying the flyers more closely, it appears the only difference between the venue's various nights is the price of the drinks. Every night the same music is played, but only on 'Chic' nights can you get two bottles of WKD for the price of one (on 'Fantom Funk' nights, bottles of Becks cost just £1).

However, neither the promise of retro music nor the cheap drinks appear to have lured the good folk of Wolverhampton from their homes this evening; by 11 o'clock there are still less than twenty people in the place. On a full night, I suppose a hundred and twenty would be a good crowd. There are just two (smallish) rooms, both with walls painted with giant swirls of red, yellow and blue (the fire door is bright purple). Random words in a glib *Austin Powers* font are projected onto the walls ('Boogie', 'Fab' and 'Glam'), as well as peace signs and silhouettes of girls in platform shoes. The venue has a couple of gaming machines and a host of disco lights. With a bit of imagination (but not much), I would guess that any pub could do a makeover like this for less than £200.

Two school-age girls are dancing (they seem to know the DJ; he's perched in a box high in one corner and appears to be wearing some kind of purple wig). The two oldest people are a couple in their fifties, clearly the worse for wear. As the DJ spins 'Dancing Queen' and 'Rivers of Babylon', the woman dances like someone's set fire to one of Pan's People; it's all sudden skips and hops and urgent hand gestures.

Watching the dancers are five businessmen who aren't happy and will blame each other in the morning, and a group of teenagers. As the older dancer does her thing to 'Hot Stuff', the younger kids are laughing at her, but then that's what young kids do. She could be the best, most proficient and athletic Northern Soul dancer on the planet, and they'd still take the piss. She's oblivious, lost in music.

I make my way up to the DJ's perch to ask if he takes requests and he says he does, but each time I ask him for something by Bad Company, or X-Ray Spex, or Hawkwind, he sorrowfully shakes his wig. Then he puts me in my place. 'I play party records. People are here to have a good time.'

I know I'm being a bit daft visiting a theme bar in search of enlightenment, instead of just for a good time, and I'm trying to enjoy this, and the truth is that the DJ is playing some of my favourite records – at one point up pops 'Best of My Love' by The Emotions – and the first half an hour was fun, but it's just relentless, thrown together disco hits and boogie-oogie-oogie and it soon just feels very, very depressing.

A few teenage lads have arrived and they're singing along to 'Mighty Real'. No-one's wearing flares or an afro wig, so I'm glad I didn't get dressed up. The fifty-something woman is loving it, though; after one of her bunny hops she nearly lands on top of a fruit machine.

I make my excuses and leave. The truth is, Flares is neither 'Fab' nor 'Glam'. It's so unconvincing it doesn't even work as nostalgia. Instead of demonstrating the supposed joys of the decade, Flares sells the Seventies short; after one night here, far from feeling the joys of the boogie wonderland, you'd be better off escaping nostalgia for good and jumping on that number 529 bus to Walsall.

I'm tempted to offer the manager some suggestions to make the Seventies experience offered by his bar just a little more authentic: David Bowie and Led Zeppelin on the playlist; Babycham and Double Diamond at the bar; projections on the walls of Patty Hearst standing in front of the Symbionese Liberation Army flag, or a big colour slide of Bob Marley puffing on a massive spliff, or shop steward Derek 'Red Robbo' Robinson calling for a show of hands at a strikers' meeting at British Leyland. And the evening's entertainment could be topped off with a fight involving football fans in extraordinary trousers (wide, with twenty-six buttons), a strike by the bar staff, a bomb threat or a power cut.

Over the next ten chapters I can't promise an encyclopaedic experience, but I can promise something closer to the reality, something less second hand. I'll draw together music, memories, undercurrents, politics and films from the decade. I'll discuss it all with several eye witnesses, an array of people who grew up in different parts of England in the 1970s: people like Alan Jones, who escaped to London from Portsmouth dressed like Mick Ronson, and took a boat ride with the Sex Pistols; Alex Patton, the biggest Doors fan in Stockton-on-Tees; and Jayne Casey, who shaved her head and got chased through the streets of Liverpool. The focus will mostly be in England because I want to write about life close to home, but there's plenty of widely shared culture on offer, and be assured there won't be any celebrities you've never heard of talking about space hoppers and Showaddywaddy. We won't privilege the memories of the rich and famous; we'll be seeing the story from the perspective of people who lived in cities like Birmingham, Manchester, Liverpool and Sheffield; people close to the grain of ordinary life, wearing hand-me-downs, taping posters to their walls, queuing for gigs or sitting in the pub.

It's intriguing and instructive to go back, join the dots and try to figure out what it was that created and defined the 1970s, but the most pressing need is to rewrite the rewriting of history. Our history is our past is our identity, our character; as people, as a nation. And it's also our present; how we got here.

CHAPTER ONE

'Lola' (1970)

On 1 January 1970 ten council refuse collectors in Abingdon went on strike after being asked to transport dead dogs from a vet's surgery to a nearby rubbish tip, and estate agents Frank Dawson were selling a three-bedroomed semi-detached house in the Manchester suburb of Chorlton for £2,750 (the particulars made much of the newly-installed pink bathroom suite). The New Year's Day newspapers were predicting a bleak few years for British manufacturers, especially car makers; *Magpie* (ITV) and *Blue Peter* (BBC1) went head-to-head on children's TV; the six members of the European Economic Community continued negotiations prior to agreeing the terms of Britain's entry into the Common Market; and George Best was banned from the Manchester United team for twenty-eight days after knocking a football out of a referee's hand.

A hero from the Sixties, George Best would have some great days ahead in the early Seventies, but many wretched ones too, as his career began a messy decline. For the next few years, children would divide into *Magpie* fans and *Blue Peter* followers, Britain's status in Europe would continue to be debated, and, as the economy faltered, the world of work in Britain would be beset with trouble and stoppages.

The situation in Vietnam had been preoccupying America

for years, even before the first troops were officially sent there
in 1965, but no end to the death and destruction was in sight.
America had moved troops into the country fearing increasing
Communist influence in the area, and throughout they'd been
able to count on the support of Britain's Labour Government.
Casualty numbers were rising inexorably, but the media could
still find space for some cheerful news: on New Year's Day
1970, Miss World, Eva Reuber Staier, was pictured at Heathrow Airport on her way home from Vietnam after visiting US
troops (she was wearing a military policeman's helmet she'd
been given as a souvenir).

Whether it's the war in Vietnam, the decline of British
manufacturing or the career of George Best, stories criss-cross
decades. To understand the 1970s – and to give us a better
sense of how to sift the million details, the random memories
– we'll have to go further back than 1 January 1970; back to
the Second World War perhaps, or to the mid-1950s and the
beginnings of rock & roll. We'll go back to the Sixties to track
the beginning of some of the big stories of the Seventies, and,
of course, we'll end up using hindsight too.

Ideas take time to filter through, first influencing an individual or two, then a small cell, but often finding the wider
community less porous, more resistant to change. Music has
often had a role to play, picking up an undercurrent, an idea
somewhere deep in the world, channelling it and propelling
it forward into the future. At the beginning of the Seventies,
The Velvet Underground were still relatively undiscovered,
years after their first LP was released back in 1967, but the
album had an edge, a disharmony, and a drug-addled darkness which set the tone for the Seventies. It's an example of
the predictive, productive power of music; according to Jon
Savage in *England's Dreaming*, 'The Seventies began with the
first Velvet Underground LP.'

It's never a case of fresh starts and full stops. Underlining
this sense of futures past, many of the big films in the early

years of the 1970s were versions of novels published in the previous decade, including *Catch 22* and *One Flew Over the Cuckoo's Nest*. In the case of *A Clockwork Orange*, at the publication of Anthony Burgess's novel in 1962, the story seemed like a far-fetched, dystopian, sci-fi tale, but in 1971 it was finally released as a film and seemed all too at home.

In Britain it would take David Bowie's advocacy of the band to bring Lou Reed and The Velvet Underground to the notice of a wider public. In January 1970 Bowie himself was mostly known for his 'Space Oddity' single of the previous year, which, released during the first successful manned mission to the moon, was considered something of a novelty hit. After this stumbling start, it seemed unlikely that Bowie was going to be one of the biggest influences on the decade to come.

At the start of the year, another musician who would play a key role in the Seventies, Bob Marley, was working with The Wailers and Lee 'Scratch' Perry (and together, later in the year, they would have success in Jamaica with the 'Little Axe' single). Other characters were not even half a step towards their iconic status; Debbie Harry – who was to be one of the decade's ace faces in her band Blondie – had temporarily given up on New York, left her job as a Playboy bunny and moved upstate outside Woodstock in Phoenicia with a pregnant friend. Martin Scorsese had just released *Who's That Knocking At My Door*, his first full-length film, over three years in the making, but hadn't yet started on another project. Mid-Ulster MP Bernadette Devlin was in the process of appealing against her six-month jail sentence for her part in the Bogside riots of August 1969. At the end of January 1970, Johnny Rotten celebrated his fourteenth birthday, cycling to school wearing a leather jacket to stay dry under the rainy sky, arriving there with his long hair plastered against his pale skin. He didn't enjoy his time at William of York, a comprehensive school near Pentonville: 'I learnt hate and resentment there,' he later claimed.

In 1970, posters of Sixties icons like Che Guevara and Jimi Hendrix were still stuck on bedroom walls, we had a Prime Minister we'd first elected in 1964, and the England football manager Alf Ramsey was still in charge after seven years in the job. In the first weeks of the year, rising numbers of households were trading black and white television sets for colour, and the most popular programmes on the two available channels were long-established favourites like *Coronation Street* and *Softly Softly*. Forty-six-year-old DJ Jimmy Young, who'd been at Radio One since it first broadcast in 1967, dominated the morning schedules with what he called the 'JY prog'.

Queen Victoria was regularly invoked as a monarch who'd presided over a greater Britain. The Second World War was far more than just a memory: city centres were still blitz damaged, bomb sites littered the suburbs, and the grey fog of austerity still covered many parts of the country. In 1970 you'd also see groups of Teddy boys on the streets, some of them revivalists, but many of them the original rebellious rock & rollers who'd ripped up cinema seats a generation or two before; they'd grown older, of course, in their drapes and slicked-back hair, giving their kids a clip round the ear or parading around like it was the 1950s and they were dodging national service.

The past was ever present, but the future was unfolding. Within a few years any fragile alliances between the trade unions, the business community and the Labour Party would collapse, England's national football team would go into a depressing decline, and the Che Guevara posters on the wall would slowly fade, along with the optimism of the Sixties. The Seventies were in part defined by this process of the Sixties unravelling, creating a generation that would never lay claim to never having it so good.

Entering a new decade, it was symbolic that the career of The Beatles, the favourite sons of the Sixties, was unravelling too. On 3 January 1970 they finished what turned out to be their last recording session together as a group, almost eight years after their rise had contributed to a new spirit in Britain. Before Beatlemania exploded, American idols like James Cagney or Elvis Presley had dominated teenage dreams. Then skiffle star Lonnie Donegan had gone close to breaking this pattern, and singers like Cliff Richard and Billy Fury had won over the teenyboppers, but the street corner kids – who were never going to be happy living solely on a diet of Cliff and The Shadows – looked for something less tame. Enter The Beatles, in 1962, with their first single 'Love Me Do'.

Those early 1960s were boom years. Heavy industry – from the chemical factories on Teesside to the Liverpool docks – appeared to offer jobs for life, and no doom-merchants questioned the future of the car factories in Birmingham and Coventry. In 1964, football fans at Liverpool's Anfield ground were filmed by the BBC's *Panorama* programme, and those in the Kop are captured on film in full cry singing 'She Loves You' by The Beatles, belting out the 'yeah yeah yeah' choruses joyously, en masse. In an age of full employment, it was all good news; confidence, peace and prosperity poured from the terraces. Swaying in the packed Kop, swaggering down Carnaby Street, emerging beautifully coiffured from a unisex salon with a bob like Mary Quant's – this confidence was underpinned by Britain's economic success.

The Koppites were part of a blessed generation. A new era had emerged from the grey, austere, constricted 1950s, breaking out of unquestioning conformity – suits and ties, cloth caps for the workers, trilbies to the office, and a top hat for the bosses – and entering a colourful era of high fashion, mass consumption and good times, triggering decades of informality and experimentation with clothes.

This burst of social nonconformity would have repercussions in the Seventies. In the second half of the 1950s rock & roll had played an important part in loosening the shackles, but the stirrings of unconstricted life had emerged in novels, plays and films in the late 1950s too; *A Taste of Honey*, *Room at the Top* and *Billy Liar* had given a voice to dissent, and a taste of dirty realism. From a very different background, but similarly expressive, the poetry of Sylvia Plath explored the roots of raw feeling which challenged formal, strait-laced traditions.

But the new spirit at the beginning of the Sixties didn't go unchallenged by the guardians of traditional, deferential, establishment Britain. Books, films and plays at the time were subject to censorship. Penguin Books were prosecuted for publishing an unexpurgated version of *Lady Chatterley's Lover* in November 1960, although this time liberalism won and the jury acquitted Penguin of obscenity charges. But attempts to control even the most mildly subversive ideas were clearly in evidence. The Beatles themselves were denounced by church-men, and, on occasion, by editorials in the popular press. The Board of Film Censors routinely objected to displays of physical intimacy between unmarried couples, and the use of what was then called 'coarse' language.

High on liberation, freed from the constrictions of the post-war generations, the young had a sense of adventure and lacked subservience. This teen revolution was about more than just a few 7-inch singles on a Dansette; the music was central to deep changes. The developments were obvious, even to those a few removes from the cutting edge of youth culture. In his poem 'Annus Mirabilis', Philip Larkin makes a connection between the beginnings of the sexual revolution, the Chatterley ban, and the release of the first Beatles LP in 1963. There's also a curious, untitled L.S. Lowry work from 1965 which illustrates the impact of social changes. After decades painting isolated houses, forlorn mill towns, be-draggled crowds and disfigured and downcast figures, he turns his gaze to a new subject and paints four girls, three of them in mini-skirts, their outfits shockingly colourful. Suddenly a new generation was on the Salford streets, dressing in ways

Lowry had never seen before. He's bewitched by the young girls' legs.

The teenage liberation then being experienced was also having an impact on family life. A weakening of the ties binding the traditional family together would become a feature of the Seventies, but in the early 1960s the process had already begun. Women were gaining independence and the young were asking questions. In 1963 an investigation in Sheffield reported: 'There are signs that some girls are tending towards more independence in their dealings with men. They are not prepared to be bowed down with lots of children, and they will expect their husbands to take a fuller share than their fathers in the running of the home.'

In the wake of The Beatles, other bands, like The Animals and The Kinks, emerged out of the beat boom, setting up stages in coffee bars and basement clubs. In the autumn of 1964, the Kinks single 'You Really Got Me' stood out, driven by Dave Davies' unique guitar sound. It was to herald the start of major success for the band. Their subsequent history, and the relationship between Dave Davies and his brother, Ray, the band's singer, was fraught to say the least, but The Kinks had longevity and survived well into the 1970s.

In January 1970 Ray Davies began work on a retrospective album of Kinks material, and made plans for a book about the life of the band going back to their early days as a successful beat group with a clutch of classic singles and a controversial reputation. The Kinks were a bunch of working class kids from Muswell Hill in North London, always asking questions, provoking. When the band formed, their name alone was guaranteed to attract controversy, like mini-skirts on the streets of Salford. In those days, when a homosexual act was a crime, 'kinky' was a kind of slang. 'Pansy' was more obvious, and 'sailor' a more oblique code word, but you'd hear them all being used – usually in an accusatory way – of homosexuals.

The Kinks never confirmed or denied anything, but they'd grown their hair a little – Dave Davies, especially, was handsomely coiffured – and had a thing for wearing red hunting jackets, white frilly shirts, black riding trousers and Chelsea boots. In New York in 1965 they were harassed backstage at a TV show by anti-Communists, and Ray Davies was accosted on the street by a redneck who demanded to know, 'Are you a Beatle or a girl?'

We have moved on a long way since then, but hair length, at the time, was gender-specific: tradition and national service dictated that young men would wear their hair short. Generally it was thought of as effeminate and outrageous for a man to take pride in his appearance, but change was fuelled by the entertainers, the likes of The Kinks and The Rolling Stones, and disc jockeys like Jimmy Savile. By the mid-1960s, in some circles at least, men were encouraged to be narcissistic, playful, unfettered by potential disapproval from wider society. Back in the 1950s, when the Teddy boys slicked their hair back and put on their drainpipe trousers, moral panic ensued. Clothes continued to have this incendiary potential: in the late 1960s Angela Carter described clothes as 'our weapons, our challenges, our visible insults'.

Not wearing a suit, not wearing a tie – this could be seen as a social threat, even into the Seventies. The suit in particular carried with it the values of uniformity, conformity and capitalism. Although the hippies cast off their suits with gay abandon, the most vivid example is probably the character Reggie Perrin, in the opening credits of the TV series *The Fall and Rise of Reginald Perrin*, leaving his crumpled suit on the beach as he fakes his suicide and tries to leave his life as a suburban businessman behind.

In every town in every decade there are magistrates and civic leaders desperate to keep everyone in line, and some citizens too, intolerant, scared, taking offence at anyone who dares to be different. These guardians of conformity were out in force in the Seventies. I've heard tales of Mancunian long hairs getting chased down the street by Irish navvies in the early 1970s. Marvin Gaye, on his 1971 *What's Going On* LP, deals with social issues, ecology, inner city blues and war, but also bemoans the harassment of people simply because their hair is long. Hair length defined where you stood in the big ideological battles of the age; by the mid-1960s, long hair had become an unmistakable sign of rebellion.

Clearly there were tensions in society in the Sixties. And if we're going to question the commonly-presented version of the 1970s, we should begin by making ourselves aware of deficiencies in received views of the Sixties too. By believing exclusively in the notion of the universal happiness and undying optimism of the Swinging Sixties, we lose a host of ideas and complications. The alleged excitement of Carnaby Street, for instance, didn't extend down every terraced street and through every housing estate.

Socially, in the mid-1960s in many parts of Britain, the black community was under siege and received no legal protection from discrimination in the search for housing and jobs. There could be hostility on the streets and widespread discrimination and prejudice, including the shocking campaign slogan 'If you want a nigger neighbour, vote Labour' employed by the Conservative Party candidate for Smethwick at the 1964 election.

In April 1968, less than a year after the formation of the National Front (NF), came the most unforgettable moment in British race relations: an inflammatory speech by Enoch Powell claiming that the increasing black population was a threat to the social and cultural wellbeing of Britain. There was no sign of the subcultural exuberance and political optimism of the Sixties, as Powell described black settlement as a 'preventable evil', couching his words in the clear language of conflict. 'In fifteen or twenty years' time, the black man will have the whip hand,' he declared.

Powell's words, and his presence, haunted the 1970s. Paul Gilroy will be one of our eye witnesses through the decade. He'll be in Brighton during the Rock Against Racism era and in Birmingham just a few years after the pub bombings. In the late 1960s he was in North London, but racism boxed him in. As a young teenager he remembers the fear he felt trying to move around parts of the city. He got friendly with a girl in Hackney, so he used to have to catch a bus, the 253, all the way across North London; getting there and back without any hassle was a major achievement. In the early 1970s he remembers random intimidation by gangs, particularly Teds and skinheads. 'We weren't so far away from Enoch Powell and in that sense there was a feeling that there was some sort of war being played out,' he says. 'People really did get hurt and in that sense I was spared the worst of it because I was a very fast runner at the time. There were certain places you avoided; I mean, I laugh now when I look at Hoxton and see what's going on there because back then that was a place you did not want to go.'

In addition to this street-level antagonism, relations between young blacks and the police were deteriorating in the early 1970s. A number of events, including confrontations at the Mangrove restaurant and the Metro youth club in Notting Hill in 1971, set the pattern for the decade, culminating in bonfire night riots in Chapeltown in Leeds over successive years from 1973, and trouble at Notting Hill Carnival.

There were other sources of discontent. According to the Child Poverty Action Group, three million children were living in poverty in 1970; the affluent society had passed them by. Thousands of families in the 1960s were also forced to cope with slum clearance. In cities like Birmingham, Sheffield, Manchester and Newcastle, housing stock was insanitary and inadequate, and plans to replace decaying terraced streets with modern housing were overdue and, at first, welcome. But throughout the Sixties planners and local authorities misjudged urban renewal, and uprooted settled neighbourhoods without adequate consultation with the residents. These experiences were reflected in songs by The Kinks, notably on the 1971 LP *Muswell Hillbillies*, a bleak, quirky record, shot through with Ray Davies' growing mistrust of the establishment and the bureaucrats. The working class inhabitants of Muswell Hill were having little say in the choices made for them; they shared this fate with countless communities up and down the country.

In the creation of high-rise estates like Hyde Park in Sheffield, Broadwater Farm in Tottenham, and Hulme in Manchester, architects and developers used time-saving and cost-cutting methods. In Hulme, factory-built concrete panels were transported in and slotted together like a child's construction toy, and under budget and on time, John Laing Concrete Limited built a dozen three-storey maisonettes and a number of giant, crescent-shaped blocks. One of the architects responsible for the new Hulme, Lewis Wormersley, celebrated his scheme's 'skilful landscaping and extensive tree planting', and the 'quality' of the buildings. Work on Broadwater Farm began in 1967 and was finally completed six years later; the estate consisted of twelve blocks housing a total of 3,000 people. During work on the site it won a Department of the Environment award, and on its completion, the chairman of Haringey's planning committee announced that 'Broadwater Farm will be an everlasting memorial to my committee'.

Throughout the 1970s urban public space and the built environment deteriorated alarmingly, as the mistaken visions of the planners unravelled, in Hulme and elsewhere. Resentment at the break-up of communities and the lack of control and consultation was compounded by glaring faults soon revealed in the new estates. Often within just a few months, families were facing broken lifts, stinking stairwells, cockroach infestation and damp and condensation percolating through concrete walls. Flawed design and inadequate building materials dragged the new estates into despair and recession, and vandalism did the rest. By the mid-1970s, most of those housed in the new Hulme had fled, and repair bills to the housing blocks had rocketed; already demolition seemed the only answer. Meanwhile, Broadwater Farm had become an everlasting memorial to the folly of the Haringey planning committee, and within five years of its completion, the Department of the Environment had changed its tune, describing conditions on Broadwater Farm as 'catastrophic'.

In every era, including our own, a good proportion of the media get caught up in the hype, fall for the same face, follow the same trend, but in every era, including our own, there are people suspicious of the story that's being fed to us. Jayne Casey will be another of our eye witnesses through the Seventies. She was born in 1956 and lived in Liverpool through the 1960s, 1970s and beyond, to the present day, and her story makes clear that there are darker sides to the Sixties; it wasn't all 'Strawberry Fields Forever'.

Her early life was scarred by her mother's death when Jayne was just five years old. She grew up in an environment that was virtually untouched by the affluent society and the Swinging Sixties: 'I remember being aware of The Beatles, and you knew all these things were happening, but it was just so far away from the life you were living and the people around you.'

In the house with her dad there were no electric lights. 'I know, it's hard to believe,' she says, 'but for the whole of my childhood there was no electric lights in the house, not a television. When the power cuts came in the 1970s, you know, I wasn't bothered. And I don't really remember them to be honest; that's what I was used to.'

Even if she'd seen the fans in the Kop singing on *Panorama*, it's not clear she would have understood the euphoria. 'My 1960s were like the 1950s, it was still post-war in Liverpool, absolutely. When I was growing up you kept chickens that laid eggs and your nan knitted your socks.'

Jayne's distance from the euphoria of the time wasn't just down to poverty and the claustrophobia of the Liverpool streets, but was intensified by the circumstances of her mother's death. She tells me the story of what happened in 1961, about how her mother's death was the result of beatings by her father. 'He'd beat her up, but at the time there wasn't much you could do about domestic violence, so he'd beat her up and it wouldn't stop and then the police used to come and beat him up. And my mother hadn't married my father, which at the time wasn't a socially acceptable thing. She'd had three children out of wedlock, so that didn't help.'

One night he beat her really badly, hitting her with a chair. She was hospitalised, and her injuries forced surgeons to amputate her leg. Within days she was diagnosed with cancer, but weak and ill and in no state to fight the disease she had no chance to recover. Six months later, she was dead. Jayne's family was broken up: she lived with her dad, and her brothers went to live with her aunt. Jayne looks back at how she experienced the 1960s in Liverpool. The big stories of the decade – swinging London, student protests, free love – were from a different world. 'That's right, it was so far away. It was so far away!'

Generally, jobs were plentiful and the young felt empowered in the Sixties, but there were plenty of people unaffected by the boom times. In *X-Ray*, his semi-fictional autobiography, Ray Davies insists he could see the Seventies coming, that there were communities who would be 'left behind without work' when 'the party was over'. In his words, 'I think the Sixties were a con; the establishment still ruled the country.'

Nevertheless, The Kinks were in fashion. Even his songs mocking the latest fancy trends were seldom off the radio, and their working class/art school background was exactly what the fashion police required. One evening in March 1966, Ray Davies watched himself on *Top of the Pops* and felt compelled to attack the screen and hide the TV in the gas oven. He then went to bed for a week and grew a beard. The next single the band released was called 'Dead End Street'.

One of the most obvious ways in which the Sixties were more complicated, and less universally optimistic than the received story of the decade suggests, is the sea-change in the second half of the decade. There was no single turning point, but the circumstances surrounding England's World Cup win in 1966 are worth recalling.

England's 1966 victory didn't herald the beginnings of greater success. In fact the national team failed to reach such heights again, and 1970 was the year in which the decades of hurt really began. That year the World Cup was held in Mexico, and, as holders, England didn't need to play in the qualifying rounds. They departed full of confidence, but within days of arriving in South America the campaign descended into farce when Bobby Moore, the England captain, was arrested in Bogota and accused of stealing from a jewellery shop. The team was knocked out of the competition in the quarter-final, losing to Germany 3–2. England had been two goals up at half-time, but Alf Ramsey made a couple of injudicious substitutions and England snatched defeat from the jaws of victory.

Sir Alf's reign continued, however, but in the years that followed the team's fortunes dipped further, including an infamous night in October 1973 when a draw at Wembley against Poland denied England a place in the 1974 World Cup Finals. The team also failed to qualify for the 1978 Championships. England's demise in the 1970s had the country looking back to the golden age of 1966, and helped to define and reinforce the nation's sense of social and industrial decline.

But even back in 1966 not everybody was convinced that England would go on to achieve greater glory. The Kinks challenged this euphoria with 'Dead End Street', not only the first single released after Ray Davies had suffered a breakdown, but also their first single after the World Cup win. 'Dead End Street' was a tale of poverty and failure, complemented by a short promotional film (they weren't called 'videos' then) in which The Kinks were filmed carrying a coffin through the London streets. 'Dead End Street' expressed the downside of the Sixties, but some of the gatekeepers of popular culture didn't want to listen, either to the music or the message. Radio One DJ Tony Blackburn declared that the subject matter of 'Dead End Street' was too depressing for a pop record and resisted playing it.

After 1966 the Sixties began to swing in a different direction. The world of the first half of the decade – sharp beat groups, mods, purple hearts and black bombers, *Ready Steady Go!* – was being left behind, replaced by hallucinogenic drugs, long hair, rambling songs and a different line-up of musical heroes: The Yardbirds, The Doors, Cream, Pink Floyd and Jimi Hendrix. The emerging force at the time among the young on the streets, at the universities and art colleges would become known as the counter culture, and in time would wash its influence over the Seventies, in particular the first half of the decade.

Which culture the counter culture was counter to was variously defined and described: the establishment, the rat race, straights, squares, the system. It was a scornful revolt against conformist aspirations of the older generations, a scepticism of mainstream ideas, and a rejection of the power wielded by the traditional ruling class (especially in the fields of media and education), but allegiance to the counter culture was demonstrated in many different, and sometimes conflicting ways, from fleeing to India in a haze of marijuana, to pursuing hard-headed political revolution on the streets of Western cities. Those in the counter culture who were looking for political change, even revolution, took strength from groups opposing the arms race, from the black civil rights movement, and from a resurgence of student activism, and the primary focus for their dissent was the war in Vietnam.

At home in North London, Paul Gilroy read a lot, including the writings of Eldridge Cleaver and journalists on *Rolling Stone* magazine, and gradually he discovered the counter culture and its underground, international flavour. Marginal voices found alliances, networks developed using favoured media (especially film and the underground press), and the word spread via the global language of rock & roll. Paul was young at the time, barely a teenager, and it took some finding. 'Yes, it was "underground", that was the word and that was the practice; and in some ways it didn't seek to be discovered.'

He remembers getting sucked into it, the excitement of underground London. 'Late 1968 going into 1969 there were a lot of free concerts. There was Blind Faith and The Stones and various things on Parliament Hill; Jefferson Airplane played there. There were all those kinds of things going on, and to someone of that youth it all seemed very attractive because of the way it enacted some of the things I was beginning to read about.'

Paul went from watching bands to forming bands within a matter of months – there was no going back. When we talk about music, however, he only tells half a story. In conversation, he can't recall ever hearing the likes of Brotherhood of Man, or the majority of Sweet's singles, but he can remember the day MC5 came to town. He's not untypical of those times, in the early 1970s, when there was a gaping gulf between mainstream pop and the world of the underground counter culture. A number of acoustic, introspective singer songwriters created masterpieces unheralded in the mainstream: Tim Buckley's 1969 LP *Blue Afternoon*, for example, and Nick Drake's *Five Leaves Left* (1970). It's likely too that some music fans bought the Crosby, Stills, Nash & Young LP

Déjà Vu in 1970 and became so engrossed in that acoustic West Coast sound that even glam passed them by.

The notion of an underground drew on an established belief that the authorities invariably attempt to suppress unhelpful or subversive opinions, but that discontented people still find ways to protest and ways of getting unheard opinions out onto the streets by whatever means are available; now it might be via the worldwide web, but back in the late 1960s it was via the underground press. Previous generations had even used primitive forms of graffiti: in 1800 the Manchester magistrate Thomas Butterworth complained that 'the public eye is daily saluted with sedition in chalk characters on our walls'.

As the acquittal of the publishers of *Lady Chatterley's Lover* in 1960, and the end of theatre censorship in 1968 both demonstrated, legal sanctions against unpopular opinions and obscenity were falling out of favour, but during the Sixties and early Seventies there was also a view that, in practice, relaxing censorship laws made little difference, and that liberal democracies had subtle but effective strategies for ensuring that questioning attitudes had no platform. Those in America who opposed the war in Vietnam, for example, enjoyed little support in the mainstream media, network television and the established press. So too civil rights activists. In what was being called a 'repressive democracy', dissenting opinions struggled to be heard and the underground press stepped into the information vacuum.

The underground press thrived in many countries, especially America and Britain, and the increased availability of primitive but effective printing methods, especially offset lithography and Xerox technology, made possible the proliferation of a large number of publications, free sheets and manifestos. In 1966, *International Times* was first published in London and found a ready audience; within eighteen months *IT* was selling 40,000 copies a month, with a mixture of political and cultural issues and a pin-up (an *IT* girl).

Oz was launched in 1967, and like *International Times* and other early underground publications, it appeared to be primarily concerned with disseminating information, particularly about drugs, and interested in music only in the context of dope and acid. The underground press soon spread outside London, with one notable example Manchester's *Grass Eye*, founded in 1968 by Salford Grammar School sixth-former Chris Dixon and inspired by *IT* and *Oz*. He was later joined by student Dave Clark, who had previously been involved with *Guerrilla*, an underground paper produced by members of the International Socialists at Manchester University.

The full range of counter culture positions was represented, with some of the publications more interested in covering art 'happenings' than hard politics, and others closely connected to pseudo-mystical, or feminist, or activist groups, although all were united in their antipathy to the hard line against soft drugs taken by the authorities; the clearest defining and dividing line between the counter culture and the mainstream involved attitudes to drug taking, especially marijuana, amphetamines and LSD. From 1967 we were in the psychedelic era; underground publications, graphic art, clothes and music were all dipped in a brew of hallucinogenic drugs. The concentration on lifestyle, politics and drugs was enhanced by the use of acid-inspired visuals. Designers made an enthusiastic use of colour, and, in contrast to the smooth edges of the mainstream press, the prose was urgent and informal. Ideas and images were included with the clear aim of shocking the bourgeoisie; for example, well-known cartoon characters like Mickey Mouse or Donald Duck often appeared in collages or mocking cartoons, often up to no good.

The period from 1967 to 1970 was particularly frustrating for The Kinks: they released some of their best work but achieved poor sales. True to form, they were going against the grain. While most British and American acts were soaking themselves in the warmth of psychedelia, The Kinks and Ray

Davies stayed in touch with a colder reality. With releases like 'Sunny Afternoon' the hits continued, as did the droll class caricatures like 'David Watts'. In 1967, when the band released the sad, regretful classic 'Waterloo Sunset', Davies was looking out over the dirty River Thames at sunset rather than California dreaming. The lyrics had a special resonance for British audiences, particularly those on the band's last two LPs of the Sixties, *The Village Green Preservation Society* and *Arthur*, which included 'Mr Churchill Says', 'Picture Book' and 'Victoria', the latter a caustic attack on empty eulogies to Queen Victoria and the British Empire.

The ideological struggles of the Sixties remained significant; through into the Seventies the conflict between the forces of change and the authorities never disappeared, as subsequent chapters will reveal. The era was marked by dissenters hurling themselves at the last bastions of hierarchy and deference, challenging norms, whether in the realm of sexual expression or in the theatre, the cinema or music. We'll discover many of these significant events on our journey through the Seventies, some of which thread back to symbolic moments in the Sixties: the Chatterley trial, the May 1968 uprisings in Paris, and the police brutality at the Democratic Party convention in Chicago, when hundreds of anti-Vietnam war protesters clashed with 12,000 police and 15,000 troops in the city's streets and parks over five days. By the very beginning of the Seventies we were a long way from the days of 'She Loves You'. 'Yeah, yeah, yeah' was being replaced by 'no, no, no', protest by rejection.

In August 1970 the Isle of Wight festival featured The Who (magnificent, by all accounts), Free, Leonard Cohen, The Doors and Jimi Hendrix. It was clear how much the music scene had changed from the early days of The Beatles and The Kinks. At the end of the 1960s, the prevailing trend was LPs rather than singles, and outdoor festivals rather than dance-halls and basements. By the middle of 1970, The Beatles were finished and creative power lay in the hands of the likes of Jimi Hendrix. His crowning moment came at the Isle of Wight festival.

Paul Gilroy had been exploring the world of the counter culture in London, but there was another part of his life. 'The other axis was the black one really,' he says. 'In that sense, for me the 1970s began seeing Hendrix playing at the Isle of Wight because there was some way in which he could hold those things together; at least, we imagined that's what he could do. Yeah, because he made my blackness cool, actually.' At one point Paul remembers Hendrix talking about skinheads. 'When he came to the Isle of Wight and started mumbling on about skinheads and all this kind of stuff, it was a very big deal for us because it suggested he understood why we have to run for our lives through Highbury and Finsbury Park. What he said spoke to us in some way.'

Clearly the times were changing, and youth culture's latest direction had appeared to set The Kinks adrift again. It's understandable that Ray Davies had been planning a retrospective of The Kinks, but 1970 was to turn out to be a great year for the band, with a massive hit and a successful LP entitled *Lola Vs. Powerman and the Money-Go-Round*.

The LP revolved around Ray's embittered tales of the music industry. Songs like 'Denmark Street' and 'Top of the Pops' detail particular areas of the music business, and 'Get in Line' the distortions of a world run by marketing men. 'Lola' is the big hit single from the LP, an irresistible, melodic, singalong song given extra impact through the way it goes to the heart of the gender and fashion hostilities of the early 1970s.

Ray Davies tells the tale straight, an encounter with Lola in a pub in Soho, who we first assume is a brazen young woman, asking him to dance, intent on seducing the singer. Davies plays the role of the naive narrator brilliantly, but as the story unfolds there's obviously something unusual going on, and when she hugs him she nearly breaks his spine. Soon the listener understands that Lola is a transvestite – who walks like a woman but talks like a man – and the encounter leaves the narrator questioning his own sexuality, but celebrating Lola's survival in a mixed-up, muddled world.

Foppishness had become a feature of rock music by the end of the 1960s. The Rolling Stones dressed like dandies, and a languid, unmacho demeanour had become part of characteristic hippy male behaviour. 'Lola' takes all this a stage further, squeezing gender issues as tight as Lola's grip. Within two or three years, thanks to artists like David Bowie, blurred gender roles were to play an even bigger role in rock music, but in the late 1960s there were few songs that covered similar ground to 'Lola', aside from The Who's 'I'm a Boy' (1966). Gore Vidal's novel *Myra Breckinridge* also questioned macho roles by revealing a character's sexual ambiguity (the book was a best-seller in 1968, despite *Time* magazine complaining, 'Has literary decency fallen so low?').

'Lola' also reflected and boosted the higher profile of homosexuality in the period. Before 1967 homosexual acts were criminal offences, and the gay world was furtive and dangerous, but homosexual acts between consenting adults in private were decriminalised through the work of Labour MP Leo Abse, who piloted the Sexual Offences Act of 1967 through Parliament. 'Lola' dug itself deeper into social consciousness than an abstract debate ever could, and became an anthem of sexual liberation.

In the last years of the Sixties, the Labour Government's Home Secretary Roy Jenkins, as well as loosening censorship on the arts and giving tacit support to the Sexual Offences Act, presided over other liberal new laws. These included a 1967 Bill put forward by Liberal MP David Steel which set out the terms that made legalised abortions available, and the NHS (Family Planning) Act which enabled local authorities to provide birth control advisory centres. Divorce laws were also adjusted, making divorce in many ways easier to obtain, but also reflecting a more equal status of women in marriage, and the impact of modern feminism on political debate. To an extent, feminism in England took its cue from America, but was also able to draw on homegrown Suffragette traditions, by 1970 campaigning for equal pay; for free birth control and abortion on demand; for the reassessment of roles in the home; and for action against the exploitation of women as 'sex objects'.

Family structures had been considered the bedrock of society, lauded by conservative commentators, but the idealised 1950s image of the self-sacrificing housewife, with a working husband and obedient kids, had been questioned in the Sixties, particularly in Betty Friedan's book *The Feminine Mystique,* which argued that in the traditional role of a housewife, women could feel subservient, contained, and in some cases be the target of extreme violence. The urgent need for equality and liberation in the domestic sphere was an early demand of the new feminist movement.

Ken Loach's 1970 film *Family Life* questioned basic beliefs in family values by playing up the claustrophobia of family life and the demeaning role of the wife. Writing in 1970, Juliet Mitchell, one of the foremost feminist writers in England, declared that 'the family appears as a natural object, but is actually a cultural creation. There is nothing inevitable about the form or role of the family.'

Jayne Casey's is a grim story, atypical in its extreme violence, but not unique. Statistics from some parts of Britain suggest that over a quarter of all violent incidents in the era were attacks on wives. More than half of all women murdered between 1962 and 1971 were killed by the man closest to them, either their husband or their lover. Domestic violence remained a powerful issue, and one feature of the Seventies was the establishment of homes and sheltered hostels for battered wives. In 1972 Erin Pizzey established Britain's first women's refuge in Chiswick, London, and such was the growth in their numbers that in 1974 the Women's Aid Foundation created a formal network for refuges nationwide.

Also by 1970 there was a sense in the women's movement that progressive legislation and the apparent support for female values among male radicals still wasn't going to deliver progress for women, and a radical separatist agenda gained credence. This could take various forms, but often focused on 'consciousness raising' groups: women-only meetings where the deepest personal experiences could be shared and collective strategies discussed.

As well as reassessing the role of women in the home, work was being done to reclaim the role of women in history. During the last weekend of February 1970 a national conference met in Oxford. Initially conceived as a meeting of female historians, it attracted disparate groups from all over the country, six hundred women convinced of the urgent need for debate and action. In 1970, in fact, the drive for ideas in the women's movement reached a crescendo. There had been an instinctive grasp for equal rights and independence, but in 1970 there was a flood of provocative books spreading ideas and searching for explanations, including Germaine Greer's *The Female Eunuch*, *The Dialectic of Sex* by Shulamith Firestone, and *Sexual Politics* by Kate Millett, in which Ms Millett laid out persuasive definitions of 'patriarchy', describing how 'male chauvinism' was emblematic of power relations deep in the social and political traditions of society. These heavyweight ideas were complemented by an increase in high-profile direct action. Among such incidents, Women's Liberation demonstrators disrupted the Miss World contest at the Albert Hall in November 1970 by throwing flour, tomatoes and stink bombs, and chanting, 'We're not beautiful, we're not ugly, we're angry.'

At the beginning of the 1970s there were already clear tensions in the women's movement. Separatist arguments were one part of this, but so were problems being encountered as a result of the way the counter culture had become especially drawn to the notion of sexual liberation. 'Sex, by the early 1970s, had become a cause,' according to Sheila Rowbotham. Crusaders like Ken Tynan and Germaine Greer were eager to break down sexual repression, abolish boundaries and challenge taboos. Some women at the time enthusiastically flaunted and celebrated their sexual power, or, to be exact, what Germaine Greer called 'Cunt Power'. In the words of Sheila Rowbotham again, Greer 'saw the expression of female erotic desire as the subversive force which would dissolve "patriarchy"'.

Others, however, resisted being defined by their private parts and took a different route, notably by de-glamming, dressing down, looking for shapeless, anti-erotic clothes. All through the Seventies this was an influential look, working alongside other attempts to find purer, anti-commercial, non-competitive lifestyles, like attempts to set up rural communes and an interest in organic and 'whole' foods, and self-sufficiency.

Female assertiveness was becoming a feature throughout society. There were also female singer songwriters working in an introspective, often confessional, acoustic folk tradition, including Joni Mitchell, Carly Simon and Carole King. A number of publishing houses were founded in England in the Seventies, among them Virago, which began publishing in September 1973 and was soon producing reprints, classics, works of feminist theory and history, always strong on semi-autobiographical, coming-of-age novels. 'The personal is political' was a core feminist belief, and similar semi-autobiographical works featured in the output of the Women's Press (founded in 1978). In 1971 *Observer* journalist Beata Lipman met a woman in Swansea who was leading a campaign against a local factory that habitually polluted the area with industrial waste. 'Twenty years ago we just accepted our lot,' she told Ms Lipman. 'We wouldn't have thought

about protesting, but things have changed and we won't stand
for it any longer.'

1970 also witnessed further steps in the emergence of gay
liberation, after a significant turning point in June 1969 when
a police raid on a New York gay bar, the Stonewall Inn, was
resisted by rioting gay men, drag queens and a small number
of lesbians. The image of all those Lolas fighting the powermen
reflected another struggle for liberation. But, against a background of war in Vietnam, there was also a need to define
the nature of the society being championed in America. For
the gay community no less than the black community, there
appeared to be no equal stake in the freedoms of the 'free
world'. Mohammad Ali had refused to fight in Vietnam, pointing out, 'No Vietcong ever called me nigger', and his words
were echoed on a flyer distributed in California in 1969: 'No
Vietnamese ever called me queer'.

The first meeting of the Gay Liberation Front in England
was held at the London School of Economics in October 1970.
Their manifesto acknowledged the gay community's solidarity
with other 'oppressed people', and called for an end to discrimination in the workplace and an end to the demonisation
of homosexuality in sex education in schools and in psychiatry
(calling on doctors to 'stop treating homosexuality as though
it were a problem or sickness').

'Lola' emerged out of this world of experimentation and
gender ambiguity, but did so without appearing to shock or
confront. Although the subject matter went beyond what was
usually accepted on mainstream radio, the song escaped a
BBC ban (although radio bosses insisted The Kinks had to
re-record the song, replacing a reference to Coca-Cola with
the brand-free phrase 'cherry cola' in order to avoid giving
free advertising).

The LP clearly recognises and illustrates the conflict
between the forces of change and the reactionary mainstream;
that's the importance of the 'Vs' in the title. For the good

souls, life is a battle, and in that grey, conformist world, dominated by the powermen – the men in suits with uniform,
obvious ideas – Lola is the most decent, creative and creditable
person on the record, the antidote.

'Lola' sold well, but The Kinks were staggering into the
1970s. Ray and Dave Davies had a disagreement over some
French fries which led to a stabbing. The lawsuits, especially
with regard to publishing monies, dragged on. Ray's rocky
marriage intensified his belief that things had spun beyond
his control. But, as if to underline their continuing relevance,
songs written by The Kinks were covered by a number of
post-punk groups, including a version of 'Lola' by The Raincoats, 'David Watts' by The Jam, and 'Victoria' by The Fall.
Influences that had informed the work of The Kinks in the
later years of the 1960s and the beginning of the Seventies – a
sense of social conflict, creeping disillusionment, an awareness
that things have got left behind, the tightening grip of big
business and the corporate world – spread through the 1970s.

The Seventies was also a heady decade for fashion. During
the Sixties there'd been a move towards an end to deference
and conformity, in social attitudes, but in dress too. Once the
buttoned-up formalities of the Fifties had broken down, the
combination of possibilities was endless, and by 1970 women
were being tempted by a new look almost weekly, and men
had a bewildering and unprecedented combination of choices:
long-haired or crew-cut, flared, tie-dyed, sharp or shoddy.
Formality and uniformity was disappearing so quickly, the
loss of faith in the suit so complete, that when Gilbert &
George toured their art show in 1970 and appeared in suits
they were the craziest artists around.

With the breakdown of the fragile unity of the counter
culture emerged one of the hallmarks of the Seventies: the
unprecedented tribalism. Just as the mods and rockers in the
mid-1960s had defined themselves as enemies, triggering violence, so the tribalism of the Seventies was more than just

about clothes or music. In a continual ebb and flow of revolution and reaction, by 1970 there were a number of youth cults antagonistic towards hippies, including skinheads. Skinhead haircuts and clothes demonstrated their difference, but also their aggression. Originally, skinheads – like mods – had been fans of ska and other early forms of reggae, but through time this purist vision had become distorted. For example, anecdotal evidence would suggest that while not all skinheads were racists, many of the most violent racists were skinheads.

Through the late Sixties and into the early Seventies, a split became obvious between the soft-focused peace and love world of the hippies, and the hardliners who advocated major social change; the latter, calling themselves 'yippies', believed that the counter culture was in danger of being commercialised out of existence. Or in the words of Jerry Rubin in 1970, 'Beware the psychedelic businessman who talks love on his way to Chase Manhattan. He grows his hair long and puts on a brightly colored shirt because that's where it's at – the money, that is. He has a big pile of cash and a short soul. A hip capitalist is a pig capitalist . . . They are traitors to their long hair.'

For Jayne Casey, however, her haircut had an even deeper significance. Following her mother's death, she remembers demanding a haircut. She had long hair down her back, massive curls. She just screamed and cried until eventually her dad took her to the barber's and had it all cut off. 'I knew I wanted to get rid of my femininity because I was so scared of him, so terrified.'

In the chapters that follow we'll see how Jayne got through all this, established her own business running a small clothes shop in Liverpool in the mid-1970s, then became part of the post-punk music scene. We'll also track down Paul Gilroy to a dodgy pub in Brighton, and a third eye witness, Alan Jones, we'll find working for Vivienne Westwood and Malcolm McLaren at their famous shop, Sex. That job, and punk, were a long way off in 1970, when Alan was relatively new in London: 'I moved from Portsmouth, my hometown, in September 1969. I couldn't wait to get out, I hated it so much.'

He was looking for a job in the fashion industry and remembers walking down Carnaby Street, which dazzled him even though its best days were over: 'I had always been a fashion victim, even in Portsmouth.'

The rise of a fashion industry catering to this new-found freedom to dress up made progressive movements uneasy. In addition, for some women the new pressures of the fashion parade were just another form of oppression. To them, liberation from traditional home and family roles allied to endless talk of sexual freedom had created a new kind of pressure: to be fashionably dressed, sexually active and subject to the male gaze like those legs Lowry loved. This was something that concerned Juliet Mitchell: 'For women, as to a lesser extent for men, the "sexual revolution" has meant a positive increase in the amount of their sexual (and hence social) freedom; it has also meant an increase in their "use" as sexual objects.'

Voices grew louder from within the counter culture raising concerns about increasing consumer pressures, that ideas were too quickly turning into products as big business and the merchandisers moved in. It was as if the young had been liberated by shifts in social attitudes, only to allow themselves to be sucked into a money-go-round.

There was also a degree of disillusion with the political direction of the Labour Party. To the political left and the radical underground, the progress made by Roy Jenkins enacting liberal laws was outweighed by a subsequent drift to the right in 1969 and early 1970: continuing support for America in Vietnam; Home Secretary James Callaghan's decision to limit the entry into the country of Asians with UK passports fleeing Kenya in 1968; the introduction of prescription charges; rising unemployment; and cutbacks in social services spending. Manchester's *Grass Eye* reflected some of this enmity: 'The Labour Party is no alternative . . . non-involvement in politics is a better option than trying to turn the Labour Party into a left-wing party. It should either be smashed or ignored. The revolution happens here, not tomorrow, but now. It's us versus capitalism.'

Most controversially of all, the Labour Government was on a collision course with elements of the left on the issue of industrial relations. During 1969, more working days were lost due to strike action than any other year in the 1960s. This rise in both official disputes and so-called 'wildcat' strikes, especially in the Midlands motor trade, convinced Prime Minister Harold Wilson and the Employment Secretary Barbara Castle that they should try to come to some arrangement with the trade unions to limit union power. In January 1969 they published a draft White Paper, 'In Place of Strife', which threatened legal sanctions against unions who failed to comply with compulsory ballots and cooling-off periods. The White Paper was opposed by large numbers of the parliamentary Labour Party, and by the TUC who published their own 'Programme of Action'. Wilson met with union leaders, including Vic Feather, Hugh Scanlon and Jack Jones, in an attempt to find agreement. Eventually the Government was forced to backtrack when it was clear that attempts to impose penalties and legal sanctions on the unions would not be carried in the Commons.

Conflicts between the trade unions and the Government were destined to recur throughout the 1970s, and battlelines were being drawn elsewhere too. As the 1960s turned into the 1970s, there was evidence that out on the fringes of the counter culture, permissiveness, dope and rock & roll had become a malevolent force, including the Tate–LaBianca killings by Charles Manson and his followers, and the killing of Meredith Hunter by Hell's Angels at a Rolling Stones concert in December 1969 at the Sears Point Raceway, Altamont. At Altamont, flower power was trampled in the dirt, and it's hard to disagree with Harry Shapiro in his book *Waiting for the Man*: 'As the life ebbed away from Meredith Hunter, the spirit of the Sixties went with it.'

Battlelines hardened and extremism increased. The Power-man was threatened by armed terror groups in Western Europe and America, and it wasn't always easy to see where the counter culture ended and terror networks began. In America, for example, the Weathermen emerged out of groups demonstrating at the Chicago convention. In Germany, Ulrike Meinhof was a journalist with far-left sympathies who became part of an urban terror group. In England in 1970, the Angry Brigade bombed the Italian Consulate in Manchester, the Spanish Embassy in London, and set off an explosive device under a BBC van parked outside the Miss World contest at the Albert Hall (on the same evening as the event was invaded by women's liberationists). A number of those who were later arrested as part of a round-up of suspected Angry Brigade members, including Angie Weir, Hilary Creek, Jim Greenfield and Chris Bott, had worked on underground publications like the London-based *Frendz*, and *Strike* in Liverpool.

The challenge for the authorities was how to manage demands for change. In many significant cases, the response of the authorities to dissident voices was brutality. In America, in May 1970, four students were shot dead by the National Guard during an anti-Vietnam demo at Kent State University. The subject of Crosby, Stills, Nash & Young's 'Ohio', the four deaths deepened the splits in American society. They also provided the motivation for Martin Scorsese's new film project. Together with some friends, including Harvey Keitel, and a crew of New York University film students, he documented popular reactions to events in Vietnam, including demon-strations and raging arguments on the street. *Street Scenes* reveals deep divisions and raw emotion, and a generation politicised by the war in Vietnam.

Escalation of conflict was also evident in Northern Ireland.

The Bogside riots in Derry in August 1969 were a major turning point, when the British troops – who had originally had a role defending the Catholic minority – came to be perceived as an occupying force by the Catholic Nationalists. This sense of a society being dragged into violence was underlined by the Army's first use of rubber bullets in Northern Ireland in August 1970.

Paul Gilroy remembers the death of Jimi Hendrix, just three weeks after the Isle of Wight festival, as a 'terrible, terrible thing'. It was a blow, a turning point, and over the next couple of years more music would reflect conflict, tracking darker twists of fate. Two English groups in particular, Led Zeppelin and Black Sabbath, would strike a chord with the post-Beatles, post-Hendrix generation. Both had a background in the West Midlands. Led Zeppelin had already made a name for themselves cranking up the blues. Black Sabbath, meanwhile, were the new kids on the block in 1970.

The Seventies began like a bad trip. The darkness and disharmony was reflected in louder, more aggressive music, the heavy times soundtracked by heavy music. Later it would mutate, become a cliché, become heavy metal, but back in 1970 no-one knew what to call the new rock style, although it definitely, defiantly distanced itself from the Sixties. 'We got tired of all the bullshit – love your brother and flower power forever, meeting a little chick on the corner and you're hung up on her and all this,' explained Black Sabbath singer Ozzy Osbourne at the time. He liked to call it 'slum rock'. 'Perhaps it's the way our environment evolved our minds,' he said.

In the run-up to the 1970 election, Harold Wilson described his wish to be part of the 'exciting new world of the Seventies'. Not only did Edward Heath become Prime Minister when Wilson's Labour Government was voted out of office on 18 June 1970, but the Seventies turned out to be a bleak decade. Wilson had misjudged the mood of the times. Things weren't bright and breezy; a storm was brewing.

CHAPTER TWO

'Riders on the Storm' (1971)

In January 1971 *Rolling Stone* magazine published a long interview with John Lennon. For the Sixties generation there was
no greater sign of time passing than the inescapable fact that
it was all over for The Beatles; by the end of 1971 Ringo Starr
had released a solo LP, George Harrison had had a hit with
'My Sweet Lord', and Paul McCartney had unveiled his new
group, Wings. In July 1971 John Lennon finished recording
the song 'Imagine'. Things had changed to such a degree that
a French underground paper, *L'Idiot Liberté*, called into question all notions of the progressive role of music, calling pop
'soporific' and 'counter revolutionary' and inviting its readers
to 'fall asleep to the sound of The Beatles'.

In most of his interviews, even up to the end of 1969,
Lennon was full of enthusiasm and optimism. But once into
the 1970s he seemed to lose this. In the *Rolling Stone* interview
he says it's no fun being an artist and he'd sooner be in the
audience. He talks about growing up in Liverpool, his favourite songs, and his relationship with Yoko Ono. He calls hippies
'uptight maniacs going round wearing fucking peace symbols',
and he's asked to consider the effect The Beatles had on the
history of Britain, at which point his despair becomes clear:
'Nothing happened except we all dressed up,' he says. 'The

same bastards are in control, the same people are runnin' everything, it's exactly the same.'

Notions of peace and love advanced in the 1960s – and the dream that we can all live as one – had been swept away by the slaughter of Vietnam, the proliferation of nuclear weapons, and disillusionment post-Manson and -Altamont. It's perhaps a callous thing to suggest, but the well-meaning, soft-centred message of 'Imagine' was an inadequate response to the world in 1971. Perhaps Lennon knew this too, telling *Rolling Stone*, 'We've all grown up a little, all of us, and there's been a change and we're a bit freer and all that, but it's the same game. The dream is over.'

John Lennon had not had a good couple of years. In February 1970 he'd had a nervous breakdown and checked into a private hospital the following month. After attempts to withdraw from heroin the previous year (a process he described in the song 'Cold Turkey'), he was now dependent on methadone. A Hare Krishna group was helping refurbish his seven-bedroom Georgian mansion, Tittenhurst Park, and making a hash of it in more ways than one. Lennon was in therapy for several months.

In the face of such a troubled life, 'Imagine' seemed a superficial response, and the hollowness at the song's heart is exacerbated by the millionaire musician extolling the virtues of living without possessions. When 'Imagine' was released, John and Yoko had temporarily moved from Tittenhurst Park to New York, where they lived in private, palatial splendour in the best rooms at the St Regis Hotel.

By 1971, disillusionment with mainstream politics was growing, but established counter cultural strategies for change were also under attack. John Lennon was part of a generation who found the world shifting under its feet. A number of songs by musicians raging on the edge of imminent tragedy were released in 1971, including 'Riders on the Storm' by The Doors. Other figureheads from the Sixties were being dragged down by personal angst or drug-propelled breakdowns, including Pete Townshend of The Who; in 1971 his work included 'Baba O'Riley', 'I Don't Know Myself' and 'Won't Get Fooled Again'.

In that same year it appeared that optimism and dreams were being replaced by hardcore negativity and sullen defiance. There was an escalation in the activities of urban terrorist groups like the Brigate Rosse in Italy, the Angry Brigade in Britain, and the Weathermen in America. In Germany the Red Army Faction (RAF), particularly its core faction, the Baader Meinhof gang, was fast becoming notorious. In May 1970, when the organisation, led by lawyer Horst Mahler, was still in its infancy, Ulrike Meinhof helped spring Andreas Baader from prison after he'd been arrested with Astrid Proll. Together with other members of the group, they fled first to East Germany and then on to a Palestinian training camp in Jordan; Palestinian groups had been responsible for many of the most ambitious terrorist operations over the previous eighteen months, including the destruction of three hi-jacked aircraft at an airfield in Jordan in September 1970. By the end of 1971, Mahler had been caught and imprisoned, but the Red Army Faction was now firmly committed to terrorism and the press dubbed the group 'the Baader Meinhof gang'. A decade of bombings and kidnappings was just beginning.

A sense of the uncertainty and violence of 1971 is plain to see in films of that year, like *Klute*, *A Clockwork Orange* and *Straw Dogs*; in the deaths of Edie Sedgwick and Jim Morrison; in the title and content of Marvin Gaye's LP *What's Going On*; and in the fear and loathing charted by Hunter S. Thompson in his drugged-up chronicle of life on the road serialised over two issues of *Rolling Stone* in November 1971.

The United States, supporting the South Vietnamese government in Saigon in attempting to prevent the North Vietnamese from extending Communism into South Vietnam, were taking, and inflicting, heavy losses. By 1971, official

casualty figures were confirming that over 50,000 American
soldiers had died since the war began, with nearly 300,000
sustaining serious injuries. B-52 bombers had dropped six
million tons of bombs on Vietnam (which amounted to two
hundred tons for every man, woman and child in the
country). As well as explosive bombs, the American Air
Force had also been using a variety of incendiary and anti-
personnel devices, including the skin-burning chemical
napalm, pineapple (cluster) bombs, and the carcinogenic
defoliant Agent Orange. Curtis LeMay, the Commander of
the Air Force, enthusiastically embraced new weapons technology. For him the aim was to blast North Vietnam 'back
into the Stone Age'.

In *The British Counter Culture 1966–73*, Elizabeth Nelson
writes about the underground press in this era, describing a
change in the atmosphere, a feeling that history was accelerating, and that the Sixties counter culture was helpless, dying:
'A new note of viciousness crept into the underground press,
a deepened sense of helplessness and despair, and an accom-
panying willingness to countenance violence and terrorism.'

It was time to wake up and smell the napalm. The counter
culture was stumbling into an era of rising drug use and widespread anger and despair, a bombed, stoned, fucked-up, tripping, going up, coming down world. Art was reflecting reality,
and extremism and terror. Ideologues – in the worlds of art,
film-making, music and the underground press – created a
decadent, outlaw culture motivated by a defiant, oppositional
attitude. There was a spirit of confrontation and experiment
in works by the likes of Living Theatre Company, and performance art also dramatised the sickness of the times: Chris
Burden crawled across floors covered with broken glass, while
Dennis Oppenheim encouraged audiences to throw stones at
him. In his 1971 work 'Trappings', Vito Acconci dressed his
penis in doll's clothes and spent three hours talking to it.

The driving forces in rock & roll in 1971 were noise, anger

and drugs. This was not only a vindication of the vision of
acts like The Velvet Underground, MC5, The Doors and The
Stooges, who had all been reacting against soft-centred hippy
attitudes on the margins of music for three, four years, but
also a great era for bands like Black Sabbath. The fuzzy anger
of their slum rock burst out of their lives in Aston, on the
outskirts of Birmingham city centre, where the band grew up,
tight knit, like a gang, all within one mile of each other. When
he was a teenager, singer Ozzy Osbourne spent a short time
in Winson Green prison for burglary, then worked in a slaugh-
terhouse before taking a job in a car horn factory.

There weren't any good jobs around. In the Victorian age,
Birmingham's factories and industrial workshops financed
grand buildings and civic pride, but in 1971 those days were
long gone. Crucial to this, the car plants of the West Midlands
– which had given cities like Birmingham and Coventry misplaced confidence and fragile prosperity in the 1960s – were
already in crisis. As the Seventies unfolded, increased and
efficient foreign competition, and rising energy prices, would
reveal the extent of the under-investment in car factories over
the decades, and leave the industry susceptible to a series
of damaging blows delivered by over-manning, trade union
disputes and poor management.

By the early 1970s, the West Midlands had a reputation
for far-right politics, with Enoch Powell arguably the most
influential politician locally. But the sense of despair in a
city adrift in the Seventies was heightened by the state of
Birmingham's built environment. As elsewhere, most of the
inner city was either boarded-up, blitz-damaged terraced
streets, or new estates of high rises and low expectations, but
the planners whose flawed visions had destroyed old terraced
street communities like Muswell Hill and Hulme in the 1960s
had also intervened in town and city centres. Birmingham
was the most depressing example in the country; during the
boom of the 1960s, the city centre had been flattened and

replaced by brutal office blocks and shopping precincts clad in grey concrete. An inner ring road strangled the heart of the city with flyovers and intrusive road systems, and pedestrians and shoppers were left to pick their way through windswept, damp underpasses.

To anyone growing up in Birmingham even in the late 1960s, it was obvious how far away the spirit of the city was from Carnaby Street or San Francisco. When the Seventies arrived, the city was on the skids. Blitzed and bombed-out, Black Sabbath's music was a powerful soundtrack to the wet fog and rain-washed concrete, but it also struck a chord more widely. The Black Sabbath track 'War Pigs' – from the 1971 LP *Paranoid* – wasn't the most precise analysis of American foreign policy in East Asia, but it had threat and doom, winding itself up with air raid sirens before launching into a relentless blitzkrieg of huge guitar riffs from Tony Iommi and apocalyptic vocals from Ozzy Osbourne.

In 1971 some of the brutality of Vietnam was revealed during the court martial of Lieutenant William Calley. He'd been investigated and arrested in connection with a massacre by American soldiers at My Lai in 1968, which for three years had grown from a dark rumour to a national scandal. At the end of March 1971, the conclusion of the court martial found him guilty of the premeditated killing of twenty-two Vietnamese civilians (altogether, it's believed that one hundred and nine civilians died in the massacre). Although twenty-five US soldiers were charged with war crimes in these years, Calley was the only one found guilty. It was said that violent abuse of civilians by US troops was endemic in the Army, and that the line between legitimate and illegitimate killing had been blurred.

Opposition to American involvement in Vietnam was growing, motivated by the suffering and the political drift, but also by a widely held suspicion that America and her allies were telling lies. America was confused, and the continuing slaughter and chaos in Vietnam, the horrific high-profile assassinations of the Sixties, and grim events like those at My Lai and Kent State, reinforced a view that somehow violence was at the heart of the American dream. In the words of Jim Morrison of The Doors, 'America was conceived in violence. Americans are attracted to violence.'

In the early 1970s an armed struggle was also being waged in Ireland. British troops were employed in increasing numbers against civilians, but civilians were also targeted by bombers. In Northern Ireland it seemed like both sides had signed up to the same strategy: for the state, and its opponents, violence was a solution.

The situation in Northern Ireland was just one of the problems for Edward Heath's Conservative administration. 'In Place of Strife' had broken down in the last few months of the Labour Government, and, as a result, and in an attempt to shore up electoral support, Wilson had relaxed wage restraints in the months leading up to the 1970 election. This had the effect of triggering an explosion of wage demands. So now Heath had to deal with inflationary pressures, alongside other, continuing threats to economic stability; notably wild-cat strikes, rising unemployment and a balance of payments deficit.

Tory plans to get to grips with the situation suffered a blow in July 1970 with the death of Iain Macleod, the Chancellor of the Exchequer. He was succeeded by Anthony Barber, who delivered a series of announcements in October 1970 which set out Tory policy for 1971 and beyond, coming down hard on inflation, cutting public expenditure and putting a freeze on wages. This hardline policy was reinforced by the Secretary of State for Employment, Robert Carr, who laid the groundwork for the Industrial Relations Bill, with its array of provisions aimed at reducing the effectiveness of the trade unions.

The boom years were gone, swinging London and full employment were finished, and industrial disputes were on the rise. The Bill was set for implementation in the first quarter of 1971, and in that period, days lost through strikes were four times the number in the same period the year before, and involved a wide variety of the workforce, including dockers, miners and electrical power workers. On 12 January 1971, the same day demonstrators in London were marching against the Industrial Relations Bill, the Angry Brigade bombed Robert Carr's home.

At the beginning of a year up to its throat in despair, violence and extremism, it's bordering on the absurd that the first No. 1 single of 1971 was something as tame as 'Grandad' by Clive Dunn, with its insistent mantra 'Grandad, you're lovely', although it would be unfair to blame Clive Dunn for the sickliness of the song; its co-writers were, in fact, Herbie Flowers and Ken Pickett (Pickett had been a member of the 1960s act The Creation and was also a Led Zeppelin roadie). Dunn later told the whole story to *Record Collector*: 'I was booked into every possible children's show. It was all plug-plug-plug, and Tony Blackburn decided it was his favourite record.'

There are various ways we could meet the challenge of accounting for the record's success in Britain, however, the first being the timing of its release – November 1970 – which aimed it squarely at the Christmas market, notorious for its love of sentimental or novelty records. It only missed topping the charts at Christmas because its sales surge was temporarily halted when striking power workers caused the closure of factories, including EMI's pressing plant.

Clive Dunn starred as Corporal Jones in the popular comedy series *Dad's Army*, and his prime time TV profile also boosted interest in the record. BBC TV helped push the record further, with a succession of *Top of the Pops* appearances by Dunn dressed as a croaky old grandad with a small choir of angelic children at his feet, which accentuated the reassuring wholesomeness of the project. There was appeal too in the record's nostalgic evocation of a sanitised, semi-mythical England. At a time when society was racked by conflict, those people who bought 'Grandad' for themselves or their children undoubtedly found the pull of a happy illusion – bowling hoops and spinning tops, innocent and respectful kids and contented old men – hard to resist. Worth remembering too is the status of grandads at the time; in many cases they were war veterans, which explains the warmth of feeling towards them. It's possible, too, that the record simply struck a chord because many grandads are indeed lovely.

1971 was a good year for bad records. Picking diamonds out of the dross has never been easy, but among the big-sellers, 'Brown Sugar' by The Rolling Stones, 'Stoned Love' by The Supremes, and 'Double Barrel' by Dave and Ansel Collins were worth cheering, as were brilliant singles by T-Rex, including 'Hot Love', 'Get it On' and 'Jeepster'. But the year that gave us records like 'Chirpy Chirpy Cheep Cheep' by Middle of the Road had started with 'Grandad' and ended with Benny Hill's 'Ernie (The Fastest Milkman in the West)', giving the lie to the nostalgic view that the music you'd hear all day on the radio was better back then.

In 1971 – according to musician, activist and rock & roll addict Mick Farren, in his memoir *Give the Anarchist a Cigarette* – the first Velvet Underground LP was 'starting to make a lot of sense', four years after the LP was released, and, ironically, a few months after the band had broken up (shortly after the release of their *Loaded* LP in September 1970). They had emerged via their connections with the bohemian artists, underground film-makers and drug addicts at Andy Warhol's Factory, and made their live debut in 1966 at 'Uptight', an evening presented by Andy Warhol which began with a showing of *Lupe* starring Edie Sedgwick (her eighth Warhol film).

The ten years from the late 1960s to the late 1970s saw a marked increase in the use of drugs, the spread of marijuana and LSD, the recreational use of tranquillisers and hallucinogens, the rise in cocaine use, and the arrival of new highs like angel dust (PCP). The California dreamers had flowers in their hair, but The Velvet Underground came out of New York with needles in their veins. Songs like 'Heroin' and 'The Black Angel's Death Song' replaced the promise of peace and harmony with discord and despair. *New Musical Express* described the band's music as 'the quintessential amphetamine soundtrack'. Injected methedrine, producing an ultra-strong charge of amphetamine, was a favoured drug of the band and their Warhol associates. In the film *Ciao Manhattan*, Edie is heard trying to describe both the nightmare and the ecstasy of the methedrine experience. It's a vicious high, she says, and 'fantabulous sexual exhilaration'.

Drugs had changed, society had changed, and just as music from the margins made an impact on the mainstream, so drug use penetrated the wider world, reflected and encouraged by the underground press. LSD, for example, had made an impact in 1965, then something of a breakthrough in 1967, around the time of the Monterey pop festival, when Jimi Hendrix performed high on double strength LSD especially made for him by Augustus Owsley Stanley III. The underground in England enjoyed Timothy Leary's light shows and the release of *Piper at the Gates of Dawn* by Pink Floyd, but Harry Shapiro in *Waiting for the Man* credits the Beatles LP *Sgt Pepper's Lonely Hearts Club Band* in June 1967 with galvanising the acid subculture and giving LSD an international profile. He also points to groups like The Grateful Dead who, he says, 'played music that was quite specifically aimed at those who used psychedelic drugs and marijuana'.

Other bands too – including Love and Jefferson Airplane – were a product and, to some extent, an embodiment of the drug culture. The Doors also had a close association with drugs, taking their name and influences from Aldous Huxley's psychedelic classic *The Doors of Perception*. Morrison had been studying theatre and film at college in Los Angeles; he wasn't a very successful student and was thrown off the course after a year. After college he took to swallowing acid like candy and began his first collaborations with Ray Manzarek. Together they enlisted drummer John Densmore, but on hearing the material Morrison and Manzarek had been working on, Densmore wasn't sure it was going to work. 'Their songs were really far out to me. I didn't understand very much,' he later recalled.

Jim Morrison perfected a studied sulk and pouty angst, railed against social hypocrisy and sexual repression, and loved to name-drop Rimbaud, Artaud and Céline. He was also influenced by Nietzsche's *The Birth of Tragedy* and claimed to identify with the qualities Nietzsche describes as 'Dionysian': disorder, permissiveness, emotional and social recklessness. Doors songs inhabited an idiosyncratic, warped world, somewhere between the dreams of Morrison's mind and the sleazy, uptight, druggy streets of Los Angeles.

The Doors appeared alongside The Who and Jimi Hendrix and the Band of Gypsies at the Isle of Wight in 1970, but their reputation in England was still mixed. They never received unanimous critical praise, although they have had support among some notable figures of the era, including the late Jeff Nuttall, author of *Bomb Culture*, who found them 'genuinely inspirational'. Mick Farren too; the Isle of Wight was the second time he'd seen The Doors and he loved their sense of theatre, intoxicated by Morrison's 'cocktail of shaman mysticism, Freudian darkness, radical politics, and horny guy in leather pants'.

The conscious attempts to cast off chains and experience extreme liberation included a belief that sexual repression was a burden that could be disturbed or removed by breaking taboos and shocking the bourgeoisie. The White Panthers had emerged in Detroit in 1968 and spread their beliefs via the MC5 and a manifesto; Clause Three declared 'Total Assault

on the Culture by any means necessary, including Rock
& Roll, Dope, and Fucking in the Streets'. John Lennon
viewed nudity as a political act, and Germaine Greer had
been extolling the virtues of 'Cunt Power'.

Certainly the puritan strain in mainstream society was so
strong that sexual display or sexual openness could cause
havoc. In Miami, in 1969, even more drunk than usual, Jim
Morrison was said to have whipped his cock out of his trousers
onstage. The FBI issued a warrant for his arrest, over thirty
Doors gigs were pulled by promoters across America, and
sensationalised versions of the story took the band to the front
pages of the newspapers. Moral disgust erupted, although perhaps Morrison would have got away with it if he'd done a
Vito Acconci and dressed his cock in doll's clothes and had a
conversation with it.

Jim Morrison revelled in the world of LSD, brandishing his
self-image as a dark poet, filling his songs with images of sex,
death, deserts, actors and the city at night. His music and
drugs were in unholy matrimony. One of the motivations for
the use of drugs in this era – especially LSD – was a desire to
break on through to the other side; psychedelic society was
founded on the promise of a drug experience which could
open up the doors of perception, reveal a great adventure,
new sensations, and another, better world beyond the dull-
ness of conformity and the easy choices of the mainstream.
There's a great Robert Crumb cartoon of two characters stuck
in a tiny box surrounded by rolling hills and far horizons, but
they're too hesitant to cut a hole and explore the world.

Live, The Doors hoped to achieve revelation and liberation
and discover a world of fantabulous sexual exhilaration. 'It's
a search, an opening of one door after another,' said Jim
Morrison. 'Through our music, we're striving, trying to break
through to a cleaner, freer realm.'

From 1967 to 1971, dangerous drug offences in Great
Britain doubled. By 1971 acid was endemic, having created

huge hopes but also an undercurrent of psychosis. It contributed to darkening skies and darker times, but it was embraced
by a new generation, treated with reverence, worshipped.
Paul Gilroy recalls the way LSD consumed the culture in the
early years of the Seventies. 'My hippie friends I was in bands
with, a lot of people, were tripping and it wasn't casual, it
wasn't just a casual adjunct to everyday life; they would
organise their weekends around their tripping adventures.'

The acid heads treated drug taking as something approaching a sacred rite, and believed in the life- and world-changing
powers of LSD. They would choose the most conducive venue,
the lighting, the music, the company. 'They would provide
elaborate entertainment and diversions that could support
that,' says Paul. 'And the music was really central to that.'

In 1971 Richard Nixon declared drugs to be 'America's
Public Enemy Number One'. In Britain, the last time drug
laws had been changed was 1966, when modifications were
made in order to outlaw LSD, but in 1971 the increasing
availability and range of drugs led to a major overhaul. The
Misuse of Drugs Act 1971 remains the cornerstone of Britain's
drug laws, superseding all previous legislation and setting out
a classification system for controlled substances which has
only recently been challenged and amended.

In the underground, the so-called 'head shops' were opening – stalls or stores where posters, drug-taking paraphernalia
and underground magazines were available. The underground press spread information about drugs, side effects, and
legal advice for any users arrested, and slang phrases, with
hidden and obscure meanings, had developed. Eugene E.
Landy's *The Underground Dictionary*, interpreting the doper
codes of the freaks and the soul brothers, was published in
1971 to enlighten the lames and squares of the mainstream.

But tensions were always present in the counter culture,
like those offstage at the Isle of Wight festival in 1970. Admission was £3 for five days of music, but the purists were

convinced that festivals should be free and that any kind of commercial intent seemed to contradict the ideals of the counter culture. A chapter of the White Panther Party was established specifically to oppose the Isle of Wight, and issued their own manifesto which claimed that the festival was 'an obvious example of capitalist interests, seeking to exploit the energy of the People's music'.

Half a million people attended, but only about a tenth of them had paid and the festival was marred by a series of violent stand-offs, with anarchists and Hell's Angels pulling down fences, fighting with security and avoiding the guard dogs. Even at the time these scenes were considered a symbol of the chaotic end of the counter culture.

The soft centre ideals of peace and love had been destroyed by pressure from two directions. On the one hand were those impatient, confrontational, nihilistic purveyors of what Nelson calls the 'new viciousness', but on the other a backlash was gathering, fuelled by the forces of reaction; from Mary Whitehouse to Richard Nixon. Elements in the underground press – let alone the likes of the Baader Meinhof gang – may have thought society in the Sixties had not changed enough, but deep in the establishment and the traditional mainstream, voices were arguing that the questioning, libertarian ideals of the Sixties had, in fact, gone too far. In 1971 we got a snapshot of these polarised attitudes during the *Oz* trial: *Time Out* called *Oz* 'the best and truest underground paper in the world', whereas to the *Sunday Express*, *Oz* was 'crude, nasty, erotic and debasing'.

Throughout the 1970s – and to the present day – the progressive, permissive Sixties have been targeted by traditional elements among the authorities, the police, and conservative and morally censorious Christian groups antagonistic to liberal law, who prefer hierarchy to equality and deference to dissent. As the backlash began, organisations emerged on the fringes of the Conservative Party specifically formed to counter attack, like the volunteer 'militia' Civil Assistance and the National Association for Freedom. In America, meanwhile, President Nixon harnessed the reactionary strain in the culture, and films like *Dirty Harry* played on populist aversion to pinkos and weirdos. It wasn't quite civil war, but it wasn't far off; in response to the early activities of the Weathermen, one police official declared, 'We now feel that it is kill or be killed.'

The new liberal laws were no guarantee of tolerance on the streets: gay bars were still secretive, and politicians and actors still feared being outed. The sense of a backlash against the women's liberation movement was also inescapable. In 1972 the gifted feminist poet Adrienne Rich was writing in the *New York Review of Books* about the emergence of fiercely anti-feminist, traditional, family-oriented female voices in academia and in the media.

One significant event in 1971 was a rally at Westminster Central Hall by the Christian group Festival of Light, campaigning against what it called 'the moral darkness of pornography, homosexuality and abortion'. Various figureheads of the morally censorious were present at the Festival of Light rally, including Mary Whitehouse of the National Viewers and Listeners Association, alongside Malcolm Muggeridge and Lord Longford. Mary Whitehouse – who had set up the National Viewers and Listeners Association in 1965 – appeared to stay up late every night throughout the 1970s, watching TV or reading every issue of *Gay News* in the search for something to offend her. She'd taken upon herself the role of defending Western democracy, which she defined using her own version of Christian values and moral purity rather than through the traditions of free speech and social pluralism.

With *Grass Eye* declaring, 'It's Us versus capitalism', the value of Lola and the Powerman as symbolic characters was increasing, as polarisation became more apparent. The confrontational stance taken by the Conservative Government revealed that there was nothing to replace strife; in Ireland sectarianism was murderous. On the shopfloor, on the streets, centrist positions were abandoned in favour of extremism, and the middle ground was pulled apart as radicals and reactionaries battled it out. The spirit of the 1970s was being defined by Loyalists versus Republicans, Richard Nixon versus Adrienne Rich, the FBI versus the Black Panthers, Regina versus *Oz*, and the White Panthers versus Mary Whitehouse. The freaks got freakier and the straights got tough.

When the Angry Brigade bombed the Biba boutique on 1 May 1971 it was a curious target, and an action unlikely to win them much support from any section of society. But the Angries believed that the revolution had been neutered by consumerism and that too many indifferent, politically unengaged hippies had replaced a commitment to cultural openness and anti-war politics with a trivial pursuit of cash, sex and drugs. Jerry Rubin had warned about the 'psychedelic businessman'. After the Biba bombing, the Angry Brigade issued a communiqué twisting a line from Bob Dylan: 'If you're not busy being born you're busy buying.'

A new generation of extremists took on not just the mainstream, but also the kind of soft-centred beliefs of the established counter culture as soundtracked by 'Imagine'. Clive Dunn was at the top of the charts for three weeks, and 'Chirpy Chirpy Cheep Cheep' was in the charts for more than six months, but out in the shadows there were performers projecting rage and a desire to challenge, though not all of them were as practised in the rhetoric of the times as Jim Morrison. 'Right now', he said, 'we're more interested in the dark side of life, the evil thing, the night time.'

Outrageous, roaring and incendiary rebel music had been made by the likes of The Velvet Underground, MC5, Black Sabbath and Led Zeppelin. Then there was Hawkwind; in 1971 they recruited Lemmy to the band. But possibly the group that best represents the years 1969 to 1971, certainly in America, is Iggy Pop and The Stooges. The American rock critic Lester Bangs was a big fan of The Stooges. On the release of their somewhat ironically titled second LP *Funhouse* in 1970, he could feel the full force of the group's visceral pull, their powerful remaking of rock & roll. The Stooges weren't just making a great noise; for Bangs, their music 'mirrors the absurdity, confusion and doubt of the times'.

They were soundtracking a state of emergency. Contributing to the appeal of The Stooges was singer Iggy Pop. The Stooges looked like a biker gang, enhanced by Iggy Pop's slightly faggy swagger and psychotic body language onstage. And among their fans in the early 1970s was one of our eye witnesses, Bob Dickinson. He was born in Reading in 1955 and moved to Congleton in Cheshire in 1970. At Sandbach School, Bob used to get beaten up: 'They didn't like me and kept on about me being a cockney. I come from fucking Reading!'

While at school he formed a band with his brother and some mates called House of Wax. 'In Congleton we couldn't get the drugs we read about,' he says, but they went to see Love play live and their music changed, got heavier and then heavier still. 'We were into the American stuff. The Stooges; it was just raw, it just felt like you felt.'

This rawness was a sign of the times, and a feature of films like Sam Peckinpah's *Straw Dogs* (1971) which went further than movies were expected to in its portrayal of rape and violence. The release of *A Clockwork Orange* was another indication of how viciousness was seeping through the culture. And in 1971, Roman Polanski was working on his film version of *Macbeth*, which would emerge as one of the darkest, most gory versions of Shakespeare ever produced.

Outside the cinemas, live venues, recording studios, performance spaces and arts labs, violence was at large. For decades, deference to authority was part of the mechanism that maintained order, but another sign of the times was how this was now breaking down. One of the causes of this process lay in the hands of the authorities themselves; the Vietnam war, the Kent State massacre, and ongoing scandals and institutional corruption had brought the police, democratic governments and the secret services into disrepute. Once flaws were exposed, these institutions looked fragile, untrustworthy and open to challenge.

Threatened, the authorities tried to face down the subversives, on the streets, in the media and in courtrooms. *International Times* was busted by a team of officers with a warrant issued under the Obscene Publications Act, who took away works by William Burroughs as well as manuscripts, subscriber lists and back copies of the paper. Two years later it was the turn of Special Branch, who raided *IT* under the impression that it was a front for the Angry Brigade. Mick Farren's memoirs include his account of the night the venue Middle Earth was raided by the Drug Squad, an incident he describes as 'social control': 'A preference for the "wrong" intoxicants was being used as an excuse to put a free-form cultural breakout back into the ordered box.'

In 1971 the English edition of Soren Hansen and Jesper Jensen's *The Little Red Schoolbook* faced prosecution. Aimed at teenagers, the book dispensed unconventional advice about drugs and sexual relations, and offered various challenges to the education system, established religion, capitalism and mainstream politics. Lawyer John Mortimer represented *The Little Red Schoolbook*'s publisher, Richard Handyside, in court, and drew parallels with the way the blasphemy laws had been used to imprison Chartists who sold the works of Thomas Paine. In any clash of ideas, the battle for the hearts and minds of the young is especially important, and schools, colleges and universities in this period were in flux.

At Sandbach School, not only was Bob Dickinson in the middle of a conflict between long hairs and soul boys, but he also stirred up trouble with a publication he put together with some friends, inspired by the underground and rejoicing in the title *Baggins*. The magazine satirised the school and was especially critical of the cadet force; Bob says: 'And we connected this with the militaristic style of the day, Northern Ireland, Vietnam.'

They published ten or fifteen issues of *Baggins* irregularly, for about a year, and Bob laughs a little about it all now. 'Some of it was a bit airy-fairy and some of it was hard-hitting, and there were poems, and record reviews as well, of course. It was modelled on many of the magazines you'd see around in the underground, although there was no "What's On" section or anything because there actually wasn't anything going on where we lived.'

The headmaster, Mr Bowles, took offence and banned *Baggins* from being sold in the school, so Bob and his friends took to selling it just outside the school gates. Eventually the headmaster began to publish his own, high-gloss, official magazine, extolling the school ('It was full of collaborationist nonsense,' according to Bob), and he also complained to Bob's mother. She was bewildered by the whole episode and said that Bob had fallen in with the wrong crowd.

Over thirty years later Bob is amused by the story, but unrepentant. 'It taught me what cans of worms could be opened if you knew how to do it.'

At school in Liverpool, Jayne Casey was moved to try other forms of rebellion. 'Oh God, I used to wear the shortest skirts and bend over in front of the teachers! I left school when I was fourteen. I was really naughty but I always used to come top in the exams and it used to drive the teachers crazy. They couldn't get it, they couldn't get hold of me but they knew I was really clever. And I left at fourteen and ran away from home.'

She ran away to New Brighton. 'It was the only place I'd ever seen with bright lights, away from the house that I lived in with my dad.'

She remembers there were still hippies around, and the first single mothers, and the first wave of heroin was just hitting Birkenhead. Boats still came in to Liverpool and Jayne came across a group of girls. 'They used to shag on the boats and they were all single mums and I used to babysit for them. I just used to move around between their houses. There was another girl who was a single mum who was a heroin addict and I used to look after her kids.'

On a night out Jayne used to go to a club called the Chelsea Reach in New Brighton and dance to T-Rex. She was angry with the ways of the world and could feel it, but had no real means of channelling those feelings. She tried out haircuts and tried to control her physical appearance. Later in the Seventies we would feast our eyes on Farrah Fawcett Majors, and adverts for Harmony Hairspray would be everywhere, so the pressure to be well groomed and easy on the eye increased, but Jayne would continue to prefer what she calls 'annoying haircuts'. Over the next few years she'll cut her hair in spikes, shave it all off again, get it dyed red, and then shaved again.

Over on the North-East side of England, Alex Patton was at school in Stockton-on-Tees. He was fifteen at the beginning of 1970. 'It's the weird thing because nowadays you look at it and all the young kids are supposed to have Darius and Will Young posters on their wall, but when I was at school in 1970 a lot of kids were into the likes of ELP, Genesis. They were into that sort of stuff. And I was a Doors fan.'

Looking back now, he thinks the majority of the lads were into what he calls 'avant-garde rock', even aged fifteen. 'Probably even before, when we were younger, 1969; I knew people then who were into Led Zeppelin.'

He'd already been drawn into the world beyond the Top 30. 'My sister got married and her husband was a total hippy and he used to bring me things like Frank Zappa albums, and got me into people like King Crimson in the Sixties, so even when I was fourteen or so I was into the weirder stuff. I even preferred The Byrds to The Beatles, and I never liked The Stones either.'

If that's what the lads were into, then Alex remembers how the girls were totally turned on by Marc Bolan and T-Rex. Bolan had taken a successful new direction in his career, jettisoning the Tolkien-soaked folk with, first, 'Ride a White Swan' in 1970, and then the 1971 singles, bursts of thrilling showbiz rock. His appearance wearing make-up on *Top of the Pops* in February 1971, when 'Hot Love' topped the charts, marked the beginning of the glam era.

1971 was also the year the music played at all-nighters in basement clubs and big halls in the Midlands, and the North of England was given the label 'Northern Soul'. Northern Soul fans were a significant tribe for the first half of the decade at least, but Alex never came across lads into soul music. 'No, I don't think there was anyone into Otis Redding or anything like that. We were pretty much all rockers. I never really met anybody into soul music; if they were they must have kept it quiet.'

Radio listeners had always had to work hard to find good music, tuning into the American Forces Network in the 1950s, Radio Caroline in the 1960s, and other pirate radio stations, including Radio London (which hosted John Peel's 'Perfumed Garden' show in 1967 before the station closed and Peel went to Radio One). Alex got into a lot of music via Radio Luxemburg. 'I got into a band called Audience; they were a great Seventies band, and the first time I heard Lindisfarne was when they played "Lady Eleanor" on Radio Luxemburg the first time it got released.'

In the early 1970s he was loyal to Luxemburg. 'I wasn't a big fan of Radio One, but people like Johnny Walker I had respect for – especially when he smashed a Bay City Rollers record live on radio – and "Fluff" Freeman, Alan Freeman, he was really popular – that was his Saturday show – and at night you'd have people like John Peel, Alan Black and Anne Nightingale. They were great, but still for me it was Radio Luxemburg.'

Conflict between youth tribes was intense in the Seventies, but in 1971 it was almost as if Alex was in a tribe of one: the biggest Doors fan in Stockton-on-Tees. Alex had heard 'Hello I Love You' by The Doors on Radio Luxemburg in 1968 and followed the band without ever becoming a devotee (he couldn't afford to buy LPs at the time). By 1971 he'd heard enough to know they were his favourite band. 'They were totally different to the other rock bands at the time, very dramatic.'

Like thousands of other record buyers, Alex was reacting to music on an instinctive level, but at first he knew little about The Doors. People like Jim Morrison and Lou Reed took rebellious attitudes to an extreme – a real bohemian, druggy, anti-authoritarian extreme – but not all of this communicated straightaway, and in any case, there's no certainty that Dionysian excess would necessarily make sense in Stockton-on-Tees, where a more prosaic view might be taken of some of Morrison's beliefs. Morrison liked to quote Blake's dictum that 'the road of excess leads to the palace of wisdom', but in the prosaic real world, the road of excess usually leads directly to the gutter.

Every week Alex read *Sounds*, *NME*, *Disc* and *Melody Maker*, but he had a sense that The Doors were outsiders. 'They still sell a lot of records and everyone has seen posters of Morrison, but The Doors were never that popular here at that time. Britain didn't need them, and then on the radio it was just poppy stuff; underground bands never seemed to get a look in. I'd go to teen parties and nobody even wanted to hear "Light My Fire".'

At teen parties you'd hear The Stones, T-Rex, Bowie, Led Zeppelin or The Faces (who, in 1971, had hits with 'Maggie May' and 'Stay With Me'). Britain also had its underground bands like Pink Floyd and the Edgar Broughton Band, some of whom were clearly influenced by The Doors, but some, like Yes, were soon travelling in a different direction when psychedelic went progressive.

In the months before his death, Jim Morrison and The Doors finished the *LA Woman* LP, and the last track the band recorded with him was 'Riders on the Storm', a tingling, atmospheric, hypnotic track and one of the band's best works. Morrison's 'rider' is the poet figure, the wanderer, an actor out on loan, carried along, surfing the storm; a Nietzschean 'übermensch' surviving the clash of cultures, halfway between Ziggy Stardust and Charles Manson.

Jim Morrison died in Paris on 3 July 1971 aged twenty-seven, suffering a heart attack in the bath, with suggestions that both heroin and alcohol had a part to play in his demise. He's one of a number of drug deaths in these years. Out of the public eye there were probably thousands of casualties; in the public eye, musicians like Gregg Allman and Eric Clapton were struggling with heroin habits, and others didn't survive. Brian Jones, Jimi Hendrix and Janis Joplin, for example, had already suffered drug-related deaths. In 1971, Neil Young wrote 'The Needle and the Damage Done'. Over the next three or four years, far from finding a freer realm and fantabulous sexual exhilaration, the following would all succumb to accidental deaths connected with drug use: Billy Murcia of The New York Dolls, Gram Parsons and Tim Buckley.

News of Jim Morrison's death emerged just after the first week of the *Oz* trial in London. In the capital, the summer of 1971 had been tense as the Angry Brigade bombings continued; the police computer at Tintagel House was hit, and, during a dispute at Ford's, the company's managing director's home was bombed. And in July, after it was announced that Upper Clyde Shipbuilders would close, the home of John Davies, the Secretary of State for Trade and Industry, was bombed.

The twenty-eighth issue of *Oz* had included a team of four-teen- and eighteen-year-olds in the art, editorial and writing processes. As usual with *Oz*, the tone was anti-authoritarian and questioning, and followed the usual formula: a mix of opinions, cartoons and features. The special issue featured writing by school pupils on subjects like music, drugs, sexual freedom and the education system.

The *Oz* obscenity trial was a clash of two Britains: the dissenting subversives and the authoritarian repressives. It also revealed the double standards and the political agenda of the police; the Obscene Publications Squad had clearly come to an arrangement with established Soho pornbrokers, allowing their shops free rein to trade in exchange for regular cash payments and other favours, whereas they had come down hard on *Oz*, *IT*, and the publishers of *The Little Red Schoolbook*.

On 23 June 1971, the trial started at the Old Bailey in front of Judge Michael Argyle QC (a relatively inexperienced judge who had twice attempted to become a Conservative MP without success). The editors, Jim Anderson, Felix Dennis and Richard Neville, were charged with conspiring to 'corrupt the morals of young children and other young persons' by producing and distributing 'obscene articles', and with publishing obscene articles for gain. Sentences for obscenity were relatively lenient, but the conspiracy charges raised the stakes; there was no limit on the fine or sentence that could be imposed.

The prosecution focused on one particular cartoon strip that had been put together by Vivian Berger, a fifteen-year-old schoolboy. He'd used part of a Rupert Bear cartoon which he'd fused with a strip by Robert Crumb. Defacing, using and abusing the likes of Mickey Mouse and Donald Duck had become accepted practice. In the hands of the young Berger, a sexually excited Rupert Bear is seen violating an (unconscious) mature female. Vivian Berger was matter of fact on the witness stand. 'I subconsciously wanted to shock your generation. Also, I thought it was funny,' he declared.

Once again, it was John Mortimer defending, and once again he tried to put the charge of 'obscenity' into context, calling his clients 'dissenters', believers in the freedom of expression and opponents of hypocrisy and social taboos. Over the next months, defence witnesses included George Melly, Feliks Topolski, Caroline Coon and John Peel, but some women felt that they couldn't support the cartoon. Nigel Fountain reports the views of Louise Ferrier in his book *Underground: the London Alternative Press 1966–74*: 'The arrogant, male, aggressive style of drawing that appeared in the name of revolution worried me.'

The jury retired to consider their verdict on 28 July, after a summing up by the judge, and found the defendants guilty. On 5 August 1971, after being refused bail, given haircuts, and kept in prison for a week while medical and psychiatric reports were prepared, the three editors were given a variety of fines, and prison sentences ranging from nine to fifteen months, but within a week the sentences were quashed on appeal and the judge's original summing up criticised for its partiality.

In the aftermath of the *Oz* trial it was clear that the authorities made a tactical error; persecuting dissenters can often make outlaw activity seem more attractive, and there was widespread public unease about the trial, even from those not normally disposed to support radical publications.

In retrospect, the trial also seemed to mark the end of an era for *Oz*; the magazine had had its day, and the dissenters and subversives had taken a wrong turn. In the underground, *Oz* was looking old fashioned, unable to keep pace with ever-evolving attitudes, especially the developing strength of feminism. The underground was changing, the world was changing. Late in 1973, the final issue of *Oz* included a piece entitled 'What Went Wrong?' by David Widgery: 'What finally knackered the underground was its complete inability to deal with women's liberation.'

The *Oz* defendants hadn't been unanimously supported by the underground, and the Biba bombing had been divisive; the splits in the counter culture had become debilitating. For example, tensions between the hedonists and the politicos at *Grass Eye* soon led to a splinter group of disenchanted contributors, including Sue Lear, Mike Don and Steve Curry, forming a new publication, *Moul Express* (it was soon renamed *Mole Express*). After several issues, *Mole Express* found its circulation dropping, and posted a request for comment and advice on the noticeboard at a shop called On the Eighth Day, and in issue fourteen reported back on the results. Readers had asked for more coverage of some of the music heroes, particularly Captain Beefheart, and had other requests – notably 'more porn' – which suggested that the agenda of revolutionary groups like the Angry Brigade wasn't widely shared. Other publications focused their political coverage on practicalities, like housing action, feminism or gay liberation. *Oz* had appealed to a wide readership, but the counter culture was now split into political factions, co-ops, communes, campaigning organisations and special interest groups. By the end of 1971, for example, *Gay Times* had a higher circulation than *International Times*.

Those struggling for political change were now in retreat. In August 1971 eight suspected members of the Angry Brigade were arrested, although the bombings continued with attacks on Albany Street army barracks and the Post Office Tower in London, and a bomb at the home of Chris Bryant, head of a building company in Birmingham, then in dispute with his workers. Meanwhile, Special Branch and MI5 made concerted efforts to infiltrate student groups, the Campaign for Nuclear Disarmament, and the National Union of Mineworkers.

In Western democracies, it's not unusual for those in political and economic power to label those questioning their legitimacy as 'subversive' or even 'unpatriotic'. In Britain and America, the security services considered Communists and pacifists the enemy within, and routinely harassed them with phone taps, surveillance and covert access to computer records and social security files. In America, COINTELPRO had been set up in 1956 by J. Edgar Hoover to monitor subversive elements within the USA; by the late 1960s they were focussing their attention on Communists and the Black Panthers (the latter were targeted with extreme violence; in December 1969, the FBI killed Fred Hampton and Mark Clark on a raid on a Black Panther HQ in Chicago, acting on information supplied by a government informer). In Northern Ireland, the secret services made a number of scandalous, not to say murderous interventions. In 1971 Alan Pakula's film *Klute*, starring Jane Fonda and Donald Sutherland, reflected a shadowy world of unseen forces and paranoia. The Angry Brigade communiqué had also railed against 'technology used against the people'. In their work 'Mean Machine', the Last Poets explored the use of what they called 'tricknology' to replace the truth with lies and to defeat free expression.

It took the Watergate scandal to reveal the true extent of surveillance culture. In June 1972 five burglars were charged with breaking into the Democratic National Committee HQ in the Watergate complex. Republican leader Richard Nixon denied knowledge of the break-in, but it emerged that it was part of a dirty tricks campaign in the election and that it had CIA help. For two years the scandal hung over America, until Nixon resigned the presidency in August 1974.

Western governments had told lies about Vietnam, but the Watergate scandal did most to encourage the spread of cynicism about politics and the belief that traditional institutions harboured corruption. In 1973, the film *Serpico*, about bent cops, struck a chord with cinema audiences and helped to launch the career of Al Pacino. Some of the covert activity proved ineffective, however; many of those involved in the Weathermen never served prison sentences as the evidence against them was deemed to have been gathered by COINTEL-PRO using illegal methods. Hoover was forced to realign his forces, announcing the official termination of COINTELPRO operations in April 1971.

Scandal and corruption in public institutions increased the cynicism of the citizens. In the months and years following the *Oz* trial, for example, the Obscene Publications Squad came under intense scrutiny. Home Secretary Reginald Maudling responded to accusations that the police were chasing down counter culture publications like *The Little Red Schoolbook* and *Oz* while leaving Soho pornographers untouched, by ordering an immediate inquiry. Head of the 'dirty squad', Detective Chief Inspector George Fenwick, responded by sending Maudling a confidential report justifying his action by claiming that the underground press was aimed at children and advocated 'the alternative society'; admitting, in effect, the political context of his pursuit of *Oz*.

Home Office civil servants, however, concluded that Fenwick's submission left a good deal to be desired, and then a further unofficial inquiry named seven Soho porn merchants who were said to be bribing senior police officers. Scotland Yard was forced to embark on a major anti-corruption drive, in which four hundred police officers were either imprisoned or suspended from the force. In addition, in 1973 several leading officers from the Drug Squad in London were charged with corruption; they were using tactics including favouring certain dealers in exchange for information on others, and rewarding informers with confiscated drugs.

Eventually, once Robert Mark became Commissioner of the Metropolitan Police, the Obscene Publications Squad was disbanded following a number of corruption trials which revealed how the squad had put old material seized in raids back into the trade, as well as accepting bribes.

Mr Justice Mars-Jones named George Fenwick as the 'chief architect' of the corruption ring and jailed him for ten years.

During the first few years of the Seventies, offshoots of the underground press, the counter culture, collectives and communes were developed, but a sense of the underground's failure hardened. This failure was the subject of Howard Brenton's 1973 play *Magnificence*. *The Party* by Trevor Griffiths, in the same year, also concerned itself with the unravelling of the Sixties generation. The dream of an 'alternative culture' was over, according to Brenton, who said it had been 'strangled to death'.

As well as laying themselves open to charges of using anti-democratic means to maintain democracy, throughout the 1970s Conservative politicians continually exploited fears that liberal permissiveness was causing social chaos. The backlash represented by the Festival of Light would find a champion later in the decade in the form of Margaret Thatcher.

Meanwhile, after the decline of *Oz*, the failure of the Angry Brigade, commercialisation neutering alternative culture, and splits and fragmentation, another turning point came in 1972 when the miners' strike revealed fundamental differences between the underground and traditional Labour left politics. Mick Farren knew that working class guardians of conformity had enjoyed beating up long hairs, and, even more significantly, he claimed that the miners were missing the point, later defining his position like this: 'Why destroy ourselves in the dark satanic mills when the new Jerusalem was so obviously there for the building?' For Farren there's no innate virtue and no dignity in 'mind-numbing labour', and he even accuses the old left of 'homophobia and cultural benightedness'.

Later in the decade, Alex Patton, having begun a career as a civil engineer in Stockton-on-Tees, would encounter industrial strife routinely, but in 1971 he was more preoccupied by the news of Jim Morrison's death, which he heard from a friend who had read that week's copy of *Sounds*. 'He showed me the front cover and to be honest I didn't believe it, I was like "No chance!" I mean, at the time rumours would fly around every week that Paul McCartney had died!'

When he heard the news confirmed on the radio a day or two later, he was annoyed. He'd put a lot of emotional investment into the band and then the guy went and died. 'Yeah, and I think it was because I wanted to see them play and the chance had gone.'

Within weeks of Morrison's death, 'Riders on the Storm' was in the Top 20 singles chart. Alex recalls the record's appeal. 'I came across the full seven-minute version on a jukebox in a big rock pub in Newcastle called the Haymarket. When I heard the seven-minute version it blew my mind away. Of all The Doors' songs I think "Riders on the Storm" is the one that made the biggest impression on this country.'

Heavy psychedelic rock, the works of The Doors, Iggy Pop, and The Velvet Underground, were all crucial inspirations for post-punk in the last years of the Seventies. The Velvet Underground were certainly one of the most influential acts of the decade, and singer Lou Reed remains an iconic figure. Lester Bangs once said that he belonged to the generation for whom The Velvet Underground were 'our Beatles and Dylan combined'.

The evening of 'Uptight' was the beginning of Warhol's alliance with The Velvet Underground, but the end of his relationship with Edie; she slid away into psychiatric troubles and struggles with drug dependency. Her final film, *Ciao Manhattan*, was finished in 1971, just a few months before she died of 'acute barbiturate intoxication', according to the coroner, who wasn't able to establish the exact circumstances of her death.

By 1971, Andy Warhol had become proprietor of *Interview* magazine. An early issue featured Patti Smith, who we'll later see had a role to play in bridging the beatnik, bohemian world of the Warhol years with the beginnings of punk with her 1975 debut LP *Horses*. In 1971 her act was a mixture of confrontational poetry, dissonant music and performance art. She was becoming a recognisable figure in New York's boho circles: 'I was pretty infamous at the time; there wasn't anybody hotter looking than me in New York in 1971, you ask anybody. It was the Keith Richards look.'

After his death, interest in Jim Morrison's theories and philosophies grew. However, not everything his fans discovered was convincing, as Alex admits. 'I'm still not really into his poetry and I'm not into the more philosophical side of Morrison, and to me a lot of it is garbage, but now I know what a smart guy he was. At the time nobody was interested in whether the rock stars were smart or not. The Doors, Led Zeppelin; they were bands who were young, sexy, with great stage shows playing kick ass rock music. That's what we were into; that was it.'

From Newcastle to Liverpool, Manchester to Birmingham, bands like Led Zeppelin and Black Sabbath flourished, bands clearly not in the business of making silly love songs. Their appeal was possibly too raw for some of the more cerebral music critics to appreciate, but in 1973 journalist Andrew Weiner went to see Black Sabbath at the Rainbow and reported back to *Rock File*. He defined Sabbath as one of the 'ultimate teenage wasteland bands', and analysed their thrilling appeal to a young generation of lads working in 'dead-end factory jobs'. 'England always was a teenage wasteland, particularly in places like Birmingham and all points north,' he writes, relating Black Sabbath to 'the English experience' (which he defines as 'casual street fighting and mind-numbing boredom').

Led Zep would go on to become one of the biggest-selling LP bands in history. Black Sabbath's 'Paranoid' would remain an anthem for the rest of the decade, while 'War Pigs' would come to be regarded as one of heavy metal's first great classic tracks. Meanwhile, posthumously, the profile of Jim Morrison would rise. Alex understands this: 'It's always the same. Everyone says that the best career move an artist can make is to die; it's stupid but it's true.'

'The End' by The Doors made a stunning contribution to the 1979 film *Apocalypse Now*, and the band were the subject of a biopic treatment in the hands of film-maker Oliver Stone. Morrison posters and t-shirts are on sale from Tokyo department stores to Balearic street markets, and his grave in a Paris cemetery has become a place of pilgrimage. The music of The Doors has crossed borders and generations, and, in some countries, Jim Morrison's life and look is still the classic definition, even the classic cliché, of a rock star: the pout, the leather trousers and the druggy excess. A version of The Doors, featuring original members Ray Manzarek and Robbie Krieger, has been on a barely-acclaimed tour in recent years, with Ian Astbury taking the Jim Morrison role, although back in 1971 Iggy Pop was considered a possible replacement for the late singer. Iggy Pop never did get that particular gig, although he later revealed that he'd been given a suitcase full of Morrison's clothes, including the hat Morrison wore in Miami in 1969 and various pairs of trousers; he ended up selling them for methadone.

CHAPTER THREE

'Freddie's Dead' (1972)

In the 1960s the civil rights struggle in America was a significant story, but as the promises of the decade started to unravel, another chapter in the story began, without the optimism and idealism. The late 1960s and early 1970s were momentous years for the black community in America, but the ideas and images also crossed the Atlantic. No-one could ignore the cultural impact of the black power salutes of athletes Tommie Smith and John Carlos at the Mexico Olympics in 1968, or the swaggering pimp and gangster attitudes in the 1972 film *Superfly*; the assassination of Dr Martin Luther King in Memphis in 1968; or the trial in California of activist Angela Davis in February 1972. The soul music of that era articulated the turbulent times, and the likes of James Brown, Aretha Franklin, Marvin Gaye and Curtis Mayfield made a sacred, enduring connection with British youth.

That the civil rights movement was unable to sustain the high ideals of the Sixties was part of the drift away from optimism towards negativity that we've already seen developing in the first years of the 1970s. The war in Vietnam – a worldwide symbol of the violence and conflict of the times – was a significant factor, destroying hopes and heightening despair. Throughout the world, powerful images from South-

East Asia appeared nightly on news broadcasts; so too the activities of the anti-war movement in America, burning up the campuses, marching against war.

At home in North London, as far as Paul Gilroy was concerned, being drawn into the counter culture and the music of the time – reading *Rolling Stone*, seeing Jimi Hendrix at the Isle of Wight – a sense of the war in Vietnam was always present: 'And that sense of America as the big beast – in many ways like the America that's emerged now – the big beast in the world, and us being in solidarity with the people who were trying to defeat that military machine.'

Most soldiers who went to serve in Vietnam were from working class rather than middle class backgrounds, and black Americans served in disproportionate numbers; during some periods of the war, 60 per cent of all eligible blacks were serving, but only 31 per cent of whites. The 1970s witnessed some of the repercussions of this racial inequality, as the atmosphere in the ghettos of the USA deteriorated, and economic recession, post-Vietnam trauma, drugs and crime took hold, creating one of the defining features of life in the 1970s: the ruinous state of urban neighbourhoods.

Soul music tracked the concerns of the black community through all these changes. Ten years ago, Chuck D of Public Enemy described hip hop as 'the CNN of black America', but, under-represented in the mainstream press and television, the black population of America had long before discovered the value of music as a means of disseminating ideas. Writer and critic Nelson George, for example, describes black radio stations in the 1950s as 'bulletin boards'. Modern jazz had always found significance deep in society. Miles Davis once described what the music of John Coltrane in the mid-1960s represented to the young black intellectuals and revolutionaries of that time: 'He played what they felt inside and were expressing through riots. Coltrane was their symbol, their pride; their beautiful black revolutionary pride.'

In the mid-1960s, soul music's messages were generally upbeat – soul music in that period reflected a dream that change was gonna come – whereas the blues had represented desperation and a struggle for assertion, and the new jazz had represented revolution. Coltrane himself had a genuine belief in the emancipatory power of music, telling Frank Kofsky in 1967, 'Music is an instrument. It can create the initial thought patterns that can change the thinking of the people.'

Although the soul singers of black America were articulating concerns close to home, their music made an impression far afield. In the 1960s, James Brown had iconic status in the black community in Britain, even though his music had a low profile in the mainstream. Paul Gilroy remembers how difficult it was to hear what he wanted on the radio, and how few places catered for this demand until the 1970s. 'I started going out into that world in the early 1970s when funk had a shape to it and became very attractive.'

As the young Paul Gilroy moved through these worlds of music, he was aware that some of the most enthusiastic consumers of funk and soul music were white listeners. The connection between tracks recorded by black musicians on the other side of the Atlantic and young British whites has deep roots, partly produced by a perception that the dominant culture in English life is complacent, safe, passionless. In the 1920s, the young took to jazz, revelling in its urban exuberance. Forty years later, The Rolling Stones grew up in an environment where blues musicians like Chuck Berry and Muddy Waters were worshipped.

The blues had a passionate following, particularly among white middle class lads, eager young men attracted to the songs and stories of Robert Johnson, Muddy Waters and Son House. 'It was a remarkable feature for that time, a lot of people defining their distance from the centre of English life by that,' says Paul Gilroy. 'I can remember going round to my friend's house around Christmas 1968 and his brother was still asleep at twelve o'clock and his big brother wakes up and puts on a Son House record.'

In the early 1960s, mods revered jazz, r&b, soul and reggae, and The Beatles had obviously spent months listening to Motown and Chuck Berry. Otis Redding was a star turn on *Ready Steady Go!*, and a network of semi-secret soul clubs in London, Liverpool and Manchester thrived, among them the Twisted Wheel in Manchester. The Wheel opened in 1963 on Brazennose Street, hosted by Roger Eagle. He booked acts like John Lee Hooker and Screaming Jay Hawkins, and his record selection – a mix of r&b and reggae – was devoured with enthusiasm by music aficionados.

Over in Detroit, Motown HQ was aware of the enthusiasm for r&b and soul among musically-minded kids of Britain; this compared favourably with the situation in the USA where record buying was likely to take place along clearly defined racial lines. Not that Britain was a particularly tolerant place. In fact, at a time when landlords could advertise accommodation with the sign 'No Blacks', employers could discriminate against black job seekers, and police surveillance of multi-racial areas was encouraged by the authorities, the development of such a passion for soul music among white working class youth in basement clubs in London, Liverpool and Manchester is remarkable.

If anything, the alliance between black music and white youth strengthened in the early 1970s. Youth culture had taken a new, psychedelic rock direction in 1967, but a good number of mods, r&b fans and Twisted Wheel regulars resisted the lure of long hair, LSD and The Grateful Dead, and instead maintained a purist devotion to the hard-driving dance beats of the Detroit soul sound. The Twisted Wheel moved to new premises at 6 Whitworth Street, and Roger Eagle departed, but the Wheel was thriving in the first years of the Seventies, a warren of dark rooms full of dedicated dancers and amphetamines. During a visit to the Twisted Wheel in 1971, journalist

Dave Godin coined the phrase 'Northern Soul'; he'd picked up on the enthusiasm of white soul music fans, especially in the Midlands and the North of England.

Into the 1970s, many Northern Soul fans would address themselves as 'brothers' and 'sisters', and the International Soul Club (based in Staffordshire) produced cloth badges for its 40,000 members which depicted Black Power's clenched fist salute. Some of this may have been naive, but in the context of a decade in which Enoch Powell had a major influence and the National Front made electoral gains, it's another sign of how disparate attitudes could be.

Meanwhile, after establishing and then leaving the Wheel, Roger Eagle first moved to a venue called the Blue Note, and then on to the Stax Club on Fountain Street, named in honour of the Stax label. Stax had a low profile in Britain – although, up until his death, Otis Redding had been a big star – and even later Stax releases, like singles by The Dramatics, or Jean Knight's classic 'Mr Big Stuff', missed out on radio play in Britain. But Stax, rather than Motown, was one of the labels of choice for the soul cognoscenti.

Stax Records, originally white-owned, was founded in Memphis in 1960 by Jim Stewart and his sister Estelle Axton (the label was named using the first two letters of their respective surnames). Memphis wasn't some music backwater; in the 1950s, local white hillbilly and rhythm & blues from the black side of the tracks had come together, and the resulting musical miscegenation fed early rock & roll as young white stars like Elvis Presley were drawn to the city to record for Sam Philips at Sun Studios. At Stax, white musicians – guitarist Steve Cropper and bass player Duck Dunn – joined black organist Booker T. Jones and drummer Al Jackson in the Stax in-house band, Booker T & the MGs. They backed Otis Redding and Wilson Pickett, and built Stax a reputation for soul music that was rawer than Motown. In the words of Steve Cropper, 'It was a Southern sound, a below-the-Bible-belt sound. It was righteous and nasty. Which to our way of thinking was pretty close to life itself.'

By the mid-1960s there were other voices being heard alongside the hopeful, gospel-tinged soul of 'A Change is Gonna Come' and 'People Get Ready'. Nina Simone's song 'Mississippi Goddam', for example – written in the wake of the 1964 Civil Rights Bill which dismantled some of the structures of apartheid in America – is a passionate plea reflecting the same angry impatience that lit the fires of rebellion in areas like the Watts district of Los Angeles, the scene of major riots in 1965. Precipitated by police brutality, the Watts riots resulted in three weeks of conflict, rioters chanting 'Burn, baby, burn', huge devastation of property and thirty-four deaths.

Attitudes hardened in the wake of the assassination of Martin Luther King on the balcony of the Lorraine Motel in Memphis on 4 April 1968 (coincidentally, just a few blocks from the Stax headquarters). Just three days after Dr King was killed, Nina Simone recorded 'Why? The King of Love is Dead'. Unsettling reverberations can be heard in much of the soul and funk of the post-King era, echoes and whispers of spacey psychedelia, fear and paranoia down in the darkest depths; and in the productions of Norman Whitfield for The Temptations, Tony Hester for The Dramatics, in the work of Sly Stone, and in songs like '(Don't Worry) If There's a Hell Below We're All Going to Go' by Curtis Mayfield.

Curtis Mayfield had shifted focus. Whereas many of the songs he had written for The Impressions in 1964 and 1965 – 'Keep on Pushing' and 'People Get Ready' – were clearly driven by the optimistic gospel of black betterment, songs like 'This is My Country' and 'Choice of Colors' revealed new notes of bitterness, a sense of the promised land disappearing, and a hardened heart in the face of the unyielding nature of US society. Curtis Mayfield had an engagement with the world and a musical gift which would also deliver potent songs, describing and defining the deteriorating conditions of life in American cities in the first years of the 1970s.

In Britain, the death of Martin Luther King was a blow to the idealists of all persuasions, but was naturally felt especially hard in the black community. Although Enoch Powell didn't hold back from his message of racial conflict, other voices mourned Dr King's death; after a CND demo in Trafalgar Square, hundreds of marchers went to an impromptu tribute at St Paul's Cathedral. In Germany, however, a man 'inspired' by the assassination shot dead student leader Rudi Dutschke, sparking major riots by left-wing students.

James Brown kept his fans in South London on the dancefloor with great party music, but the messages in songs like 'Say It Loud (I'm Black and I'm Proud)' were darker and less carefree than his earlier work. One of the most irresistible James Brown grooves in this era, the 1969 track 'I Don't Want Nobody to Give Me Nothing (Open Up the Door I'll Get It Myself)' is clear in its assertiveness and impatience, looking not just for a way out of the ghetto, but demanding tangible change, and a slice of the capitalist cake.

One man who shared this faith in black capitalism was Al Bell. Stax had employed Bell as promotions manager, nurturing the good will of radio stations and shop owners, and he emerged as a key player in the company after a slump in their fortunes. By 1968, a distribution deal with Atlantic had proved problematic, Otis Redding had died, and, following the death of Dr King, the atmosphere at Stax HQ had changed. Cropper felt excluded. Isaac Hayes, who had marched in Memphis with Dr King, was despairing: 'I went blank. I couldn't write for about a year; I was filled with so much bitterness and anguish I couldn't deal with it.'

A wedge had been driven between the black and white members of the Stax family. In 1969 Estelle Axton severed her connections with the company and Jim Stewart began to take a back seat. Some other key characters began to drift away, and rumours surfaced of gang-related violence and intimidation; Bell himself was at various times said to be a victim of racketeers. Stax adopted a new logo and made a new start as a black-owned label, with Bell taking Stax towards a more politically engaged position, financing a reprint of the SNCC's manifesto 'All Roads Must Lead to Revolution', and using a Stax subsidiary label, Respect, to release a spoken-word featuring Reverend Jesse Jackson.

After Dr King's death, the Christian community's vision of non-violence seemed inadequate, and the Black Panthers came centre stage, although they had already been gathering support from those seeking radical solutions. Angela Davis, for example, had already joined the organisation, having experienced the extreme racism of the Ku Klux Klan growing up in Birmingham, Alabama. Writer Mark Anthony Neal expressed it like this: 'The Panthers articulated the rage that King was either incapable or unwilling to expose.'

In the last year of the Sixties, a total of twenty-seven Black Panther party members were killed by the police in a series of murders, shootings and assaults on black prisoners. Suppression of African-American dissenters, and the Black Panthers in particular, continued into the Seventies. In January 1970, three black prisoners were shot dead when a prison guard opened fire during a fight in the exercise yard at Soledad prison. When an investigation into the three deaths announced a verdict of 'justifiable homicide', a riot erupted and a white guard was set upon and killed. Three prisoners were arrested for his murder; they became known as the Soledad Brothers, and one, George Jackson, was sentenced to death. Then, some seven months later, as part of a plan to force the release of the Soledad Brothers, Jonathan Jackson (George Jackson's brother) led an attempt to kidnap Judge Harold Haley and take four other hostages in a courtroom in California. The police moved in and during the gunfight

Jackson and two of his accomplices were shot dead; the judge also died during the shoot-out.

The backdrop to all this, the Vietnam war, demanded a direct response too, and the burning of draft cards, demonstrations and dissent built steadily through the Sixties. In the music fraternity, by 1970 even those not known for their political beliefs were responding. Motown, for example, had been releasing some of the sweetest two-and-a-half-minute singles ever released – the likes of 'Stop! In the Name of Love' and 'Bernadette' – but an edge appeared in their output, although the new direction was pioneered by producer Norman Whitfield rather than Motown boss Berry Gordy. Whitfield was the power behind Edwin Starr's classic anti-Vietnam song 'War' (1970), and with The Temptations he addressed a world of segregation and humiliation in songs like 'Ball of Confusion (That's What the World is Today)'.

The anger on the streets was reflected throughout the soul world. Largely powered by the vision of the Chicago-born songwriter and producer Eugene Record, The Chi-Lites had hits in 1969 with ballads like 'The Twelfth of Never', but the changing atmosphere got to them. Marshall Thompson from the group was interviewed in 1974 by journalist Tony Cummings, and explained the change of direction in 1970 which had led to the release of the band's single '(For God's Sake) Give More Power to the People': 'We needed to broaden our sound. Up until then we'd choose mainly ballads. Sweet things. There was a lot of unrest and injustice in the world and we all felt that artists couldn't ignore that situation and sing just about love.'

1972 was a critical time, as the Afro-American community felt the pressure of Vietnam, riots and urban decay. With drug use rocketing and rising unemployment, civil rights protests dissolved into despair and confusion, and music documented and articulated the change. The same era is also the backdrop to the 1995 film *Dead Presidents*, an interesting and enlightening take on the black experience in urban America in the early 1970s.

We first meet the film's main character, Anthony Curtis (played by Larenz Tate), at home in the Bronx in 1968, a teenager with limited options but a zest for life. By 1971 he's in the Marine Corps in Vietnam, taking part in gruesome reconnaissance operations. Within months, the situation in Vietnam had deteriorated. American policy in the region was in disarray, with President Nixon and National Security Adviser Kissinger extending the war, including a major escalation of the bombing campaign against North Vietnamese targets. But by August 1972 Kissinger was also in secret peace talks with his North Vietnamese counterparts in Paris; over the next few months the war would stumble towards an untidy, violent conclusion.

The love for Detroit soul shown by the Twisted Wheel DJs was one small example of the way in which, throughout the Seventies, popular culture was creating links between Britain and America. There were some common experiences: pot smoking and denim were rampant internationally; manufacturing cities like Detroit and Manchester were both experiencing severe economic downturns; English rock bands like Led Zeppelin were huge in the States, while bands like Fleetwood Mac began to develop something approaching a transatlantic image; as did Rod Stewart – post-Faces – and Eric Clapton (on his *461 Ocean Boulevard* LP in 1974). Later in the decade, punk emerged out of a dialogue between malcontents in New York and London.

In the USA, however, there was one experience not shared this side of the Atlantic: the return of soldiers from Vietnam. A few lucky veterans settled back into a good life, most suffered stress and a sense of dislocation, and many also joined an organisation called Vietnam Veterans Against the War, questioning the policies of the Government. In 1972, Ron Kovich, with five other members of Vietnam Veterans Against the War, disrupted the Republican Convention in Miami in August, producing much publicity for the cause, including an extensive interview with Kovich in *Rolling Stone*.

It was also in 1972 that Paul Schrader began working on his screenplay for *Taxi Driver*; featuring a Vietnam veteran Travis Bickle – the Robert De Niro character – battling his past, the world around him and his rage. After Martin Scorsese had directed the film, he went on record with this analysis: 'It was crucial to Travis Bickle's character that he had experienced life and death around him every second he was in south-east Asia. Travis Bickle was affected by Vietnam; it's held in him and then it explodes. And although at the end of the film, he seems to be in control again, we give the impression that any second the time bomb might go off again.'

Returning veterans were unlikely to be convinced that they were back in a land fit for heroes, and Travis Bickle certainly feels this strongly, railing against the pimps and hustlers (the 'scum') on the streets of New York. Afro-American Vietnam veterans also had every reason to feel cynical, having served in disproportionate numbers, despite widespread criticism of the war by prominent black figures, including Mohammad Ali and Martin Luther King (in 1967 King criticised the way the war had directed finance and focus from inner city welfare to international warfare). In *Dead Presidents*, when Anthony Curtis announces his intention to go to Vietnam, one of the other black kids in his neighbourhood tells him, 'This ain't our war.'

By 1973 we see Anthony Curtis back in the Bronx after serving his tour of duty, but during his years away the neighbourhood has changed and he's adrift. His fellow ex-GI and best friend is in a worse state: he's a junky. If they came back at all, the black soldiers who had fought for Uncle Sam returned to hopelessness. Back in the world, Anthony Curtis – haunted by nightmares, in a last effort to support his family – turns to crime, planning an armed robbery on a cash-carrying bank truck.

The notion of a ghetto had a racial dimension in America, and a history going back at least into the 1950s, as large numbers of black workers left the Southern States for the big cities looking for work; at the same time that black families were moving into cities, so whites were moving out of the central core to the outlying suburbs. As a result there was a net loss of population in cities like Chicago and Detroit, and ghetto neighbourhoods of low-income black families became a common feature. The National Advisory Commission on Civil Disorders investigated the Detroit riots of 1967 and reported, 'The ghetto too often means men and women without jobs, families without men, and schools where children are processed instead of educated, until they return to the street – to crime, to narcotics, to dependency on welfare, and to bitterness and resentment against society in general and white society in particular.'

The further deterioration in the state of urban ghettos in the early 1970s could be tracked by statistics relating to falls in the population of the core area of cities, and rises in unemployment, one-parent families and drug use. But this despair had a soundtrack too – two classic examples are Donny Hathaway's 'The Ghetto' (1970) and 'Ghetto Child' (1972) – and it also had a physical shape; an urban landscape broken and failing.

In the first years of the 1970s there was evidence that, as a way of life or a means of organising society, cities had failed. The American ghetto had extreme and particular causes and conditions, but the ghetto experience was felt internationally. Cities had been built on the migration of workers to areas promising employment in the large scale manufacturing industries – whether those migrants were from the American South, or the hundreds of thousands of workers from rural England, Ireland, Eastern Europe and parts of Scotland who had poured into English cities in the nineteenth century – but now cities were falling apart as economic activity dwindled and those jobs disappeared. Additionally, we have already seen how poorer families had been buffeted by the experience of slum clearance in Britain, and how cities like Birmingham were subject to upheaval and urban blight. This urban trauma is key to understanding the Seventies; later in the decade we'll see how hip hop and punk – both responses to recession-hit post-industrial life – reflected, but also, crucially, remade urban experience.

Marvin Gaye's LP *What's Going On* articulated inner city blues, political and racial confusion and environmental destruction. Songs on the LP linked the demise of black family life with the destruction in Vietnam, but in all the pleas to save the children, questions to brothers, and words of comfort to mothers, there are no answers. In the ghettos, the ideologies powering civil rights had been uprooted like road signs fallen in a hurricane, and there was no clear direction.

There were always some activists in the black movement who saw their struggle as an aggressive, macho activity – the sisters were often sidelined, or even denigrated – and female soul singers had a valuable role in tempering this, although their most pressing battle was probably with male chauvinism in the music industry. Vicki Anderson, Lyn Collins, Marlena Shaw, Linda Jones and Candi Staton were all doing great work, giving witness and being heard. Jean Knight's 'Mr Big Stuff' (1971) and Betty Davis's 'Anti Love Song' (1973) were among songs that put men firmly in their place. Esther Phillips too; her 1972 LP *From a Whisper to a Scream* includes a brilliant version of Gil Scott Heron's 'Home Is Where the Hatred Is'.

Among many women writers of the time there was a determination to document and to validate their experience with personal tales and autobiographical narratives. Complementing the work of the great female soul singers was a surge in black female writing in the early 1970s, including particularly novels by Toni Morrison and poems and short stories by Alice Walker. It was an era of re-evaluation; in 1972 John Berger was rewriting the agenda and language of art criticism in *Ways of Seeing*.

One black female who hadn't been sidelined was Angela Davis. In 1972 she went on trial, charged with supplying guns to Jonathan Jackson and – in aiding Jackson's bid to free George Jackson – conspiracy to murder, and kidnapping. Davis had already become notorious, having been dismissed from her work at the University of California in San Diego after the intervention of Governor Ronald Reagan, who accused her of subversion. Davis was unashamed and unrepentant: 'When people start saying that we are subversive, we should say, "Hell, yes, we are subversive; hell, yes, and we are going to continue to be subversive until we have subverted your whole damn system of oppression – hell, yes!"'

Like the *Oz* trial in London in 1971, the Angela Davis trial in 1972 revealed a clash of cultures, but race was a key ingredient in the latter case. The Black Panthers were a controversial organisation, but the violent suppression they had suffered at the hands of the authorities had delivered them the sympathy of a wide section of the black community. Although now chiefly remembered for their belief in an armed struggle, the Panthers also ran breakfast schools in the poorer parts of the major cities which bolstered this support and drew young people to their cause. In the late 1960s, a teenager who would go on to become a soul music superstar began hanging out at a Black Panther programme in Chicago and met and admired Fred Hampton, among others. Under the influence of their teachings she changed her name from Yvette Marie Stevens to Chaka Khan.

Well before the trial itself, supporters of Angela Davis campaigned against what they considered her victimisation, citing the fact that she'd been refused bail. For fourteen months in the Marin County prison, she was forbidden from communicating with other prisoners and granted just two exercise sessions a week. *The Times* described her as 'a symbol

of resistance'. In a further twist to the story, during her detention, George Jackson was shot dead during an alleged escape
attempt, although there was a widespread belief that the
prison authorities had conspired to have him killed.

In one of the most intriguing meetings of the decade, mid-
Ulster MP Bernadette Devlin visited Angela Davis during this
pre-trial detention. Even though the visit pre-dated her high-
profile intervention after Bloody Sunday, Bernadette Devlin
was already playing a leading role in the Catholic minority's
campaign for civil rights in Northern Ireland and was visiting
the States on a lecture and fund-raising tour. She left the
meeting describing the conditions in the jail as 'scandalous',
and declared her support for the 'struggle against political
oppression' being waged by Angela Davis. 'I think we're in
the same struggle,' she said. 'Angela Davis sees it as the liberation of all people. It's a class struggle.'

Support for Davis grew in the weeks leading up to the trial.
A fifteen-year-old was arrested after an unsuccessful attempt
to hi-jack a plane; he confessed he'd intended to take hostages
and demand her release. In Paris, 60,000 marched in her
support. In London, hundreds gathered for a torchlight pro-
cession, street theatre, poetry readings and placard-waving
picketing outside the American Embassy in Grosvenor Square.

As the trial itself proceeded, the all-white jury of eight
women and four men heard accounts of the confusion outside
the courthouse during the shoot-out, a mass of technical detail
from the ballistics experts, and discussions about the FBI's
methods in procuring love letters (they were important to the
prosecutor's case after he'd taken the decision not to stress
the politics of the case, but to insist that Angela Davis was
motivated by her passionate love for George Jackson). Even
before the trial, it was accepted that she wasn't present at
the shoot-out, and she willingly confessed that guns used
by Jonathan Jackson had been purchased by her, for her
own protection and bought legally using her own ID. The

prosecutor's case seemed to ebb away, and after forty-nine days in court, the jury took just thirteen hours to find her innocent of the charges. Many conservative commentators, however, continued to claim her guilt, with some suggesting that the jury had been cowed into a not-guilty verdict by the fear of stirring up riots, but as Angela Davis talked to the press outside, the crowd took up the chant of 'Power to the people'.

Twenty-three years later, the makers of *Dead Presidents* created a role for an Angela Davis figure, Delilah, who greets Anthony on his return from Vietnam with the words 'Welcome home and welcome to the revolution'. Delilah's character isn't entirely convincing, however, partly because the world of the rest of the film has so clearly moved into a new phase; the ghetto has fallen apart and her idealism looks like an anachronism.

By 1972, many of the great female soul singers were also searching for ways to deal with fading hopes and inner city blues. Looking for answers to both personal despair and political angst, some artists embraced a mystical Afrocentric world view, while others were turning back to a gospel vision. Aretha Franklin did both, on her two LPs in 1972, *Young, Gifted and Black* and *Amazing Grace*. They were fine records, but the urgency and street-suss she'd brought to her version of 'Respect' in 1967 was missing. According to Craig Werner in his book *A Change is Gonna Come*, 'Aretha's music of the early Seventies testifies to the feeling of a community still holding on to a vision of possibility, but aware that the revolutionary moment may be slipping away.'

If the trial of Angela Davis was the most politically charged event of 1972 in black America, then a key music moment in the year was the Wattstax concert, described by critic Nelson George as 'the black Woodstock', although whereas Woodstock has come to symbolise the power of rock music to galvanise a generation, Wattstax has never had such potency. Perhaps this is a product of the marginalisation of black music in the early 1970s by a rock-obsessed underground clogged up with Grateful Dead fans. Certainly there was now a much clearer division between rock and soul; in 1967, at Monterey, Jimi Hendrix featured alongside the likes of both Otis Redding and the Mamas & the Papas, but in America in 1972 white kids weren't sharing the idols of the young blacks (for them, 1972 was all about acts like James Taylor and Carole King, or Jethro Tull – who topped the American charts in 1972 with their *Thick as a Brick* LP – or the Allman Brothers Band, or Lynyrd Skynyrd). Also, Woodstock had plugged into a vibrant energy source, but, as we have seen, Wattstax took place as soul music's political charge stumbled in the face of new challenges and confusion in the cities.

The Wattstax concert at the LA Coliseum grew out of the Watts Summer Festival, which had been operating annually as a commemoration of the Watts riots, and was developed via Stax's newly-opened office in Los Angeles. It was attended by 110,000 people, $73,000 was raised for good causes, and the crowd were entertained by an array of Stax recording stars, introduced by compères including singer William Bell and film-maker Melvin van Peebles. Jesse Jackson was also prominent onstage, dressed in a dashiki, hailing 'liberation through music' and calling on the crowd to move from 'Burn, baby, burn' to 'Learn, baby, learn'.

The headline act on the day was Isaac Hayes. With the nickname 'Black Moses', he'd become a charismatic figure-head in the black community, comfortable with his black pride and worldly success, having just taken ownership of a peacock blue, gold-plated Cadillac. He was back to being creative, and was basking in the success of his soundtrack work, having just won an Academy Award for best movie song with 'Theme from *Shaft*'.

Shaft was one of a number of blaxploitation movies that played a key role in the dissemination of black culture in the era. Despite the plots not always being watertight, blaxploit-

ation films, unapologetic and entertaining, had larger than
life leading characters – Shaft himself, the drug-dealer priest
in *Superfly* – as well as plenty of sex and a high level of violence. Many of these films featured brilliant soundtracks scored
by some of the big stars – Marvin Gaye (*Trouble Man*), Bobby
Womack (*Across 110th Street*), James Brown (*Black Caesar*) and
Curtis Mayfield (*Superfly*) – and took millions of black dollars
at the box office.

Usually from the poor and disenfranchised side of the
tracks, power was something the cinema audience had only
a tenuous hold on in the real world, but they enthusiastically
identified with the empowered, successful leading characters;
black men who succeeded in a white world. And the occasional female heroine also appeared, including, in 1974, *Foxy
Brown* – 'A chick with drive who don't take no jive' – played
by Pam Grier. Ms Brown had razor blades hidden in her afro,
and a wonderful wardrobe awash with fur coats, mini-skirts
and hot pants. Clothes were important to the blaxploitation
films, as Nelson George acknowledges in his book *Hip Hop
America*: 'In keeping with the candy-colored aesthetic of the
period, these movies dressed the stars in state-of-the-art
threads that allowed them to live as large and insolently as
we all dreamed we could.'

Somewhere in the mix, too, were connections between the
sweeping, majestic, irresponsible hold on power displayed by
the leading characters and their sexual exploits, between
sexual potency and power, and between power and money.
Characters like Goldie the pimp in *The Mack* were presented
as cool, controlling, confident heroes.

Paul Gilroy remembers how he reacted to the blaxploitation
moment in London. He went to see Curtis Mayfield play live
at the Rainbow Theatre. Paul had a girlfriend who worked as
an usherette and she told him that if he slipped the doorman
ten bob he'd let him in through a side entrance. Paul didn't
quite believe that it would work, but it did, and he took his

place in the audience, witnessing the power and presence of Mayfield: 'It was the most intense, sepulchral atmosphere.'

The blaxploitation genre never had the unanimous support of the black community in America. Civil rights groups like NAACP and CORE, as well as Jesse Jackson, were among those cynical about the commercial motives of the film producers and swift to decry the way the films appeared content to perpetuate stereotypes; for the likes of Jesse Jackson, too many blaxploitation films were brazenly anti-social, presenting a major shift in cultural values from a sense of community and solidarity to one of individual go-getting.

Aside from enjoying the music of Curtis Mayfield, Paul Gilroy also had trouble accepting many of the blaxploitation messages, describing them as 'a capitulation'. He thought they were buying into some of the worst features of capitalism, the system: 'I didn't really fall for it, it didn't really appeal to me; in a way it was too much aligned with that version of America the counter cultural thing was rejecting. Like the idea that in the case of John Shaft, he was a cop; what was that about?'

Paul doesn't deny the films had an influence, but confesses that for him the best thing about them was the blaxploitation 'look'. 'Yes, I still thought certain features of it were cool and interesting style-wise and wanted to copy that. This was in the period when I was beginning to save up for a leather jacket and we tamed and manipulated our afros with great skill, but at the same time, the world of *Superfly*, the world of *Shaft* wasn't an attractive one.'

Soon it would all be over, as films of questionable quality flooded the market – anyone for *Blacula* ('Dracula's soul brother')? – but elements of blaxploitation – the violence and the untouchable leading characters – reappeared in the next big Seventies cinema craze, the kung fu movies. But cinemagoers also had a chance to see a movie of Wattstax, released by Columbia Pictures at the beginning of 1973. *Wattstax* featured concert footage mixed with images of urban ghettos, exhortations from Jesse Jackson, and soundbites and stories from local Watts residents. Richard Pryor was filmed after the event and cut into the final movie. In an era of Black Panther activity and justifiable homicides, Pryor has the camera crew cracking up with his satirical stories and one-liners, at one point asking mockingly, 'How do the police accidentally shoot a nigger six times in the ass?'

In the intervening few months between the Wattstax festival and the movie, another film was released which reflected the changing times: *The Autobiography of Malcolm X*. Although this reawakened interest in Malcolm's life and his political philosophies, the film also loudly played up his relevance to the new situation in the early 1970s, including his demands that blacks 'get off welfare and help themselves', and 'stay away from dope, which is just for dopes'.

In the deterioration of urban neighbourhoods, breakdown of communities, and the negative experiences suffered by Vietnam veterans, the spread of drugs had a significant role. This is vividly portrayed in *Dead Presidents*; drugs have taken hold of the 'hood, and the pushers and pimps are in control, taunting Anthony Curtis and the Vietnam veterans with their wealth and status.

A connection between the Vietnam war and the spread of drugs is clear. In 1971 it was estimated that 10 per cent of soldiers in Vietnam used heroin, and so when their tour of duty ended, they brought their habits home. Criminal gangs fed this development, and corruption and collusion by the law enforcement agencies also aided the spread of the drug. The FBI were happy, and the populace were pacified. In the words of Nelson George, 'The growth of the urban drug culture stifled the civil rights movement, as heroin's vicious grip took hold.'

The prevailing mood in the ghetto was one of self-destruction. Musicians, writers and poets addressed this, most notably Gary Byrd in his astonishing cut 'Are You Really

Ready for Black Power?', which bravely questioned materialism and the motives of black brothers preying on the
vulnerable and selling out the community. This sense of a
community turning on itself was present in more commercial
tracks too: the 1972 hit single 'Backstabbers' by The O'Jays,
for example, is a tale of a personal life shattered by betrayal.

The destructive influence of the spread of drugs was beginning to become an issue in the music of the time, sidelining
the grand utopian themes of the civil rights era. In 1972 James
Brown's *There It Is* LP included the song 'King Heroin', and
songs by Curtis Mayfield like 'Pusherman' and 'Freddie's
Dead' reflected widespread self-doubt in the black community, the confusion described by The Temptations, and the
question 'What's going on?' posed by Marvin Gaye. On the
Wattstax soundtrack, Jesse Jackson articulates his bewilder-
ment: 'Brothers and sisters, I don't know what this world is
coming to.'

A Harlem coke dealer, Superfly fits the blaxploitation cliché
of the badass anti-hero, but key to the success of Curtis
Mayfield's *Superfly* soundtrack is the way the music undercuts
the swagger, giving the leading characters an ambiguity. Far
from celebration, Mayfield questions the role of the pimps
and pushermen in the ghetto. The song 'Freddie's Dead', for
example, uses the almost incidental but tragic death of a representative character to lay bare the reality of the pusher's
world. In *Dead Presidents*, Anthony Curtis is also a decent
character dragged down. The strategy of tracking political
issues through a personal story – the effects on ordinary citizens of drug use and rising crime in the deteriorating urban
ghettos – is also in evidence in the song 'Jim, What's Wrong
With Him?' by The Dramatics, who recorded for Volt, a Stax
subsidiary. Their LP *Dramatically Yours* was full of the concerns
of 1972; other song titles include 'Beware of the Man with
Candy in His Hand' and 'The Devil is Dope'.

Ironically, while criminal gangs appeared to be prospering

in the ghetto, radical elements had been policed out of existence (having been specifically and violently targeted by law
enforcement agencies over many years). But as well as confrontation, the authorities had also been careful to compromise, and the acquittal of Angela Davis was perhaps proof
that progress had been made since the bus boycotts in
Montgomery in 1956 and the early days of civil rights. By
1972, all this – together with the spread of drugs strangling
community values in the ghettos – was taking the heat out of
the revolution.

There had been some political advance – in 1972 Andrew
Young became Georgia's first African-American congressman
(and, later, Mayor of Atlanta) – and some economic advance,
too, at least for some in the black community. A black middle
class was emerging – ambitious black graduates, black politicians, and a wave of workers granted opportunities through
affirmative action – and began moving into a wider, whiter
world, often joining the white flight out into the suburbs.
The notion of a uniform 'black community' began to seem
problematic.

Black flight further weakened the ghettos, where, battered
by recession, unambiguous social progress was still a promise
away. In 1972, the Commission of the Cities followed up on
the Civil Disorders report into the 1967 riots five years earlier:
'Our basic finding is that the shameful conditions of life in the
cities have become worse; housing still a national scandal;
schools tedious and turbulent; crime, unemployment, disease,
heroin addiction higher, welfare rolls longer, minority–police
relations just as hostile.'

In the 1960s, the civil rights struggle was a significant story,
but as the movement lost momentum in the early Seventies,
other sites of conflict became apparent, especially the rising
tension in the Middle East. Violence between states, social
unrest, and the PLO's brand of international terrorism dominated international affairs in the 1970s and beyond. In 1972,

just a couple of weeks after Wattstax, came a shocking incident at the Olympic Games in Munich when members of the Palestinian Black September organisation, dressed as athletes and with weapons hidden inside sports bags, broke into rooms housing the Israeli Olympic team and took hostages.

Two of the era's sporting greats – swimmer Mark Spitz and Russian gymnast Olga Korbut – were multiple medal winners at the Olympics that year, but the carnage that followed the hostage-taking overshadowed the event. Two athletes were shot and killed in the initial raid, and nine others were taken hostage. Three hundred police officers surrounded the building and negotiations ensued. The terrorists were demanding the release of two hundred Arab prisoners, but through the seventeen-hour siege various deadlines and threats passed until, in a shoot-out at the airport, in a confrontation by all accounts desperately badly handled by the German authorities, all the Israeli hostages died, along with five Palestinians and a policeman.

At the time, the German authorities were already heavily involved in attempts to deal with the Baader Meinhof group. The terror group – who had avowed links with the PLO – never avoided soft targets, but their ability to strike at the heart of political power in Germany was phenomenal. Their attacks in the early months of 1972 included a number on various US Army headquarters in Germany, and Munich's Criminal Investigation Office, but the authorities made a major breakthrough in June 1972 when, in various locations in Frankfurt, Hamburg and Hanover, the police arrested several leading members of the gang, including Andreas Baader, Ulrike Meinhof, Gerhard Muller and Gudrun Ensslin. However, their comrades continued their activities in an effort to force their release.

In Britain, there were concerns as IRA bombs exploded on the streets of London, and, in Northern Ireland itself, sectarian violence was escalating, as the bombing of McGurk's bar on

North Queen Street in Belfast on 4 December 1971 demonstrated. The Loyalist extremists in the Ulster Volunteer Force were responsible for the outrage, and fifteen Catholics were killed. By the mid-1970s, a UVF unit known as the Shankill Butchers was engaged in horrific sectarian killings, which included the deaths of thirty-three people in bombings in Dublin and Monaghan in May 1974, and the murder of three members of the Miami Show Band in 1975.

As well as this Loyalist violence continuing unabated through the 1970s, the English mainland would become a target for IRA bombs. In the same way that Vietnam had overshadowed and distorted life in America, so in Britain the 'troubles', as they were known, would be a constant disruption and reminder. 1972 would witness one of the most infamous incidents, Bloody Sunday, on 30 January, when thirteen unarmed demonstrators were shot dead in Londonderry by the Parachute Regiment.

The killings and subsequent cover-ups of Bloody Sunday – as well as TV footage of a priest, Dr Edward Daly, waving a white handkerchief as cowering figures carried a dying man through the streets – had huge importance in feeding anti-British sentiment. The outcry was immediate. The following day, an angry Bernadette Devlin physically assaulted Home Secretary Reginald Maudling in the House of Commons, and within weeks of Bloody Sunday, the *Guardian* was describing the event as 'Britain's My Lai'.

Bloody Sunday, of course, fuelled the sense of injustice and gave credence to the view that the British Army was an oppressive force. In terms of that oppositional culture, those people who had supported *Oz* and the defendants, for example, most were naturally inclined to support the IRA. Paul Gilroy: 'There was an absolute sense that what was happening there was a colonial war like all the other ones, like South Africa; it was no different, it was a colonial thing. And in that sense you had to support the IRA.'

For people harbouring dreams of radical change, the IRA were freedom fighters, and challenges to the state from whatever source were welcome, as Paul admits: 'You can laugh at this if you like, but I would have to say that for four or five years, I really thought there was going to be a revolution. From 1969 onwards until maybe 1974, although maybe by 1974 I think I had worked out that it wasn't likely. But for a large part of the period you're talking about I really thought there was going to be a revolution and so obviously the rising up of the IRA, all of that stuff, was part of it.'

He also admits that there was a tendency to romanticise the Republican struggle. 'Obviously there were romantic aspects to that and there were aspects of it which were connected up with the fact that the Irish Nationalists had adapted motifs from the civil rights struggle, and somebody like Bernadette Devlin was the focal point of that, one of those iconic figures.'

After the killings at McGurk's and the brutal provocation of Bloody Sunday, recruitment to the IRA increased and the organisation made a significant switch in strategy. Twenty days after Bloody Sunday an IRA bomb in the Army town of Aldershot killed seven people. It was the first IRA attack on the mainland, but many more were to follow through the decade.

Paul Gilroy admits, though, that before the mid-point of the Seventies – as the optimistic spirit of the 1960s became a distant memory, black liberation struggles were sidelined and the IRA campaign turned into a catalogue of random violence – for people who had convinced themselves that positive social change could come out of the chaos of anti-Vietnam marches, free festivals, black power and urban terrorism, so the sense of revolutionary potential began to fade.

Some of this was due to the strengthening grip of corporate business on what had been symbols of oppositional culture; the hip capitalists had turned the counter culture into a product, rock music was accepted by the media, festivals were making money, and long hair and fashions which had been markers of alternative attitudes had become mainstream.

Another part of this change was that the curse of the mundane brought down dreams of social revolution. In Britain and America, with living standards falling, industries and neighbourhoods in ruin, the struggle became less about changing the world and more about just trying to get by. In many ways, the 1972 miners' strike was a sign of this.

There wasn't always common ground between the traditional left and the 1960s underground, between workers' demands for wage rises and better working conditions, and those counter cultural dreams of liberation. We've already heard Mick Farren's contention that in their struggles, trade unionists merely dug themselves further into a system that exploited them with 'mind-numbing' jobs. The miners' strike was evidence that those whose politics were utopian were giving way to the pragmatists.

The strike began on 9 January 1972, and soon over a quarter of a million miners were involved, seeking a wage rise higher than the £2 a week offered to them under the Government's pay guidelines. Participants in the strike may or may not have been questioning the system, but they certainly shook the Government with their action, forced the first widespread power cuts of the decade, and used flying pickets and secondary picketing to great effect, mobilising in order to block coal movements. On 3 February, while picketing outside Keadby power station near Scunthorpe, Fred Matthews, a thirty-seven-year-old miner, was killed under the rear wheel of a lorry driven by a non-union driver. Ten thousand people attended Fred's funeral near his home in Yorkshire, and print workers in London staged a one-hour strike in his honour. The Conservative Government decided to declare a state of emergency as a result of dwindling coal stocks.

But a confrontation at the gates of Saltley coke depot in Nechells Place in Birmingham was the turning point of the strike. In the early days of the strike, lorries had been diverted there from other distribution centres shut down by pickets, then, as the NUM arrived and began a round-the-clock picket, workers from other industries declared solidarity with the miners and a mass picket was announced for Thursday 10 February. Fifteen thousand people had gathered by the middle of Thursday morning, and faced by such a weight of numbers and a determined opposition, the Chief Constable of Birmingham, Sir Derek Capper, took the decision to instruct the Gas Board to close the gates, and announced they would remain closed for the rest of the day, handing victory to the pickets.

The day the gates were closed coincided with the first power cuts across the country. Power cuts would become a feature of life in the 1970s; the Government would announce for each area of the country a series of four-hour periods each week in which there was a likelihood of disconnection. These emergency regulations would include advice to industrial users (to shut factories) and householders (to stock up on candles). Train services would be hit. In some cities, there would be traffic chaos as breaks in the power supply disrupted traffic lights.

Attempts to conserve electricity went even further in February 1972. Over the weekend it was announced that big industrial users of electricity would only operate three days a week. On Friday 18 February, at the end of the first week of the state of emergency, a million and a half workers were laid off. With momentum running with the miners, the outcome at Saltley and the chaos in the country, Heath backed down within days of the emergency being declared.

Paul Gilroy admits that somehow the miners' strike seemed a sign of the dilution rather than the strength of the struggle for social change. 'It's curious that in my sense of what the revolution entailed I didn't include things like the miners' strike. I could see it was more economistic, or whatever. It was more to do with people trying to improve their lot within the available options; they weren't really trying to make a different system.'

He was disappointed that the world wasn't going to be turned upside down. 'I was disappointed,' he says before smiling, 'and I still am.'

Meanwhile, back in the USA, stagnation in the civil rights movement, the trauma of neighbourhood breakdown, and division in the black community appeared to draw some of the urgency from soul music. Marvin Gaye, for example, moved on from *What's Going On* to smooth-talking lust ballads like 'Let's Get it On', a song that plugged into the 'heroic' figure of the blaxploitation superstud, and also reflected that shift in the Seventies away from a communal sense of 'us' to a more individual outlook.

The adjustment in Marvin Gaye's career was mirrored by many other soul acts, as the mood and the market moved towards records like Diana Ross's hit 1973 LP *Touch Me in the Morning*. A ballad sung by The Drifters celebrating a hot date kissin' in the back row of the movies became one of the big songs of 1974. The Chi-Lites had always done love songs brilliantly, and returned to sweet things with 'Oh Girl'. Earth, Wind & Fire, who were later one of the great bands of the decade, drew on mystical and magical pan-Africanism and big basslines, and certainly steered clear of sentimentality, but never reflected any kind of street-level urgency either, wowing crowds with levitation rather than revolution.

Through the rest of the decade, we'll see how far soul and funk travelled from the social concerns of the early 1970s, as the buzz word 'ghetto' was replaced by 'disco'. Yet black American music remained influential and ever changing. As funk became absorbed into disco, the culture of black America was still being spread through various media, including films like *Carwash* (1976) and the TV show *Soul Train*. The clips of *Soul Train* we'd see on *Top of the Pops* were just the coolest TV ever. Antonio Fargas had featured in the films *Shaft* and *Across*

110th Street, and was then served up for prime time TV, starring as Huggy Bear in *Starsky & Hutch*. It was perhaps predictable that the media felt able to celebrate the dance moves of black America – as well as the clothes, the wide lapels and the floppy velvet hats – having been reluctant to show much enthusiasm for Angela Davis and '(For God's Sake) Give More Power to the People'.

However, in some neighbourhoods of Britain, close identification with the Afro-American experience loosened and the Caribbean roots of black Britain strengthened, and, as soul music drifted towards disco, reggae began to become a clearer focus for the aspirations and enthusiasm of a generation of black youngsters. The beginnings of this Rasta or 'roots' element in reggae was marked in 1972 by the release of the film *The Harder They Come*, and by Bob Marley's LP *Catch A Fire*, and was soon firmly established by small independent labels, and one or two bigger companies, notably Island Records, but also Virgin (with their *Front Line* compilations).

Nevertheless, the assertive attitudes, soul music's urge to engage with the world, the power of the groove, the urgency, and the flowering fashions of the funk and soul era still hold considerable value for musicians, music fans, designers and film-makers (notably Quentin Tarantino). In urban neighbourhoods, soul music was the messenger – perhaps even the agent – of change, and these deep links remain, and go some way to explaining why current stars like Angie Stone and Erykah Badu reach back to that era, looking to the past to help define the present.

In those intervening thirty years, gangsta values and Reaganomics have brought more despair to more neighbourhoods, and nurtured more cynical materialism, inequality and racial division. In hip hop, pimp attitudes can still be glamorised. Soul music's preoccupation – how to transform the ghetto into a community – is still urgent, the story of the blues is still unfolding. In *Dead Presidents*, the armed robbery goes horribly wrong, and Delilah – the Angela Davis character – is a casualty. At the very end of the film we hear 'Where is the Love?' by Jess and Trina, a version of the 1972 classic performed by Donny Hathaway and Roberta Flack, a meditation on an era of fading optimism and loss of hope, and a question echoed three decades later by the Black Eyed Peas. In the first decade of the twenty-first century we're still post-work, post-hope. 'Where is the Love?' plays out as the *Dead Presidents* credits roll. At the end of the story there's no happy ending.

CHAPTER FOUR

'Life on Mars' (1973)

The years 1973 and 1974 have been described as a 'watershed' by historian Eric Hobsbawm, when a post-war era of relentless economic growth, high employment and a massive rise in the ownership of material goods had clearly ended. This affluence had been driven by the developed capitalist countries – among them the USA, Britain and Germany – but was a worldwide phenomenon. Hobsbawm quotes a term used in France to describe the era: 'les trente glorieuses' ('thirty glorious years').

A prosperous, technologically-advanced, international manufacturing economy had been created, but this globalised network relied on unproblematic, cheap oil supplies, a situation thrown into doubt in October 1973 with the outbreak of the Yom Kippur war. Israel engaged Syrian troops on the Golan Heights and Egyptian forces at the Suez Canal. Fighting soon escalated and Jordan and Saudi Arabia joined the conflict. A few days into the war, the Organisation of Arab Petroleum Exporting Countries decided to cut back oil production by 5 per cent, and to continue to reduce production by 5 per cent every month until Israel withdrew from Arab lands. At the same time, a broader grouping of oil producers tore up agreements and increased price levels. These included countries that America and the West had courted for years, including

Saudi Arabia, and Iran, where the Shah was America's biggest Arab ally. The balance of power was shifting; no longer could the West rely on cheap access to the world's energy resources.

The oil crisis exposed weaknesses in many of the world's economies. America and Europe were knocked into recession and no lives were unaffected. In the face of rising raw material costs, transportation and energy prices, companies looked to cut back on labour costs, unemployment rose and working people in the mid-1970s suffered the first falls in living standards since before the Second World War. The world 'slid into instability and crisis', says Hobsbawm, describing a new era, and the arrival of what he calls the 'Crisis Decades'.

In England, a new generation embraced acts like David Bowie, T-Rex and Roxy Music, who consciously celebrated their distance from the 1960s and The Beatles and The Stones with a mix of sensational gender blurring, teenage anthems, decadence, negativity and daft clothes. Bowie especially was a key figure through the Seventies, his magpie mind picking up ideas and putting them into his music and his image, his songs reflecting some of the instability and chaos, but always with a pop sensibility. For Jayne Casey, desperate to avoid being dragged down by her troubled early life in Liverpool, dancing to 'Get it On' by T-Rex or 'Changes' by David Bowie was a first stepping stone on the way to another, better world.

The changes we were living through marked the end of the golden years. Workers who felt they deserved a bigger slice of the cake might or might not have been justified, but the cake itself was getting smaller. The international manufacturing economy, those big factories promising high employment, profits and prosperity, had, literally, run out of energy.

The Conservatives' Industrial Relations Act – which attempted to redraw union constitutions and to rein in union power by setting up legal and financial sanctions against maverick union action – poisoned the atmosphere between the Government and the unions, and failed to deliver stability.

Twenty-three million working days were lost in 1972 due to strike action, as ambulance drivers, civil servants and firemen engaged in industrial action. The scale of the miners' victory after the confrontation at Saltley had raised expectations among workers in other trades, notably the rail workers. The three rail unions – the NUR, ASLEF and the TSSA – were notoriously disunited, but this time they threatened joint action and began disrupting London's commuter services. Within days of a ballot of members which produced an over-whelming majority favouring the extension of industrial action, the Government settled the strike, with one Government adviser describing the situation as a 'humiliation'.

A feature of the era was how often and easily confrontations developed; the building workers' strike of 1972, for example, was marred by allegations of threats and intimidation by pickets, but the employers also took an uncompromising stand (at one site, the pickets were met by the contractor's son brandishing a 12-bore shotgun). In Shrewsbury local employers had formed an anti-picketing squad, which confronted a flying picket of two hundred and fifty building workers who arrived in Shrewsbury in coaches and cars, and when the pickets moved to a site in Telford fist fights broke out between pickets, site managers and strike breakers. One of the pickets was the actor Ricky Tomlinson, then a UCATT shop steward. He and his colleagues had escalated the strike without help from his trade union bosses at UCATT and the T&G head-quarters; this was another feature of disputes in the 1970s – tensions between the trade union leadership and the generally more militant shop stewards.

The extremism we saw developing in the first years of the 1970s was coming to a head in the workplace. While the rank and file workers organised, the employers' body, NFBTE, had been compiling a dossier on the activities of the pickets throughout the building workers' strike, and the views they expressed through their report unleashed a frantic demonisation of the flying pickets on the part of the Government and in some of the media. Police chief Robert Mark, for example, compared the flying pickets to Nazis: 'To some of us, the Shrewsbury pickets had committed the worst of all crimes, worse even than murder, the attempt to achieve an industrial and political objective by criminal violence, the very conduct, in fact, which helped to bring the National Socialist German Worker's Party to power in 1933.'

In July 1973 thirty-five of the pickets were tried at Mold and Shrewsbury, and six of them were charged with unlawful assembly, affray and conspiracy to intimidate. Among the six, Ricky Tomlinson was imprisoned for two years. In his speech from the dock he was unrepentant. 'I look forward to the day when the real culprits, the McAlpine's, Wimpey's, Laing's and the Bovis's and their political puppets, are in the dock facing charges of conspiracy and intimidating workers from doing what is their lawful right, picketing,' he told the court.

Robert Mark, meanwhile, had security problems to deal with as the IRA's campaign on the British mainland continued with bombs in London in March 1973, causing one fatality and injuring more than two hundred, followed later in the year by numerous letter bombs and a number of bombs in London underground stations. On 21 July 1973 the IRA detonated twenty bombs in Belfast, killing eleven people and injuring more than a hundred.

Instability was evident in the workplace, in schools and universities, and on the streets, but was also present in conflicts worldwide. The continuing Cold War loomed large, as Russia and the United States looked to extend and defend their spheres of influence in the world, and was fought on many fronts; from Vietnam in East Asia to South America (the CIA's covert activities in the early 1970s included the military overthrow of Salvador Allende's government in Chile in September 1973). Russia and the United States invariably took sides in regional disputes, even civil wars (in Angola, for example). Although a ceasefire was brokered between Israel and Syria after three months, the battles around the Suez Canal continued. Once it became clear that the Soviet Union had plans to send forces into the region to intervene on behalf of the Arab states, Nixon and Kissinger ramped up the pressure by putting America on a war footing.

Many of the potent symbols of the Cold War struggle between Washington and Moscow were individuals. During the months before the Angela Davis trial, for example, the American authorities lambasted her for her membership of both the Black Panther Party and the Communist Party, while Tass – the official Soviet news agency – took a clear, possibly predictable line: 'America is going through a period of political upheaval, and the government is striking out against all those who have the courage to speak out against the injustice and racism occurring in the United States at this time.'

Individuals in the Communist bloc were often powerless in their own country, yet became internationally known. Soviet dissident Andrei Sakharov – a nuclear scientist turned critic of the arms race – was a high-profile human rights activist; silenced and harassed by the Soviet regime, he was nominated for the Nobel Peace Prize in 1973. Alexander Solzhenitsyn too had a high profile; a former Red Army captain imprisoned for speaking out against Stalin, his accounts of the labour camps – in the works *One Day in the Life of Ivan Denisovich* and *The Gulag Archipelago* – reached massive audiences in the West. He had been banished from the Soviet Union by 1973, but frequently appeared on Western television and found a vociferous champion in the shape of Bernard Levin in *The Times*.

The stories told by the dissidents damaged the standing of the Soviet Union and its Eastern bloc allies but, on the other hand, strong performances in the gymnasium, the shot putt circle and on the athletics track at championship meetings and the Olympic Games gave a boost to Communist countries. In this battle, the use of performance enhancing drugs became commonplace and was largely undetected, or, at least, publicised. Citizens, crowds in the grandstands, and viewers on TV weren't to know, but Eastern European athletes in the Seventies were pumped full of drugs, often to great and fatal cost to their health. America was playing the same game too. Glorification of the nation was all.

In July 1972 two other Cold War gladiators met, face to face, although neither was armed, nor particularly dangerous; they were two chess players, but the match in Reykjavik between the Russian reigning world champion, Boris Spassky, and the American challenger, Bobby Fischer, became a sixty-four-square Cold War battlefield, generating public interest in a chess match unknown before or since.

As a young man growing up in Brooklyn, Fischer had spent all his waking hours studying chess and would frustrate friends with his inability to follow any kind of conversation about art or politics. However, the Sixties Cold War rhetoric did permeate his mind. In a magazine interview in 1962 he accused the Russian chess establishment of rigging tournaments, and over several years he continued to taunt the Soviets as he established himself as a major force in international chess, with a controversial, somewhat cranky reputation.

As the World Chess Championship grew closer, Fischer grew anxious, claiming that the Russians were planning to shoot down his plane, and threatened to withdraw when he discovered that his favourite TV shows were unavailable on Icelandic TV. The politics surrounding the match had become so intense that when it looked like Fischer might not show, President Nixon ordered Henry Kissinger to intervene. Kissinger telephoned Fischer but Fischer wouldn't take the call. Nevertheless, he made it to Reykjavik and the match began on 12 July 1972. Fischer, however, continued with his complaints, many of them bizarre (the chess board, he claimed, was too shiny).

Just over six weeks later, Fischer emerged victorious. He'd taken on and conquered the Soviet star, even though – in contrast to Spassky who had a sizeable entourage of helpers and chess strategists travelling with him – Fischer had just one adviser, Bill Lombardy. In any breaks in the play the Soviets would gather in huddles in Spassky's hotel room to plot the next moves, but Fischer ignored offers of help from Lombardy and was contemptuous of Spassky. 'The guy's a fish,' he would say, 'let's go bowling.'

The biggest struggle was the nuclear arms race, as NATO and the Soviet Union threatened each other with increasing stockpiles of nuclear weapons, more than enough to destroy the planet many times over. Each sought to maximise their retaliatory threat to deter the other side from using their weapons. It was a policy of Mutually Assured Destruction, with the most fitting acronym in history: MAD.

The Cold War played a major part in the space race. It might be imagined that the space race was about glory, or national pride, but shadier motives have always played a part, and links between the space race and weapons systems and espionage were barely hidden. And like any war, the Cold War had its casualties: the athletes suffering the side-effects of the drugs, and the four hundred people who died trying to cross the barbed wire, ditches and armed guards at the Berlin Wall between 1961 and 1989. In 1971, three Russian cosmonauts were found dead when their spaceship returned to earth.

Whatever the motivations for the superpowers, the story of space travel in this period transfixed the world and fired the imagination of a generation. In July 1969, when the first manned mission landed on the moon, millions of people in Britain woke early to watch the moment live on television. We were in an era when the adventure and danger of space exploration permeated everything, from sci-fi outfits on the catwalk, to religion, cinema and music. David Bowie's single 'Space Oddity' was released during that historic Apollo XI mission in 1969, telling the story of Major Tom taking his protein pills, checking his dials and jetting off into space, apparently having made the decision never to return.

Bowie had begun the Seventies looking like a cross between Lauren Bacall and Lindsay Kemp, appearing in a dress on the front of the 1971 LP *The Man Who Sold the World*, and making an idiosyncratic choice of live venues: the Purcell Rooms one week, the London Palladium the next. Some reviewers in this early phase of Bowie's career wrote him off as a dilettante, and the 1971 single 'Changes' seemed to underline his own uncertain search for a musical as well as a personal direction. But other reviewers identified his potential star quality. Tony Palmer wrote of him in 1969: 'He smiles; you melt. He winks; you disintegrate.'

The 1960s had dazzled us with advances in technology, in speed, adventure. The 'white heat of technology' had delivered truck loads of domestic appliances – washing machines, tumble dryers and colour TVs – and promised us more; a bright new, carefree tomorrow. TV presenter James Burke co-hosted *Tomorrow's World* and also played a key role in the BBC's coverage of the Apollo missions. From 1972 until 1976 he also hosted the TV series *The Burke Special*. Every week he would investigate the latest scientific and technological innovations, strapping volunteers to lie detector machines, or introducing robots who were trained to undertake all household chores. In one edition his show featured television's first computer hacker, when a guest showed how easy it was to gain illegal entry to Inland Revenue computer records, sparking a security alert.

Despite the glitz and excitement of the space race, there were also concerns about technology being out of control, and the power that technology granted to governments, and to agencies such as the FBI and the CIA. Political paranoia bled into the personal domain, and was captured brilliantly in Francis Ford Coppola's film *The Conversation*, starring Gene Hackman.

Surveillance anxiety also leaked into the Fischer/Spassky duel. Fischer complained about the presence of TV cameras and the proximity of the audience. The Soviets replied with demands of their own, claiming that Fischer had a hidden device that was distorting Spassky's thought patterns. The hall was swept for evidence, Fischer's chair and the light fittings were taken apart, but nothing suspicious was ever discovered.

Anxieties ran deep. The Last Poets had called it 'tricknology': the perception that powerful interests were perfecting various means of perpetuating their power under the cloak of technological advance. A view that there was a gap between what rulers were telling us and reality was widely held, and in an atmosphere in which all kinds of conspiracy theories thrived. Eric von Daniken, for example, found a reading audience of tens of millions for his book *Chariots of the Gods* (1968) and, subsequently, *In Search of Ancient Gods* (1973) and *Miracles of the Gods* (1974), all detailing his theories that alien astronauts had visited the ancient Egyptian and Inca civilisations, including descriptions of a giant spaceport in the Andes. And questions continued to be asked about the John F. Kennedy assassination, the Bermuda Triangle and the possibility of life on Mars.

David Bowie's song 'Life on Mars' was first heard on his 1971 *Hunky Dory* LP, on which a number of songs – like 'Starman' and 'Queen Bitch' – revealed two of Bowie's favourite subjects: space travel and gender bending. With men on the moon and spaceships on their way to the outer reaches of the galaxy, life's possibilities were being stretched and it wasn't just in Bowie's head that there was some connection between space travel and sexual exploration. Although the 1960s were reckoned to mark the height of sexual liberation, it wasn't until the early years of the 1970s that the dissemination of liberal attitudes, use of the contraceptive pill and the spread of pornography transformed sexual behaviour in the furthest reaches of the UK and the USA. Just as space exploration became an almost everyday occurrence, so sexual exploration went mainstream in the 1970s.

Some big changes in views about sex and sexuality had occurred in less than a generation; according to pollsters, three-quarters of Americans accepted the idea of premarital sex, and as many as a third thought the institution of marriage was obsolete. In 1972, one of the non-fiction books of the year was *Open Marriage: a New Lifestyle for Couples* by Nene and George O'Neill, which included chapters entitled 'Why Save Marriage At All' and 'Love & Sex Without Jealousy'.

In Britain, the scale of the social changes was marked by a rise in casual sex, shifts towards liberalisation of the law, the greater availability of 'top shelf' magazines, and the arrival of some steamy sexual shenanigans on prime time television (notably the series *A Bouquet of Barbed Wire*). Permissive attitudes and the Pill had destroyed moral and physical barriers to casual sex, and adventure seemed to be encouraged. Another best-selling book in the era was *The Joy of Sex* which detailed a choice of sexual positions.

The Joy of Sex was illustrated with line drawings of the enthusiastic couple, but more vivid depictions of the sexual act were available in magazines and films. In 1972, *Playboy* hit its all-time peak circulation: seven million copies. The same year saw the release of the porn film *Deep Throat*, starring Linda Lovelace, a hardcore film made for just $22,000, that caused a stir in its opening weeks in America. Among the most enthusiastic viewers of *Deep Throat* were TV anchormen, mainstream actors, musicians and artists. Gossip columns detailed the guest lists not at the latest restaurant or nightclub openings, but at the latest screenings of *Deep Throat*. The dirty mac brigade were there too, of course, and students, and couples, even first dates.

Deep Throat became the first porn film to take more than a million dollars at the box office (going on, finally, to net nearly six hundred million dollars). It was all the rage; *Deep Throat* got a British release, and then a load of low-rent Swedish films arrived at local Gaumont and Jacey cinemas, and they were proper porn films, featuring fornication rather than the giggly smut and unimaginative titillation of what had been offered before in high street cinemas. Into this changed environment came the first *Emmanuelle* film in 1974, with the heroine dispensing erotic goodness, as she was to continue to do through the decade. For all its fame, the *Emmanuelle* series was something of a soft-focus disappointment, and a much more valuable film in this era was *Last Tango in Paris* starring Marlon Brando and Maria Schneider. *Last Tango* had what the *Confessions* series didn't have: boredom, lust, danger, unpredictability.

This was the era of disease-free party sex and sexual experimentation. The effect of the sexual revolution in the mainstream is celebrated in Rick Moody's 1994 novel *The Ice Storm*, set in 1973 in the Connecticut suburbs (and later made into a film directed by Ang Lee and starring Kevin Kline and Sigourney Weaver). Benjamin Hood is one of the book's central characters; a work colleague, George Clair, is obsessed with *Last Tango in Paris* ('the most erotic film ever', he tells anyone who will listen).

In *The Ice Storm*, Rick Moody uncovers confusion in an era of heightened sexual expectation. Suburban reality collides with the sexual revolution, and, despite Nene and George O'Neill's promises of sex without jealousy, sexual activity is awash with betrayal and lies. Furthermore, Moody relates the complicated personal lives to the deceit and cover-up of Watergate. According to Benjamin, 'The government is unfaithful. The world is. Nothing is the way we think.'

The Ice Storm is persuasive because it acknowledges that the pleasures of casual sex are easier to celebrate in song or watch on a big screen than to enact, and that few people understood the full implications of the sexual revolution, and even fewer played an active part in it. From Stoke-on-Trent to Stockton-on-Tees, few people were overdosing on carnal pleasure. Of course changes were in the air, and new attitudes, casual sex and escalating drug use made a practical, incontrovertible difference to many people's lives, but any real story of the Seventies also has to acknowledge that often new ideas never arrive, change is just a rumour and the good life is just out of reach.

Confusion was rife in this era, with moral guardians like the Festival of Light still trying to influence public policy, yet films like *Deep Throat* were hitting the headlines, and top shelf magazines were proliferating. In February 1974 a newsagent in Bath was taken to court after police raided his shop and took away copies of magazines including *Penthouse*, *Forum*, *Adult Digest*, *Health & Efficiency*, *Mayfair*, *Playboy* and *Club International*. Millions of such magazines were in circulation, and there was little surprise when the case was dropped, yet in the same month, in the run-up to the general election, Edward Heath was promising a purge of top shelf publications with the introduction of the Indecent Displays Act after a campaign led by Mary Whitehouse of the National Viewers and Listeners Association.

Benjamin Hood in *The Ice Storm* isn't revelling in the sexual revolution, he's stumbling around in the dawn of the crisis decades, in a world which, according to Eric Hobsbawm, 'had lost its bearings'. Monogamy and marriage were questioned, and notions of sexual identity too; the early 1970s witnessed a greater acceptance of behaviour previously considered deviant. It was the era of Ray Davies singing about Lola, Al Pacino playing Sonny robbing a bank (badly) to pay for his lover's sex-change operation in *Dog Day Afternoon*, and Andrew Logan's 'Alternative Miss World' held in a converted jigsaw factory in Islington in 1972. This spirit of adventure energised David Bowie, and in January 1972 Bowie's new persona was unveiled; he'd created a character for himself –

Ziggy Stardust – and renamed his band the Spiders from Mars. Four months later, the LP *The Rise and Fall of Ziggy Stardust and the Spiders from Mars* was released.

Bowie has said that the character of Ziggy was based on Vince Taylor, an early rock & roller who had a spell in France as an Elvis impersonator in the mid-1950s, and had a smash hit with 'Brand New Cadillac' in 1959. Bowie met Vince Taylor a few times in the 1960s, when Taylor had clearly gone off the edge. Bowie says he remembered him opening a map outside Charing Cross tube station, putting it on the pavement and kneeling down with a magnifying glass. 'He pointed out all the sites where UFOs were going to land.'

While drawing on this encounter with the unhinged, spaced-out Vince Taylor to help create the character, the Ziggy name also had undeniable echoes of the model Twiggy (who was to appear on the front of Bowie's *Pin Ups* LP in 1973) and Iggy Pop. Bowie seemed to be fascinated with Iggy, and is said to have had him in mind in the songs 'Panic in Detroit' and 'Jean Genie'. Iggy had few showbiz graces, and as a performer there was no artifice. He was deliciously, sometimes disastrously, all too real.

In creating his reinvention Bowie drew on the frisson of androgyny and the sparkle and danger of space travel, but also dramatised some of the darker obsessions of the early 1970s that had already been explored in the music of The Velvet Underground, The Stooges and The Doors: apocalypse, angst, insanity and suicide. Despite these heavy themes, key to his crossover appeal was his ability to always keep his music playful, thrilling, full of choruses and pop tricks. The release of the single 'Starman' on 28 April 1972, six weeks before the LP, marked the beginning of a two-year period, through to the end of 1973, when Bowie was the biggest act in Britain, with eight Top 10 singles and four Top 5 LPs (including three that went to No. 1). It was like Bowie was some kind of emissary from the underground sent to change the mainstream, making the avant-garde pop and the world weirder.

He acknowledged confusion, but opened up possibilities, embraced deviancy. There was a sense of being an outsider about him, and until the punk years and the arrival of Johnny Rotten, Bowie was the primary role model for many disaffected young Britons, male or female, looking for rebellion and outrageousness.

In many ways his co-conspirator was Marc Bolan. Bolan was the prettiest star, the originator, but for Alan Jones, Bolan was eclipsed by Bowie. Alan had been in London since 1970 and was always looking for the fashion cutting-edge, usually at one or two of the capital's gay hangouts. 'I never liked Bolan's look, that dishevelled look,' he says. 'It was too on the cusp of hippy whereas Bowie was a bit more futuristic looking; it was such a strong image at that time.'

Bowie's influence on the young in the 1970s is hard to overstate; from beyond his commercial period and on to the *Low* LP in 1977, his music, his clothes and his attitudes touched a generation, put make-up on art students and wedge haircuts on football fans. Dozens of musicians who went on to achieve success in the 1980s drew inspiration from Bowie; in fact, a debt to Bowie is probably the only thing The Smiths and Duran Duran have in common.

Bowie's reassertion of sexual ambiguity in rock & roll was influenced by his wife Angela; it was Angela who took him to see Andy Warhol's outrageous play *Pork* and who insisted on nights out in gay bars in London, some of them the same ones Alan Jones had been frequenting. Alan recognises how Bowie, although in some ways ahead of his time, was also absorbing and refashioning various looks around at the time. 'It's very hard not to look back in retrospect and think of things differently to how they were, but what I will tell you is this: many people in those bars had the look that Bowie went on to have a year later.'

The music in gay bars at the time hadn't evolved into the

classic gay disco sound – Alan remembers dancing to Black Sabbath's 'Paranoid' – and gay men were also a long way off the clone look that began to dominate in the second half of the 1970s. 'Most of them would be wearing Alkasura, the clothes were always from Alkasura,' Alan says. 'I used to have every single outfit Alkasura ever had, red corduroy jumpsuits, brilliant stuff. It was such an important brand. And people would be wearing those tucked into boots and there were little gold tops and that's what I remember; people looking like that.'

The strength of this influence inspired Bowie to make a confession in *Melody Maker* in January 1972, claiming, 'I'm gay and always have been', although in the original interview, the journalist, Michael Watts, stresses that Bowie's amused, sly jollity undermined some of the seriousness of the confession. As Bowie's career continued, this sense of make-up and artifice remained.

Bowie was inspired by Iggy but also fed from the New York of Andy Warhol and The Velvet Underground. In New York he found sleaze, deviance and decadence, just as he would later in the decade in Berlin. According to Barney Hoskyns in his history of glam rock, 'New York was about drag queens and junkies, small-town freaks transforming themselves into gutter aristocrats as they revolted against America's repressive homophobia.'

America never took to Bowie with the same fervour that England did. England in the Seventies was the sub-culture capital of the world. Ideas, especially those disseminated through music, moved quickly, and the colour and the controversy surrounding Bowie appealed to kids who celebrated their distance from the Sixties and its music. 'Bowie offered noise and glitz and sexual ambiguity as a statement; a boot in the collective sagging denim behind of hippie singersongwhiners,' according to the sleevenotes of the Rykodisc reissue of *Sound & Vision*.

In England, music fans weren't restricting themselves to the occasional Bowie single, they were buying into his look, even his life. Jayne Casey was among those who were drawn to Bowie. She'd left home, left school and run away to New Brighton. She stayed with a number of older girls there and looked after their kids. She'd been leading this life for eighteen months or so when, one day in 1972, the headmistress from her old school knocked on the door. She told Jayne she wanted her to go back to school. 'She told me I was the brightest kid she'd ever met and she'd not forgotten me. She'd come to New Brighton. She'd asked round and she'd found me.'

She asked Jayne to go into care. 'I agreed and I packed what few things I had and she picked me up and took me to the Social Services office and I sat there until ten o'clock at night until they got me a foster home.'

Despite the opportunity for a new start, she'd get thrown out of one foster home, and then be placed in another the following week, and she seldom settled. She had few possessions, but one was precious: a copy of Simon & Garfunkel's *Bridge Over Troubled Water* album. Although she could be spikey and confrontational, the album addressed another part of Jayne's personality, embracing her with a warm blanket of melancholia. An LP of acoustic ballads, intimate and well-crafted, *Bridge Over Troubled Water* was released in 1969, although it wasn't until the 'Bridge Over Troubled Water' single broke into the charts early in 1970 that the LP began selling. By 1975 it had sold more than ten million copies; one of the best-selling albums of all time.

She accepts now that she was a handful for her foster parents. 'By that time it was too late really because I'd been brought up by my father and I hadn't been socialised properly. I didn't understand family life, I just didn't understand it at all. I wasn't trying to be difficult, it was just the person I was. I hated the world that I was in, hated the values and just thought it was so hypocritical and shit. I wanted to find boys who wore mascara and leather trousers!'

When she wasn't listening to Simon & Garfunkel, she'd be out painting the town red. The impact of those nights dancing at the Chelsea Reach strengthened as she started hearing things about Andy Warhol, The Velvet Underground and the Factory scene. Thus an instinctive enjoyment of 'Get it On' led her to a new world of exciting ideas: 'I'd become aware of Warhol, and I'd heard about the whole Velvets scene, although I don't think I'd heard much Velvets then actually, and I dyed my hair red and got it cut into spikes.'

During the summer of 1972, Bowie developed his relationships with the Velvets and Iggy Pop. At a live show at the Festival Hall, Lou Reed was Bowie's special guest, and a week later Bowie hosted a press conference at the Dorchester Hotel and invited Lou Reed and Iggy Pop along. His advocacy of their music gifted them new audiences; both of them played sell-out shows at the King's Cross Cinema during July 1972. Bowie had also taken on the role of producer for Lou Reed's LP *Transformer*. Iggy Pop, meanwhile, was working on *Raw Power*. He'd lost his lustre and sold Jim Morrison's clothes, and had been trying to give up heroin but had got stuck using Quaaludes and other tranquillisers. But London energised him.

Although their debts to New York were clear, the backgrounds of some of the era's key English icons couldn't be much further from New York's mean streets. Bowie was born in Brixton and grew up in Bromley in Kent. Roxy Music were also intriguing, in their early days especially. A brilliant band who presented sleek high art concepts in a deviant pop context, but, again, their backgrounds were far from the drug dives of New York. Brian Eno had been Social Secretary at Winchester Art College, and Bryan Ferry, son of a coal miner, had grown up in Washington in County Durham and been taught by Richard Hamilton at Newcastle Art College. In 1970 Ferry had left an r&b band called the Gas Board and formed Roxy Music.

Bowie's Ziggy Stardust persona, plugged into sci-fi fantasy and apocalyptic fear, successfully created a link between the experimental, suffering, fragile rock star – out there all alone – and an astronaut, an alien, a space adventurer. In Bowie's work at the time there also seemed to be some belief in the power of the gifted individual, an übermensch, a saviour; an idea which he developed later, the idea of a 'homo superior', a rider on the storm.

Through 1972, not content with the success of Ziggy Stardust, Bowie also found time to work with Mott the Hoople. Mott had made several LPs under the guidance of Guy Stevens, but their career was floundering and they were on the verge of breaking up. Hearing of their troubles, Bowie offered them a song he'd just written, 'All the Young Dudes'. Mott recorded a new LP during the summer, with Bowie co-producing; 'All the Young Dudes' was the title track and a massive hit in August 1972.

You'd need more than a few songs to define everything there is to be said about the generation emerging during that particular part of the Seventies, marching out from under the shadow of their hippy older brothers and sisters. Some of the rebellion and confusion is there in Alice Cooper's 'Eighteen' (1971), and some of the exhilaration is caught in T-Rex's 'Children of the Revolution', but 'All the Young Dudes' by Mott the Hoople is immense, an anthem for a post-Beatles generation ('We never got it off on that revolution stuff / What a drag'), delivered with all the swagger of a football chant. The dudes are untamed juvenile delinquent wrecks, drinking wine, feeling fine. The record and the band's image were perfect for the times: Mott managed to combine a slightly unnerving take on glam with the emotional hard rock of Led Zeppelin.

In many ways, the era of 'All the Young Dudes' was a high water mark for lad culture; lots of drinking, bovver boys stalking city streets, football hooligans causing havoc on Saturday afternoons. It all made sense twenty years later when *Loaded* and Oasis inflicted another dose of lad culture on Britain, and we had a return of stomping terrace rock as practised by Slade, and haircuts reminiscent of The Faces (1973, 'Pool Hall Richard' era).

But life for lads in 1972 and 1973 wasn't as clear cut as the image suggests; in fact, the young dudes had an identity crisis, as the loosening of authority and a lack of rules was creating self-exploration but also great confusion. There's a character mentioned in 'All the Young Dudes': 'Jimmy looking sweet / Though he dresses like a queen / he can kick like a mule.' Young hooligans would be wearing make-up, skinheads were dancing to black music. Another band of that moment, Slade, roared like rabble-rousers but kept their threat in check. In 'Vicious', on the 1973 *Transformer* LP, Lou Reed asks us to hit him with a flower. In 'Walk on the Wild Side' (on the same LP), he tells us he was a she. Half the lads at school would be fighting at football, the other half daubing peace signs on toilet walls.

Bowie spoke to this identity crisis and lads listened; the messages were mixed, but in an age of confusion they rang true. There was an ironic, skin-deep, or showbiz element to a lot of the cross-dressing in the glam era. Marc Bolan's attitudes were also less than clear cut. 'I don't really care what people think,' said Bolan. 'Anyway, I don't believe chicks like really butch guys.' But he wasn't the first man to realise that getting in touch with his feminine side was a big step to getting in touch with feminine fans.

At the same time as men were discovering new questions to answer, there was also an increased amount of activity in feminism and the women's movement. 1972 saw the launch of *Spare Rib*, established by Rosie Boycott and Marsha Rowe, who had both been around during the very first days of the Virago Press. In the underground press there had been dozens of publications – like *Shrew* and *Harpies Bizarre* – but *Spare Rib* was the first commercial and high-profile feminist-focused magazine in England. But the *Spare Rib* agenda – campaigning, consciousness-raising and discussing steps forward for radical feminism – was only part of the story of 1972; in the same year, out of the consumerist wing of the women's movement, came the first issue of *Cosmopolitan*.

The developing empowerment of women would take time to filter through nationwide, and Jayne Casey remembers little about the wider debates. A struggling teenager back in Liverpool after her few short months in New Brighton, she was, as ever, relying on her survival instincts. 'I was in children's homes and I fucking hated it and it fucking hated me, and I tried to do my A Levels, and I just couldn't stand it, it was just so awful. Oh yeah, this is what happened. They put me into some kind of approved lodging place and I was lodging with a family and the family were really cool actually, lecturers at the University. And I left school much to everyone's disgust and I got a job in a hairdresser's as a receptionist.'

It was 1973, she was seventeen. The hairdresser's was called Cut Above the Rest, a Manchester-based company with a branch in the centre of Liverpool. She was employed there not to do much, but just to be somebody. 'They employed me to sit out front because I was so gorgeous! I was a bit like a kind of Marilyn Monroe lookalike, kind of blonde and tits and gorgeous.'

Back in New Brighton she'd dreamt of meeting boys with mascara. Sitting on reception at Cut Above the Rest, she'd become used to people coming in, hanging around. One day in walked a boy wearing salmon pink trousers and mascara. His name: Pete Burns. He said he wanted a job. 'I think he was fourteen at the time, and there was like no chance.'

But Pete Burns so wanted a job that he returned again

and again, and by the end of 1974 he'd started work at Cut Above the Rest. Jayne was soon to meet other lads who were to form a kind of family for her. After Pete Burns came Holly Johnson, and then Paul Rutherford hot on his high heels.

Jayne remembers some of the staff at the hairdresser's were out on the town one night without her, and they came in the next morning and said, 'We met this kid last night who was so fantastic and he had red tights on, and his name was Holly.' 'I was really pissed off that I hadn't met him. Habitat was next door to us and some time later they all came running in shouting, "The boy Holly's next door in Habitat; come and have a look!" and I did and there he was in Habitat, I saw this creature!'

Jayne had met her boys in mascara in roundabout ways. It had all happened by accident, but there was no other way, says Jayne: 'You didn't meet in clubs because there wasn't a scene.'

If you looked a bit different and you were somewhere in town you eventually found each other. 'People would tell you, they'd walk up to you, tell you there's another weirdo down the road! So within a couple of years I'd got a right posse of boys with mascara. I shaved my hair off, and thought, OK, this is it, let's have a laugh!'

The Seventies generation was enjoying a burst of excitement, but that's not to say that the music coming out of the radio was uniformly wonderful. Listeners in those years endured the likes of 'Puppy Love' by The Osmonds, 'My Ding a Ling' by Chuck Berry, and a bunch of songs by John Denver. Even music industry insiders weren't very comfortable with this; in one demonstration of frustration and distress, a Los Angeles DJ, Robert W. Morgan, played 'Puppy Love' non-stop for ninety minutes. Fearing for the mental health of the DJ, listeners called the police, who broke into the station and turned the music off.

Pioneers like Bowie, Bolan and Roxy Music had been inspirational, but they'd also helped to soften the market for a host of glitter bands who absorbed some of the elements that the pioneers had displayed, perhaps even neutered them; this is a familiar process in the history of pop music. And so it was that in 1973 *Top of the Pops* became a playground for Sweet, Mud and Gary Glitter, and some of glam's attitudes and some of its clothes would reappear in the next pop sound: The Rubettes and the Bay City Rollers.

Having achieved a glorious combination of glam and pessimism, David Bowie was clearly intent on taking things further, beyond the commercial confines of the teeny bop singles of Sweet. Bowie's records had an edge, a sense of apocalypse, and a sense of time running wild. But there was a personal cost: in February 1973, on the second Ziggy tour in the USA, Bowie collapsed onstage and soon after decided to break up the band.

After the rise and rise of Ziggy, plus, of course, his work with Lou Reed and Mott the Hoople, by 3 July 1973, the Ziggy Stardust and the Spiders from Mars retirement gig, Bowie was exhausted and also suffering what he called 'a serious sort of head problem'. In 1976 he looked back: 'It was quite easy to become obsessed night and day with the character. I became Ziggy Stardust. David Bowie went totally out of the window. Everybody was convincing me that I was a Messiah, I got hopelessly lost in the fantasy . . . I really did have doubts about my sanity.'

The link between the artist and the astronaut that he'd set up had turned into a modern version of an old myth, and one he was to return to several years later (when he played the character Newton in the film *The Man Who Fell to Earth*); an individual, a wanderer, home from a quest, changed. There's possibly even a connection to be made with the returning Vietnam veteran who journeyed to places we can't imagine, witnessing the apocalypse up close.

Roxy Music were going through changes in mid-1973 too. Brilliant singles like 'Virginia Plain', 'Love is the Drug' and 'Both Ends Burning', their debut LP, Bryan Ferry's mad super-quiff, and Eno's lurid bleepy artiness had all made a big impression on music lovers, in England at least, but in June 1973, after Roxy's second LP, *For Your Pleasure*, Brian Eno left the band. Ferry began to pursue a solo career alongside Roxy Music, and Eno began to record with Robert Fripp.

In America, some of the next generation of performers took their cue from Bolan and Bowie, including Kiss, who slapped on a ton of make-up and made their debut at the end of January 1973. Kiss guitarist Ace Frehley was clearly as much a fan of James Burke as he was of David Bowie, later proclaiming, 'By the time I'm forty, inter-planetary travel will be common. I'm gonna be on Mars.'

Generally, glam never took hold in America. Roxy Music's first and second LPs made a great impact in Britain but not in the USA. In the rock world, listeners seemed to prefer the likes of the Allman Brothers, Lynyrd Skynyrd and Johnny Winter, and it was left to small scenes in big cities like New York and Los Angeles to discover Bowie. In LA the scene found a focus at Rodney Bingenheimer's English Disco. In New York, a key venue was the Mercer Arts Center, regularly featuring bands whose names promised camp confrontation: Teenage Lust, the Harlots of 42nd Street, and Ruby & the Rednecks. Pre-eminent were The New York Dolls, formed in 1971; their debut LP was released in 1973, a year after drummer Billy Murcia's death. They were a cult act from the beginning, supplementing the sort of trashy look The Rolling Stones were perfecting with confrontational, strutting, transvestite sleaze. The influence of The New York Dolls has been acknowledged since by the likes of The Smiths, The Undertones, and the Sex Pistols. 'They really didn't give a shit,' said Glen Matlock of the Pistols, approvingly.

The New York Dolls had been one of the bands most clearly

identified with the scene at the Mercer Arts Center, a part of
the Broadway Central hotel which was battered and decrepit.
The Mercer Arts Center collapsed, literally, in 1973; the walls
caved in and plaster fell from the ceilings (two members of
the band the Magic Tramps were said to have been in the
Mercer when it fell down). It was later claimed that its structural problems had been exacerbated by people vomiting on
the floors and pissing on the walls.

In 1973 Bowie released 'Life on Mars', a melodramatic,
slightly unsettling story of a young girl with mousey hair,
already world weary, which flashed high into the charts; it
had a great appeal to cynical and saddened miserabilists who
liked their music. There were obviously plenty of them
around, enough to buy hundreds of thousands of copies of a
track from a two-year-old LP.

Sometime soon after Bowie's LP *Aladdin Sane* was released
later in 1973, Alan Jones was working at the Portobello Hotel,
and the LP inspired him to go out on many occasions sporting
the same famous red and blue lightning flash make-up across
his face as Bowie wore on the LP's cover. Fashions were
going in a direction Alan loved: boys and girls in one-piece
jumpsuits, groovy jackets, rock chicks in fishnets. Although
he hasn't much memorabilia from his past, he began fishing
around until he found a picture of himself from that era, and
there he was, with a lightning flash, long blond hair and
skintight trousers. 'I had always been a fashion victim, even
in Portsmouth. At that time I had really long blond hair and
people used to mistake me for Mick Ronson because I really
had that look and I was always going to the early Bowie gigs,
the early Queen gigs.'

Queen's combination of gaudy rock, a theatrical front man,
and decadent, dramatic songs delivered them hits like 'Killer
Queen'. But, by all accounts, the most intense onstage performer in 1973 was Iggy Pop, full of personal demons and a
bucket of drugs. He was all for going to the edge and then

leaping over it, and took to lacerating his chest onstage with a broken bottle.

The glam moment was disappearing, driven out by commercialisation. At this point Marc Bolan was adamant: 'Glam rock is dead. It was a great thing, but now you have your Sweet, your Chicory Tip, and your Gary Glitter . . . what those guys are doing is circus and comedy.'

Sweet and Gary Glitter were still going strong early in 1974 (though not for long), but the pioneers had moved on, and not necessarily in happy directions. Eno had left Roxy Music, T-Rex were in decline, and Bowie, for a genius, had a crazy sense of taste and timing, and he was unfortunate when his deeply annoying 1967 'Laughing Gnome' single was rereleased and charted (later in the decade he'd release the awful Christmas single with Bing Crosby). But at least the records kept coming, releasing the *Pin Ups* LP in October 1973, cover versions of some of his favourite Sixties songs, including 'Where Have All the Good Times Gone?' by The Kinks.

In addition to a fascination with medieval myths, runes and Tolkien, progressive rock bands maintained an interest in the mystery of space and interplanetary travel. Yes had already gone intergalactic with tracks like 'Astral Traveller' and 'Starship Trooper', and in 1974 they released *Tales from Topographic Oceans*, atmospheric, ambitious, flawed and indulgent, one of progressive rock's most important LPs, with a cover by Roger Dean. Another landmark release that year was Pink Floyd's *Dark Side of the Moon* (which featured in the *Billboard* LP charts for the next fifteen years).

Spaceships, the moon and the solar system also became popular subject matter for dance music. Funk bands embraced the sci-fi angle, especially Parliament – featuring George Clinton, Bernie Worrell, Bootsy Collins and Maceo Parker – in the era of the *Mothership* LP (1975). And right through to the end of the 1970s disco was still going cosmic, with songs like 'Spacer' and 'Dancing in Outer Space', and, most intriguing of all perhaps, Gene Page's *Close Encounters* LP (1978), featuring space-themed songs (including a discofied cover version of the theme from the TV series *Star Trek*).

In the mid-1970s, space as portrayed on George Clinton LPs and Hollywood blockbusters like *Star Wars* was much more exciting than NASA's space programme. As public opinion moved on from the height of space fever, the space programme was scaled down. In December 1972 Apollo XVII became the last mission sending men to the moon, although unmanned space exploration continued; in the first half of 1973, the Soviets launched Venera 2, bound for Venus, while the Americans launched Skylab. In December 1973 the American Pioneer 10 spacecraft arrived on Jupiter and began to beam back the first close-up images of the planet before flying onwards. In the late 1980s it became the first spacecraft to leave the solar system. Nobody seems to know where it is. In 1976, a Viking probe was sent to look for life on Mars.

Economic pressures took some of the glamour from space exploration. It was beginning to look like an expensive, worthless spectacle, sucking public money into endless quests and distracting us from the mundane problems of everyday life. Gil Scott Heron had considered it as such for several years; his debut LP *Small Talk at 125th & Lenox* includes the classic 'Whitey on the Moon', which links the cost of the space programme with the deterioration of urban neighbourhoods. In 1976, the phrase 'Life on Mars' was used by Dexter Wansel as the title of an LP which included sleevenotes by Philadelphia songwriter Kenny Gamble, which also questioned the preoccupation with space exploration: 'The Viking probe will send back pictures to earth to let man see if life is on Mars. For what reason? Man has not mastered his existence here on Earth.'

We were being brought back down to earth. The spectacular potential of space travel, the bright new tomorrow promised by *The Burke Special*; those possibilities seemed closed off. The exhilaration of 'Children of the Revolution' seemed misplaced in a more mundane world, in a world of shrinking job opportunities, power cuts, *Mean Streets*, the numbing effects of heroin, and downers like Mandrax.

In America, Vietnam veterans were back, with nightmare memories and an uncertain future, but the war looked like it was finally moving towards some kind of a conclusion. In 1973 Kissinger's meetings in Paris produced a peace agreement which signalled a withdrawal of American troops from Vietnam, but no line was drawn under the Vietnam experience, as the area slid into chaos. The United States continued to arm and finance the South Vietnamese government in Saigon until August 1974. In the same month, the Watergate scandal forced the resignation of President Nixon, but even then the political, social and emotional reverberations from America's involvement in Vietnam continued to be felt – in memories, politics, books and films – and are still being felt today.

As 1973 turned into 1974, the IRA stepped up its campaign on the mainland. On 18 December 1973 a series of IRA bombs in London injured sixty people, and in the first days of the new year two bombs exploded in Birmingham (at Stephenson Square and Priory Circus), although there were no injuries. A couple of days later, five bombs were planted in London, with the Boat Show and Madame Tussauds among the targets.

The activities of the IRA were unignorable, part of the chaos and uncertainty of the times. On 11 November 1973 a peace agreement was signed between Israel and Egypt, but the oil crisis was far from over. As oil prices rose in the run-up to Christmas, Britain was especially hard hit; nearly two-thirds of its oil came from the Middle East. In the same period, industrial unrest grew. In October 1973 new arrangements for price and wage controls had come into force under Stage 3 of the Government's counter-inflationary policy, and wage increases over the winter were limited and closely linked to the cost of living.

However, the cut in oil exports from Arab countries gave strength to the National Union of Mineworkers; not only to demand higher wages but also to push for modernisation and investment in the coal industry which had become sidelined by successive governments and allowed the country to become dependent on oil. In November 1973, just eighteen months after their last successful strike, the NUM went on the offensive again, implementing an overtime ban in pursuit of a pay claim in excess of Stage 3 guidelines. This had an immediate effect on fuel supplies, which was exacerbated by industrial action by electricity power engineers, and then ASLEF rail workers banned overtime which disrupted the delivery of coal. On 13 November 1973, the Government declared a state of emergency.

During the state of emergency and beyond, however, Alan Jones maintained a state of high excitement. His job at the hotel introduced him to the Sadistic Mica Band (when they came over from Japan to support Roxy Music), the Back Street Crawlers and actors Richard Dreyfuss and Maria Schneider, the female lead in *Last Tango in Paris*.

Hobsbawm's phrase, describing a society that had 'lost its bearings', is accurate. No-one knew whether to believe Erich von Daniken, Joe Gormley, Nene and George O'Neill, James Burke or Aladdin Sane. Not everyone was enjoying sexual freedom or living a glam life, but you could get a touch of it as excess became attractive in a world with more questions than answers. Alan Jones was on the guest list when The New York Dolls came to town. Back at the hotel there'd be rock chicks, groupies, same sex trysts, and secret affairs. It was all a bit decadent, a bit daft: 'We were all really out there, I mean, I could show you some pictures of how I used to go to work in blue velvet hotpants. I don't know how I managed to walk down the street sometimes to be honest with you. When I

look back I'm amazed because I did look quite camp, I must
have done.'

His sexuality was conspicuous, but he never had any hassle
on the streets of Ladbroke Grove. 'I never had that; I never
felt persecuted. I never felt that persecution and I don't know
any of my contemporaries who did. I'm a very strong person
anyway and I've always been that way, but it wasn't just me;
all my friends felt the same.'

The glam moment was fleeting, but Alan reckons it's likely
that his self-confidence, and the sense of tolerance on the
streets, were boosted by the role of popular culture in creating
new circumstances. 'We were helped by the tenor of the
times, when you were seeing the Bowies and Marc Bolans
and there was that blurring, it was there, wasn't it? In the
zeitgeist, the ether.'

Whether the fads for coloured hair and boys in make-
up made a deep or lasting impression is hard to measure.
Liverpool, for example, wasn't Ladbroke Grove. In fact, most
places were harder and less forgiving, and the eccentric – or
the miserable, the creative, or the gay – were faced with fierce
pressure to conform to a whole other set of social and gender
norms. In those towns and cities, the sight of lads in blue
velvet hotpants was considered confrontational. Glittery guys
with girly looks were accepted on *Top of the Pops*, but not in
the queue for a taxi near Lime Street Station in Liverpool,
or in Redditch or Dewsbury, or on the bus from town to
Harpurhey.

Jayne Casey would move to London for a short while, and
then, even more briefly, live in Manchester, before moving
back to Liverpool, waking up one Thursday morning and seeing her face on the front cover of *New Musical Express*. But
back in those Bowie-fixated days, she was becoming aware of
how intolerant reactions could be. People working in offices
around Cut Above the Rest would collect fruit from the
market and throw it at the window. 'It just used to be hell.

We were in a pub one night and somebody just came up and split Pete Burns's head open with a pint glass and there was blood pouring out. He had something like twenty-eight stitches in his head.'

Her gang were beginning to thrive from all the attention of office workers, scallies and Friday night pissheads. 'You definitely wanted attention, and also you hated them all – it was "Just fuck off" – and you couldn't bear them so we were pleased to be pissing them off.'

In our current era there are frequent moral panics about urban violence, a proliferation of CCTV cameras on city streets, and film footage of drunken youths battling it out using broken bottles is served up for entertainment on Sky One. In the Seventies, before closed circuit or satellite television, city centres at night were no more secure than they are now. There were no guns, of course, but a great deal of low-level violence, even though, in contrast to today's high-octane nightlife industry, towns and cities were virtually empty most nights. There was no retail buzz and cities like Birmingham, Liverpool and Manchester had no tourist infrastructure. Instead, in old pubs, down deserted streets, round empty buildings and derelict warehouses there were people looking to batter you.

At the beginning of the crisis decades, conflict wasn't just played out by the Cold War powers, or terrorists and rogue states in the Middle East; there was conflict on the streets too. In the Seventies, life seemed raw, as tribes and football hooligans took to the streets. Jayne Casey and the weirdos – Bowie fans, and boys in mascara – were engaged in a fight for the right to be arty, for bubbly blondes to shave their hair off, and for the right of boys to wear salmon pink trousers. The guardians of conformity would be ready for them, but Jayne and her gang gave as good as they got: 'And we were well prepared to have a fight because we'd all grown up fighting. We weren't soft kids, we came from heavy working class backgrounds and we knew how to fight. Pete Burns was a fantastic fighter. We'd shock them; the scallies would come for us and we'd batter them! We attracted violence, every night, which was good; we hated the world and expected the world to hate us.'

CHAPTER FIVE

'Sad Sweet Dreamers' (1974)

On New Year's Day 1974 the International Soul Club hosted an all-dayer (starting at midday and going through until midnight) at the Top of the World in Stafford, with live acts including The Real Thing; tickets were just 88p. *Blues & Soul* magazine habitually passed information to readers, giving notice of all-dayers, all-nighters, DJs, major tours and live appearances, but during another difficult winter, journalists on the paper were just as often giving advice on travel plans.

No winters in the Seventies were free of some industrial chaos. From October 1973, the latest stage of the Conservative Government's counter-inflationary wages policy had put the Government and the unions on a collision course. The situation was greatly exacerbated by the oil crisis, as Arab producers restricted supplies and raised prices. At the beginning of 1974 the mood among political commentators was dark and doom laden. The *Guardian*, along with other papers, was only able to print limited numbers of copies due to a worldwide shortage of newsprint, but in the first issue of 1974 the paper's economics editor believed that the developed countries in the world had come to the end of an era of growth, and an editorial underlined this view, predicting continuing falls in living standards and higher unemployment, and posing the question 'Has Britain become ungovernable?'

In various parts of the country the miners were threatening to escalate their industrial action, and more increases in oil prices from Libya and Nigeria were on the way, but it wasn't just the threat of another miners' strike and the petrol shortages that created a sense of deepening crisis. At the beginning of 1974 – to give the communities of Northern Ireland a chance to govern their own affairs, and in a bid to end division – a power-sharing Executive, led by Brian Faulkner and his deputy Gerry Fitt, was established, but it received little support from the Loyalist community.

Loyalist factions – like the Ulster Freedom Fighters, a breakaway group from the Ulster Volunteer Force – were contributing to the continuing sectarian violence. At the end of January 1974, two UFF gunmen approached a gang of thirteen electricity workers laying cable in Newtownabbey, singled out Roman Catholics, took them to one side and opened fire with machine guns, killing two of the Catholic workers instantly. Meanwhile, the IRA continued to take the armed struggle to the mainland; twelve people died in February 1974 when an IRA bomb exploded on a bus carrying Army personnel and their families on the M62.

Over the first four months of 1974 the Executive struggled to provide an alternative to direct rule from Westminster, destabilised by the intense opposition of those determined not to give the Catholic Nationalists any kind of foothold; supported by Unionist MPs in Parliament, the Protestant organisation the Ulster Workers' Council initiated widespread, disruptive strike action with the intention of destroying the political initiative. Within fifteen days Faulkner had resigned and the Executive collapsed. Political discussions continued, but the likelihood of Unionist and Nationalist politicians working together seemed increasingly remote.

In January 1974, rumours that an Arab terrorist group had

the use of Soviet-made SAM 7 missiles dominated the news, and, as paranoia and uncertainty about international terrorism increased, troops and Scorpion reconnaissance vehicles were on standby at Heathrow Airport. Tensions in the Middle East, which had precipitated the oil crisis, set the agenda for decades to come. These tensions were increased by infighting amongst Palestinian terror groups; Abu Nidal's renegade Fatah Revolutionary Council broke away from Yasser Arafat's Palestinian Liberation Organisation, accusing Arafat of compromise and threatening to intensify the violence.

The year began with a three-day week in place. And as part of the state of emergency, the Government announced additional energy-saving measures: television stations were closed down at 10.30pm, and motorway speed limits were reduced to an energy efficient 50mph. Inflation was well above 20 per cent, and an election was looming. In the last week of January, challenging the Government's pay policy, the National Union of Mineworkers announced a full ballot of members as a first step to an all-out strike. The ballot revealed that 84 per cent of union members had voted for strike action; Prime Minister Edward Heath steadfastly refused to put more cash on the table, so a strike was called. Heath immediately announced an election date.

The general consensus among the writers in *Blues & Soul* during this chaotic winter was that at a time of petrol shortages it was better to travel by train. Despite travel hassles, but boosted by the low ticket price, The Real Thing's trip over to Stafford from their home in Liverpool was a success; things were beginning to come together for the band. It would be another thirty years or so before I caught up with them though, at a venue in Bradford on a bill with two other bands, Odyssey and Rose Royce. I'd seen some advertising material from Pennington's and clearly it wasn't going to be any kind of cutting-edge venue (the following week it was hosting a special onstage appearance by the presenter of *Bargain Hunt*,

David Dickinson). Pennington's was going to be buzzing later, but my Asian taxi driver told me this wasn't always the case: 'Most nights it's quiet up there, dead. It's the wrong part of town, you see.'

Surrounded by glorious hills, Bradford is home to the outstanding Museum of Film and Photography and plays host to an annual film festival the rival of any in the world. Also in the city there's the West Yorkshire Playhouse, and the home of composer Delius, and a few miles up the valley the magnificent Salts Mill galleries created by Jonathan Silver in Saltaire, the site of an old Victorian textile factory development of factories, houses, schools and churches built by Titus Salt in the mid-nineteenth century.

During the election campaign in February 1974, Saltaire played host to an anti-Common Market rally addressed by ex-Conservative minister Enoch Powell. Two days earlier, at the Mayfair Suite in Birmingham (part of the new Bull Ring development), he'd pulled 1,800 people. At Victoria Hall in Saltaire 1,000 people were inside and almost as many were locked outside. Powell was vehemently against increasing British links with Europe, and at the time it was Labour that was sceptical of the Common Market, while the Tories were pushing for greater links with Europe. As with his views on race, Powell was appealing to a narrow nationalism, defending a version of British identity. Heath's agenda, according to Powell, was to ensure that 'Britain becomes the province of a European super-state', and for this reason he urged a vote for Labour.

The old industrial site at Saltaire is a symbol of Bradford's glory days in the Victorian era, when Bradford rose with the British Empire. It was one of those cities that was a vital cog in Britain's mighty manufacturing industry, and part of a trading network that created a new monied class and put silk hats on Bradford millionaires. Now, looking backwards is what Bradford does best. Attractions at St George's Hall in recent years include appearances by comedians and orchestras, but also a huge number of visits by music acts from a bygone era, including Gene Pitney and Steeleye Span, as well as an Elvis tribute night, Björn Again, and the Kings of Swing ('recreating an era when everyone fell in love to songs like "Come Fly With Me",' according to the publicity material).

Wool textiles had been the mainstay of Bradford, but competition from low-cost imports and advances in manmade fibres had led to a major contraction of the industry. In 1964 around 50,000 people were employed in textiles in Bradford; nearly one-third of the total working in the town. Ten years later, the number of people employed in the textile trade in the area had nearly halved, the Victorian heyday had long departed, and, in 1974, Bradford, along with many other towns and cities, faced an uncertain future.

This was the major social change in the Seventies; as the crisis decades arrived, Great British hype and glory faded, an era of growth disappeared, and the post-industrial age arrived. The oil crisis had exposed structural problems in industry – connected to a host of issues, including under-investment and over-manning – and strengthened the hand of foreign competitors. Manufacturing industry had created and sustained our cities, and the post-industrial future was uncertain. The Labour Party's 1974 election manifesto promised a White Paper entitled 'The Regeneration of British Industry'.

These economic and social changes knocked the likes of Manchester and Sheffield, but at least those cities had some diversity, a university campus, and some retail strength to provide a basis for survival; one-industry or satellite areas had little to look forward to other than deterioration and dereliction. Places like Nelson, Bradford and Oldham lost their industries and their self-confidence in the 1970s. It could be argued that they were saved from extinction by the arrival of Asian immigrants, shoring up the population and creating new businesses. By 1974 nearly 10 per cent of the Bradford population was from Pakistan and India.

The death of traditional manufacturing industries left thousands of acres of derelict warehouse and factory space in northern England. Salts Mill, for example, fell into disuse, although, thanks to Jonathan Silver, it now houses an exhibition dedicated to the work of artist David Hockney, one of Bradford's other homegrown talents. Hockney had attended Bradford College of Art in the 1950s, and although he maintained local connections (returning to visit his parents two or three times a year), he yearned to escape. He moved to London, and then discovered the gay bars of New York (and the art scene there; he was befriended by Andy Warhol), travelled and taught in the USA. By the mid-1970s he was enjoying a laid back, gay-friendly lifestyle among the hedonistic art circles of Malibu Beach and the Hollywood Hills, his canvases lit by the California sun. In 1978 he bought a house in the Hollywood Hills; he'd got as far from Bradford as anyone could without making a home on the moon.

Unmoved by nostalgia and dismissive of so many of the options to experience or re-experience the sound of the Seventies, I was, admittedly, breaking all my promises when I went to see The Real Thing in Bradford. Of course there is an explanation, and not just the fact that their hit singles from the mid-1970s – 'You to Me Are Everything', 'Can't Get By Without You' and 'Can You Feel the Force', and the classic 'Children of the Ghetto' – are all irresistible; or because I'd met Eddy Amoo of the band a few months earlier for a marathon two-hour interview – during which he, brightly, very willingly, discussed racism, the disco days, and his unease with some of the versions of Seventies history – and I told him I'd try to catch The Real Thing live; or because I wanted to celebrate the lives of dance music devotees in the 1970s. My main purpose in going over to Bradford that evening was that I hoped the night would ease the nightmare of my Flares experience in Wolverhampton. There I'd been served the Seventies repackaged and reheated like some easy cook cliché, all freshness and spice removed. I wanted to get closer, if you like, to the real thing.

Back in the Seventies I'd missed out on seeing The Real Thing play live. Looking back, you realise you bought outfits you'd have been better leaving in the shop, or you'd listened to the wrong people telling you about the wrong groups. I did OK, saw some great gigs, but it was probably the wrong decision to save up to buy tickets to see Gong instead of The Rezillos, and The Boomtown Rats instead of The Ramones. I also missed Earth, Wind & Fire, and I remember the night The Real Thing came to town. The cool girls went to see them, but I sat in watching *Match of the Day*. And then all these years later, their tour was advertised and opportunity knocked one more time.

Back then, the black population seemed to be cut out of the media, and music shows like *Top of the Pops* were among the few places where black faces appeared in the public eye. There were a few sports stars, although we were still a long way from the situation today; most of the high-profile British boxers, for example, were white (Henry Cooper, Joe Bugner and Pat Cowdell), and it would be four years before a black footballer played for England, and even longer before a black footballer could play for England without the threat of racist abuse from sections of the team's fanbase.

Most of the black acts on *Top of the Pops* were American musicians, but The Real Thing were part of a select number of black British pioneers in the 1970s. From Manchester, Sweet Sensation became the first black British soul act to top the charts, in October 1974, with 'Sad Sweet Dreamer'.

In 1974 Sweet Sensation were on a similar live circuit to The Real Thing. The night before The Real Thing played that Stafford gig, Sweet Sensation were playing at a New Year's Eve special at Tiffany's in Newcastle-under-Lyne with an eight-piece soul band, on the same bill as Johnny Johnson and the Bandwagon, and DJs Colin Curtis, Ian Levine, Soul Sam and Pep. Built around the brilliant singing voice of Marcel King, Sweet Sensation had their break on the TV talent show *New Faces*, where they were picked up by the songwriter and producer Tony Hatch who was one of the panellists on the show. He guided them to the Pye label, recorded an unsuccessful single, 'Snow Fire', and then released 'Sad Sweet Dreamer', co-produced by Hatch and the songwriter Des Parton.

Out and about in 1973 and 1974 you'd hear classic black American soul everywhere; Four Tops and Smokey Robinson hits belting out, distorting, as you rode the waltzers at the fair; and wonderful Chairmen of the Board singles, or the sound of The Supremes blasting through the tannoy standing on the terraces waiting for the teams to appear at the football. The big new sound was coming from Philadelphia where producers Kenny Gamble and Leon Huff were producing luscious, string-led hits for the likes of MFSB and The O'Jays. In this climate, the infectious sound of 'Sad Sweet Dreamer' hit the soul spot.

All over the country dance clubs were filling up, from the mainstream discotheques to dozens of small venues catering to funk and soul connoisseurs, from the unashamedly cheesy to the wilfully obscure. In the long tradition of music and nightlife in England, we've already seen how black American music has been the dance music of choice since the passionate rhythms of 1920s jazz were embraced on the dancefloor. White youth had devoured releases on the Chess, Stax and Motown labels from the mod era and beyond, while bands like The Beatles and The Rolling Stones had begun their careers in the early 1960s doing cover versions of Chuck Berry and Motown. In the mid-1970s dancefloors were seeing more action than at any time since the mod explosion in 1964.

Thirty years ago, long hairs had their double LPs, but soul

fans, with short hair and short songs, had their 7-inch singles. Back in 1974, teenagers might have been buying the Bay City Rollers, but the Pennington's crew were more likely to have been buying 'Keep on Truckin'' by Eddie Kendricks, a classic version of 'Who is He and What is He to You?' by Creative Source, 'Love's Theme' by the Love Unlimited Orchestra, Johnny Bristol's 'Hang on In There', 'Rock the Boat' by the Hues Corporation, or 'Funky Nassau' by Beginning of the End. Such was the rush of records aimed at the discotheques that in one issue of *Black Music* they introduced a new category on the singles reviews pages: 'Funk, bump & boogie'.

Soul was a major force in music and had a wide influence. For example, David Bowie, using the sounds and styles of soul music, reinvented himself yet again with the *Young Americans* LP, leading to his classic appearance on *Soul Train* in November 1975 when he performed 'Golden Years' and 'Fame'. American post-Wattstax soul and the Philly sound dominated, but there were also exciting new forms of jazz featuring the likes of The Crusaders and Herbie Hancock (his classic *Head-hunters* LP was released in 1973), and a pocket of activity down in Miami. But when a *Soul Train* audience member asked him when he actually started getting into soul music, Bowie seemed to take it back to the mod era. 'Getting into it? Well, back in England you see, when I was a teenager popping 'em, you know – I don't know if it's a similar expression over here – on street corners,' he tried to explain. 'We have street corners in London,' he said, laughing a little at his own joke, while everybody else in the studio just seemed confused. 'And we used to go to a lot of clubs and James Brown was very popular about then. I was about seventeen then.'

In England in 1974, Northern Soul was also still going strong; after the closure of the Twisted Wheel late in 1971, the Torch in Tunstall, Stoke-on-Trent, briefly flourished, and then the Highland Room at the Blackpool Mecca became another favoured venue, hosted by DJs Colin Curtis and Ian

Levine. The Mecca soon had a rival, though, after DJ Russ Winstanley established Wigan Casino's all-nighter from September 1973 onwards.

The various Northern Soul nights, venues and DJs tended to define themselves against what others were doing. Thus when Wigan Casino instituted a second room in 1975 playing older classics, Blackpool Mecca moved towards funk and Philly and further away from the tried and tested beat-heavy stompers that the Casino was known for. Then there was the Pier at Cleethorpes, promoted by Mary Chapman, which caused a stir throughout 1975. All over the country, clubbers would travel to venues for one-offs, monthlies and all-nighters; this wasn't how mainstream clubbers behaved. A manager of the Mecca-owned Tiffany's club in Newcastle interviewed by Tony Cummings in 1974 during a night hosted by DJs Colin Curtis and Ian Levine said, 'We realise this Northern Soul scene is quite different from other discotheque situations. You wouldn't get kids travelling forty miles or more for an "ordinary" disco. It's a minority audience, sure, but a pretty sizeable one. And the kids are very, very dedicated.'

Then as now, records could first make an impression out in the margins and go on to transform the mainstream; thus in January 1974 'There's a Ghost in My House' by R. Dean Taylor was being played by rare soul DJs at the Central Soul Club in Leeds, the all-nighter at Samantha's in Sheffield, and on Monday nights at the Windmill Club in Kettering, but by the end of April they'd stopped playing it. Specialist DJs are often like that; taking a song out of their record box if it's all over the radio and high in the charts.

The scene mostly revolved around DJs playing their choicest tracks, but soul acts were also available live. The Exciters arrived late in the summer, playing Wigan Casino, Wolverhampton Lafayette, and American Air Force bases at Mildenhall and Lakenheath. Also in 1974, Jr Walker & the All Stars toured (incorporating venues like the Rainbow in

London and Manchester Free Trade Hall, as well as the Heavy Steam Machine in Hanley, which was run by Chris Burton who had previously been the man behind the Torch), The Detroit Emeralds appeared at Tiffany's in Hull and Barbarella's in Birmingham, and a double bill of The Four Tops and The Delfonics played everywhere from Hammersmith Odeon to the Fiesta in Stockton-on-Tees in the autumn of 1974.

There were dozens of DJs in the 1960s and 1970s who had nurtured these traditions – evangelical enthusiasts like Guy Stevens trawling record stalls in search of authentic soul and r&b. To these aficionados, the notion of imported music appealed; they didn't want the obvious or the compromised, and considered black American music the most authentic sound around. Some DJs were preciously uncommercial, like Les Spaine at the Pun Club on Seel Street in Liverpool, but even those with a populist outlook, like Chris Hill – who in 1974 was playing the Goldmine in Canvey Island, Essex – would target connoisseurs on certain nights of the week with promises that his sets included 'Latest US Imports'. By 1974 record shops like One Stop, with three branches in London, specialised in bringing music in from abroad.

Despite the efforts of Abbafication, it's unarguable that much of what was most marginalised thirty years ago is now the most influential, and, furthermore, it's gratifying that many of the most commercial acts have disappeared, or at best been consigned to the fringes of showbusiness; where oh where are The Rubettes? The combined Top 20 hits of Television, MFSB, The Clash and Kraftwerk are less than the number achieved by The Rubettes in their heyday, yet the influence of those acts is huge.

The 1970s soul scene exemplifies this. Generally, the action was in unheralded places, and soul scene followers were never surprised if their lives were changed by a trip to hear a DJ like Neil Rushton playing at the Catacombs in Wolverhampton; that's why the *Blues & Soul* listings were so important. I'm fairly sure that the best record played anywhere in England in August 1974 wouldn't have been in a high street discotheque with the DJ trapped in a pop chart playlist; more likely it would have been played at the Blue Room on Washway Road in Sale on a Thursday, or at Tiffany's in Darwen on a Thursday, or on a Friday at the Four Aces in Dalston.

The soul scene thrived away from the mainstream, and enjoyed the benefits of a specialist infrastructure – DJs, venues, promoters, shops and magazines – but it's been much neglected since. In Liverpool, if the 1960s belonged to The Beatles and the 1980s to Frankie Goes to Hollywood, The Real Thing were probably the most successful band of the 1970s. But The Real Thing are rarely mentioned in Liverpool's hall of fame, just as Sweet Sensation have frequently fallen off Manchester's music map. In fact, black British bands are probably the least well documented part of Seventies music.

That this particular episode in black British music history has been overlooked, and that the contribution specifically of The Real Thing has gone unacknowledged, isn't just my perception; it's a view shared by the band. Eddy Amoo was invited down to Albert Dock a couple of years ago: 'I was invited to an unveiling of a plaque they had put up for all the number one artists in Liverpool. I went down and I was totally ignored by the Liverpool media; the only people they were interested in were Atomic Kitten and Paul McCartney's brother!'

At the end of the Sixties, while Eddy Amoo had been in The Chants – who had played with The Beatles and been given guidance early in their career by Brian Epstein, eventually signing to Pye in 1963 – his younger brother, Chris, had declared his desire to form his own band, and The Real Thing were born. The first four members – Chris Amoo, Ray Lake, Kenny Davis and Dave Smith – all grew up together in Liverpool 8, hung out in some of the street gangs of the time and began making music together in 1970.

Back in 1972 Eddy watched as his brother's band won themselves a slot on the TV show *Opportunity Knocks*. The band made enough of an impact to release 'Vicious Circle' on Bell Records, which unfortunately flopped. They moved to EMI and 'Plastic Man' got the band their first *Top of the Pops* appearance (it was a song Eddy Amoo had originally written for The Chants). As Eddy's involvement with The Real Thing increased, the natural progression was for him to formally join the band, which he eventually did following the departure of Kenny Davis.

By 1974, another British soul group had achieved considerable success. Hot Chocolate, signed to Mickie Most's RAK record label in 1970, emerged with the brilliant 'Brother Louie' in 1973, a subtle, smoothly delivered song about an inter-racial love affair between a black girl and a white boy opposed by his racist parents. 'Brother Louie' was a hit in Britain, but the song became successful in America only after it was picked up and covered by a white group, The Stories, who took it to the top of the US charts. Hot Chocolate soon had a couple of American hits in their own right, with 'Emma' and 'You Sexy Thing' (released at the end of 1975, 'You Sexy Thing' sold two million copies worldwide). Key to the band's appeal was singer Errol Brown, who had a great shaved-head look, like a British Isaac Hayes, aspiring and well dressed.

Huddled under the awning at the front of Pennington's, lit by the rope lights running the length of the club, the crowd for The Real Thing gig is pleased to get out of the Bradford rain, impatient and expectant. It's a mixed queue, with women just in the majority, a lot of couples, some office parties. A couple of men look like they share Errol Brown's wardrobe, handsome black fellas loving it. The ladies are all gladrags and highlights. Out of a minibus come what could well be half a rugby team, every one of them in their best new shirt. It's raining, we're in what's reputed to be the wrong part of town, but nothing can dampen my spirits and those of a hundred of West Yorkshire's finest disco devotees.

In front of me a mother with her daughter is happy to talk as we wait for the doors to open. They don't usually go out together, but it's a treat tonight and the mother has paid for the tickets. They're meeting a gang of friends inside later. I'm too polite to ask them their ages, but I would guess they're something like eighteen and thirty-nine. Not many others are on a family outing. The average age of the audience is at least thirty-five. I'm sure there's an element of nostalgia among the older people, and there's curiosity among the twenty-somethings, but already it's clear we're a good few steps away from a revival night. The vinyl collections may have been sold and replaced by CDs, but no-one has forgotten what it all meant back then; there's no half-witted 'irony' and none of that 'so good it's bad' absurdity.

The doors open at nine, the queue moves quickly and we go straight in. Some tickets are on sale on the door (£15), but they're all going to go by 9.30pm. Inside, we emerge into a low-slung club, a proper discotheque. Pennington's is a blast from a recent past; it would have been lauded as the perfect venue before club fashions evolved into the warehouse look, well before chill-out rooms. There are bars along most of the walls and above them lengths of pulsing blue and red lights. More lights are suspended on giant frames from the ceiling. At one end of the venue is a stage lit by green, red and blue lights. I haven't been in a building like this since, well, the 1970s.

As well as the Central Soul Club in Leeds on Fridays, and various nights featuring DJ Kev Roberts at Samantha's in Sheffield, in 1974 the soul brothers and sisters in the Bradford area were blessed with a number of specialist soul nights within easy reach, including an occasional all-dayer at the Portcullis Club on Pitt Street in Barnsley (featuring guest appearances from Wigan Casino resident Richard Searling). An all-dayer would typically take place on a Sunday, from

1pm through until midnight; you'd expect to pay 75p in advance.

The Real Thing couldn't relate to Northern Soul at all. Firstly, the band resented the aficionado's belief that their homegrown records could never be as authentic as American imports, and secondly, Eddy seems to confirm one of the perceptions at the time: that it was reggae and funk or jazz-funk that attracted a blacker crowd. For many black kids in the 1970s, Northern Soul was a white scene that appeared to revolve around the wrong kind of drugs; amphetamine sulphate was not the drug of choice among inner city black kids.

For Eddy, Northern Soul in the 1970s was also too much about looking backwards. The Real Thing clearly took influences and inspiration from America in the same way that The Beatles, The Rolling Stones and Led Zeppelin did, and remained open-minded, eager to evolve: 'Musically we've always hung around the clubs where they played soul and r&b and stuff, so in those days it was like The Temptations, and then Sly & the Family Stone, and then along came bands like Earth, Wind & Fire.'

The rising interest in the newer black music was further fed by radio, which helped soul ballads and funk, bump & boogie cross over into the mainstream. The mid-1970s saw the arrival of some strong independent local radio stations, with some legendary specialist soul shows: Greg Edwards on Capital Radio, the influential Andy Peebles on Manchester's Piccadilly Radio, and Mark Jones on Radio City in Liverpool. But Dave McAleer was an A&R man for Pye at the time, and for him Radio One was the key: 'The great radio victory for black music in Britain wasn't getting specialist shows on the air, it was getting David Hamilton playing Barry White, and Tony Blackburn playing The Commodores.'

Around the time of Wattstax, we've seen how black American soul had shifted towards melodic break-up and make-out songs, and beautiful but sentimental ballads which were great for radio – Michael Jackson's 'Ben', Roberta Flack's 'Killing Me Softly with His Song', and Diana Ross's massive-selling soundtrack LP *Mahogany*. And there were also numerous trios and quartets: vocal groups like The Stylistics, The Drifters, The Detroit Emeralds and Gladys Knight's Pips, whose silky harmonies, slickly choreographed dance moves and brightly coloured suits made the early colour TVs throb with excitement.

Pennington's is full, with seven hundred people in within an hour of the door opening. A couple of gorgeous thirty-something black women, Gwen Dickey lookalikes, shuffle on the carpet close to the dancefloor. The Tina Charles song 'I Love to Love' is playing and a bunch of girls at the bar start singing – the first singalong of the night. Then it's 'Le Freak' and they get on the dancefloor, five of them. Whatever era, from youth clubs to all night raves, the females are always the first up. These youngsters – wearing trousers and cowboy belts, skirts and halter necks – know a good time when they read about it on a Pennington's flyer.

In our current era you get used to DJs segueing and mixing, but now there were gaps between the songs, silence. Thirty years ago you'd have undoubtedly had some DJ shouting and bantering, but there was none of that, at least not at first, although eventually, halfway through 'Le Freak', the DJ starts whooping and cajoling the crowd into dancing. These people want to dance – they put hours in at the discotheques twenty-five or thirty years ago, learning the words to all the big records on the youth club scene – and his is an easy job. The youngsters in their cowboy belts are soon joined by a few maturer, but even more enthusiastic dancers, a couple of dozen all told. Then the DJ plays 'Who's That Lady' by the Isley Brothers and the dancefloor fills even more. Older punters are up and dancing, although the younger ones carry themselves slightly better – there's more bend in the knees.

The rise of dancefloors and discotheques through the 1970s

defies a certain logic. As the decade unfolded, the Bradford that Hockney had left behind – the Britain that Hockney had left behind – became even less attractive. In Bradford the activities of the serial killer Peter Sutcliffe – the Yorkshire Ripper – would blight thousands of lives, and the effects of mass unemployment would hit hard. What was there to celebrate? But then a lust for life is always there somewhere; when bleakness descends, it's a joy to escape. Generations will always want to go out dancing, drinking, grabbing tight to any bits of joy, looking for a better life, or at least a great night out. In desperate times, the dancefloor is always better than the dole queue.

The uncertainty of living in a collapsing economy was exacerbated by the results of the general election in February 1974. After a bitter campaign, no party achieved an overall majority, and Enoch Powell's intervention had a small but significant effect, especially in marginal seats in the West Midlands. Both of the main parties lost a considerable number of votes; despite a higher turnout, the Tories lost 1.2 million votes, but Labour lost half a million as well. The Liberals, a refuge for the disenchanted, gained hundreds of thousands of votes but few extra seats. Minority independence parties like the SNP and Plaid Cymru also gained votes. Immediately after the results were announced, there were some discussions between Heath and Thorpe, with a view to the Liberals supporting a minority Conservative Government, but no agreement was reached and Labour took power. Heath's confrontational politics had ended in failure.

On becoming Prime Minister, Wilson looked to move fast on a key proposal in the 'Regeneration of British Industry' White Paper: the creation of the National Enterprise Board. The NEB was established with the belief that private enterprise had failed to develop and nurture British industry, and that public funds should be available in order to intervene in particular industries and extend public ownership where appropriate (parts of the NEB initiative also intended to establish greater democracy in the workplace). Over the next two years, with the economic crisis deepening, Labour's NEB would be forced to assist a number of Britain's most well-known companies.

There's evidence that communities under pressure during a period of economic distress have a tendency to seek scapegoats, and during the recessions of the mid-1970s, the National Front, under the leadership of John Tyndall and Martin Webster, proved to be an influential political and social force. The NF could always count on a traditional following among those happy to use violence and intimidation against ethnic minorities, but their strategy in the 1970s was to present themselves as a respectable political party. During the February 1974 election, the NF were among the smaller parties who took votes away from the main parties.

Britain in the 1970s was riven by big ideological battles, and the race issue was conspicuous on the streets. The 1971 Commonwealth Immigration Act effectively blocked new entrants from the old Empire, although dependants of those already in Britain still had rights to join them. But by this time, the NF had already begun to turn against the second generation immigrant communities; ie those born here. In 1974, roughly a third of the one and a half million non-white people in Britain were second generation rather than primary immigrants.

The NF made headway in an era when the political process looked flawed and the major parties lacked credibility. In the mid-1970s there was also less awareness and less respect for minority. For example, in the majority white community there was a wide tolerance of racist jokes, discrimination, racist chanting at football matches, and even race attacks and so-called Paki bashing.

In terms of raising media interest and sowing the seeds of disharmony, part of the National Front's strategy was to stage provocative marches in areas with a high immigrant population or ones with a history of racial tension. Communities looking to defend themselves from NF action, and anti-racist and left-leaning groups mobilised to counter the threat. Most followed a set pattern; by giving the NF protection, the police became a target of violence too and the day descended into mayhem and pitched battles. In the 1970s, areas like Haringey and Lewisham in London; Ladywood in Birmingham; and Manningham Lane in Leeds became the sites of violent clashes between the National Front, the police, and counter demonstrators. Protesters picketing an NF meeting at the Conway Hall in Red Lion Square in June 1974 clashed with police, and one protester, Warwick University student Kevin Gately, was killed by a mounted policeman's truncheon.

Labour had taken power after the February election, but without a clear majority, and later in the year Harold Wilson was forced to call a second election, looking for a stronger mandate. In 1970 the National Front had fielded just ten candidates in the general election; in February 1974 they had fifty-four candidates, and then ninety in the October 1974 election, which entitled them to an official party political broadcast on TV.

Eddy Amoo is well placed to describe the influence and profile of the National Front in the 1970s, and specifically how race impacted on life in Liverpool. Significantly, unlike The Beatles, The Real Thing never moved from their home-town to taste the joys, or otherwise, of London. Eddy now lives barely a mile from the house in which he grew up in Toxteth, and in our interview we were to return a number of times to his memories of the city and Toxteth (or Liverpool 8 as the district was known back in the 1970s, then, as now, home to many people from the city's black community).

In the early 1970s Liverpool was suffering tough times, and the grim economics of the decade created poverty and conflict.

Eddy Amoo remembers the atmosphere of the times, with the National Front gaining electoral credibility in some pockets of the country and pressure building through the decade on the streets of Liverpool 8. Racism wasn't always overt, but it was often accepted. 'From my personal point of view, Liverpool was OK. It's always been pretty racist – not racist so much in the people that you meet on the streets, but the institutions of Liverpool are racist; they were then and they still are. If you're black in Liverpool it's well nigh impossible to make any headway in any business; you've really got to fight and fight hard.'

Over in Manchester, Sweet Sensation followed 'Sad Sweet Dreamer' with another single, 'Purely by Coincidence', and an LP. The latter included smoochy ballads, an uptempo, Wigan Casino-style track ('Please Excuse Me') and the two hits. 1974 was the high point for Sweet Sensation, but turned out to be the beginning of the end for them too; success was fleeting.

In 1974, though, success for The Real Thing still wasn't even assured. They had also signed to Pye, and in the studio had recorded some songs written and produced by heart-throb pop star David Essex, among them 'Watch Out Carolina', which is slightly too obviously indebted to Essex's own 'Rock On'. The single flopped, and Pye were still in search of that elusive hit.

Late in 1975 a songwriting and production team, Ken Gold and Mickey Denne, played the band and their manager, Tony Hall, some demos of five songs they'd written. One song in particular impressed them: 'You to Me Are Everything'. Recorded with Ken Gold at the Roundhouse Studios, 'You to Me Are Everything' is a warm, catchy, stirring dance single with perfect soul strings and a singalong chorus; a classic that topped the charts in June 1976. The follow up was another Gold/Denne number, 'Can't Get By Without You'. The Real Thing had arrived, confirming that showbiz adage that it takes years of hard work to become an overnight success. Four long years after *Opportunity Knocks*, The Real Thing picked up the *Daily Mirror* 'Best New Group' award.

The band's debut LP, *The Real Thing* – including the two successful Gold/Denne singles – was released in October 1976. Whereas Sweet Sensation had been recording tracks provided for them by Tony Hatch, The Real Thing were pushing their own songs alongside the Gold/Denne numbers, but this produced a tension between their instincts and commercial pressures. Hot Chocolate had found themselves in a similarly compromised position, trying to push songs about race (in their case, songs like 'Amazing Skin Song'), while also locked into a continuing search for more plush, unchallenging hits.

The Real Thing's own songs on their first LP included a couple which had some of soul's social consciousness ('Flash' seems to owe something to Curtis Mayfield's 'Superfly'), which sit a little uneasily with songs that reveal the influence of some of the spangly-jacketed groups of the era, like The Stylistics. And 1976 was a fertile year for their music; another hit that year was 'Car Wash', a big-selling song from one of their co-stars at Pennington's, Rose Royce.

There are no examples of ironic Seventies fashions in the crowd at Pennington's, which is probably a relief for Eddy Amoo. The Real Thing have played many arena shows with the likes of Shalamar and Rose Royce, experiences that have made Eddy wary. During our interview he expressed dismay at the way a lot of music that came out of the Seventies is misrepresented, and perhaps even mocked: 'You get these twits turning up in these big stupid wigs and all these stupid clothes. That has nothing to do with the Seventies scene we were into and sometimes it does annoy me that we get rubbished in with that.'

All the best clubs are semi-secret, and open-minded, with sexual and racial diversity. Even if shopping centres and inner city streets were sites of tension – and despite racist door policies in many high street clubs – the best dancefloors could achieve this in the towns and cities of England in the mid-1970s. The Enoch Powell fans would never have believed their eyes if they'd seen the mix of people groovin' to James Brown, Earth, Wind & Fire, and 'Keep on Truckin''. In fact, in 1979, a youth publication from the BNP, *The Young Nationalist*, couldn't comprehend, and certainly didn't like what was going on, demanding that 'Disco and its melting pot pseudo-philosophy must be fought or Britain's streets will be full of black-worshipping soul boys.'

If the fragmentation of society and the tribalism of youth culture produced many different Seventies generations, then it's probably the case that a sizeable number of people in Pennington's for The Real Thing show were present on the soul scene in Britain in the mid-1970s. This part of the Seventies generation had a fondness for Motown, perhaps flirted with glam, rejoiced when Bowie went soul, worked hard all week, loved the sexiness of Saturday nights out, and didn't read *Sounds*. Maybe it was just the way these things happen; with a hippy older sister and punk younger brother, maybe they were just the funked-up middle child.

The Pennington's stage is deep, with plenty of room for a band who will provide backing for all the acts tonight. The members of The Real Thing – the two Amoo brothers and Dave Smith – emerge, in matching white trousers, black t-shirts and shiny black jackets, and the show opens with 'Can You Feel the Force?', a lovely slice of sci-fi jazz-funk with a 'whoop-whoop' chorus and an upbeat message about unity, inspired by the film *Star Wars*. 'I remember sitting there with Chris one day and I said "Can you feel the force?" and it just dropped in,' says Eddy. 'Some things just fall together, like magic.'

Onstage, Eddy acts like a cheerleader, bubbly, confident and aware that the band's responsibilities as the opening act require some showbiz strategies. Eddy exhorts the crowd to 'Wave their hands in the air', then demands that we clap our hands above our heads, then tells us we have to say 'Yeah'. It's beginning to work; everybody says 'Yeah'.

The area near the front of the stage is full of shuffling and dancing. The twenty-something girls in tight trousers are waving and singing along. Then it's ballad time and Chris serenades us with 'Whenever You Want My Love'. When the cheering dies down – and just before they sing 'You'll Never Know What You're Missing' – the band's showbiz instincts kick in again and Chris announces, 'We'd like to dedicate this one to all the ladies in the house.' He said that, he really did. With a straight face.

Over halfway through the set, it's time for another song about heartache, and the band launches into 'Can't Get By Without You'. Chris points the microphone towards the crowd and the choruses are belted out. Eddy takes off his jacket and does a rap. He's working hard to work a crowd, and I notice that the louder he shouts, the more his Scouse accent stands out. It's an intriguing combination – a Scouser steeped in the soul of black America.

Many times in their career, Eddy and Chris Amoo wrestled with ways of bringing the Liverpool street into the music, and one product of this was a 1977 concept album entitled *4 From 8*, containing only self-penned songs, including an eleven-minute track, 'Liverpool 8 Medley', a combination of three songs: 'Children of the Ghetto', 'Liverpool 8' and 'Stanhope Street'. The LP has a great gatefold sleeve featuring photographs of the band and Liverpool 8, and the city's Anglican cathedral amid desolate streets. 'The LP was totally where we were at and what we were into,' says Eddy.

The Beatles had sung about Penny Lane, The Real Thing wrote about Stanhope Street. 'Stanhope Street was one of the main thoroughfares in Liverpool 8,' explains Eddy. 'When I was a kid we always seemed to end up walking through the streets and then maybe at ten o'clock at night we'd all end up on some corner on Stanhope Street getting chips or something like that. It summed up the whole area for me.'

We saw in 1972 how the deterioration of inner city neighbourhoods created and defined the 'ghetto' experience, and 'ghetto' was a word we'd got used to hearing on the news in an American context. But – in a process not far removed from the way Bowie gave notions of New York sleaze an English context in songs like 'Rebel Rebel' – in 'Children of the Ghetto' The Real Thing were bringing the concept much closer to home. 'In a way the word "ghetto" had become really hip to people on the streets because of Donny Hathaway and people like that and I thought it suited Liverpool 8,' says Eddy.

He's careful in what he says. He knows that historically the word 'ghetto' can carry negative connotations – 'A lot of people were a little bit upset about it, but that's what Liverpool 8 was and is; it's a ghetto' – but in the Seventies the word, and the concept, could be used in a positive sense, even in a celebratory way. 'We used "ghetto" as a togetherness term really; that was a part of it. It was poetic, in those terms. We all live in this cauldron of black, white, Chinese, African, Indian. It's like "The World is a Ghetto",' he says, namechecking War's 1972 song.

Communities are sensitive about how they are portrayed, and putting all this down on disc inevitably changed the way The Real Thing were viewed locally, although they had mainly positive reactions from the people Eddy grew up with. 'I think they were made up. But I think that when you have success – particularly if you come off the street – a lot of people expect different things and you find that you don't change, but a lot of people around you do. It's a strange feeling and I bet bands like Sweet Sensation had the same experience as us.'

But in the inner city black communities in Toxteth and Moss Side, tastes were changing. On the front line, for the young black British, reggae was now being heard alongside soul and funk at parties, dances and in the school yard. In

1972 and 1973 Paul Gilroy noticed this change: 'Reggae was skinhead music and so we'd been avoiding it and despising it, but we began to get a different sense of it really and we began to get a sense that reggae itself was changing and it began to pick up more of a Rasta influence.'

Bob Marley's *Catch A Fire* LP, the release of the film *The Harder They Come*, and the success of the movie soundtrack released by Island Records had made a major impact in 1972. Gilroy, resistant to *Superfly*, had enjoyed *The Harder They Come*, and his interest in roots reggae deepened listening to Steve Barnard's 'Reggae Time' show on Sundays on Radio London. He remembers he also got the chance to see The Wailers at the Greyhound on Fulham Palace Road: 'That was a very powerful encounter. I remember grabbing my sister's hand and rushing down the stairs so we could talk to Bob Marley on the pavement outside because I just thought it was amazing.'

Once out on the pavement a hurried encounter took place. 'I can't really remember what passed between us, but I do remember that what there was was a kind of incomprehension.'

Which, looking back, is reasonable. 'Yes, because I don't think he could have understood what we wanted to invest in him at that point. Why would he?'

In 1974, one development from 1972 was the rise of an authentic homegrown reggae scene in Britain, including the emergence of Matumbi who featured Dennis Bovell in their line-up (they recorded for Trojan during 1972 and 1973, releasing a version of Hot Chocolate's 'Brother Louie', followed by a version of Kool & the Gang's 'Funky Stuff' entitled 'Reggae Stuff'). Black Slate formed around 1974, as did Misty in Roots. Other bands, including The Cimarons, The Rudies and The Pacesetters, had been working and recording in London for several years (the debut LP by The Cimarons, *In Time*, was released in 1974). Britain also had a number of established labels, including Creole and its sister label Cactus, but pre-eminent were Trojan who controlled around 75 per cent of the reggae market, producing and licensing tracks from JA and distributing smaller labels and imported sounds.

Small, independently-owned shops and market stalls played an important part in making the all-important Jamaican imports and pre-releases available. In 1974, outlets like Black Wax and Don Christie in Birmingham, Morpheus in Croydon, and the Muzik City chain (with nine shops around London) would draw customers from a wide area looking for rare records. Some of them had been handling soul from America and extended their contacts to include reggae from the Caribbean, like Aquarius in Birmingham and Jumbo Records in Queen's Arcade in Leeds.

Dozens of shoe-string reggae record labels also emerged in the mid-1970s, many based at shops: Ethnic in Kensal Green (run by producer Larry Lawrence), Magnet in Stoke Newington, and DIP in New Cross, for example. Many record companies were small-scale and informal, and some unfortunately gained a reputation for bootlegs and mis-labelling. But the market was fragile, and even the strongest companies didn't always survive. Back in 1967 the Pama label had been set up alongside a shop in Harlesden, a local hangout, and among its staff in the early years were Adrian Sherwood (who would later go on to form On-U Sound and become a supremely creative and successful producer) and singer Delroy Washington (responsible, in the mid-1970s, for tracks like 'Give All the Praise to Jah' on Virgin Records). In 1973, however, financial pressures forced Pama to cease trading, although a second series of releases began to emerge in 1976.

The Ashanti label was founded in 1974 by Rupert Cunningham and Junior Lincoln, who had also established Bamboo Records back in 1969, an outlet for British releases of singles produced by Clement (Coxsone) Dodd by artists like Bob Andy and Alton Ellis, and the Banana label, which released early recordings by Prince Far I and the Wailing Souls. Ashanti was based in London N4, with an office behind Junior's Music Spot on Stroud Green Road. Although it was set up to represent and promote the full range of Jamaican music, including steel bands, Ashanti plugged into the new Rasta-inspired reggae – 'roots' reggae as it was being called; one of their first releases was a triple LP of Rastafarian music, *Grounation*.

In many ways, reggae music had been regarded as a cheap commercial opportunity, a novelty bandwagon widely unappreciated in the black community in Britain. Quality control was a problem and Junior Lincoln was on a mission, as he told journalist Carl Gayle in June 1974: 'The music that has been promoted in this country as reggae has been so bloody bad! I love Jamaican music but with every music you have good and bad records. It so happens that there's been a lot of bad records promoted as reggae.'

In the second half of the 1970s, roots reggae took hold and connected with a growing interest in Rastafarianism. As we'll explore in a later chapter, with black American soul losing some of its political charge, a generation of reggae musicians articulated a desire for freedom and justice which was picked up by a new generation in England. Eddy Amoo was well aware of this development. He recalls Liverpool 8 in the early 1970s as a tight-knit community: 'It was from the early Seventies onwards that people started to realise that if they stuck together politically they could achieve a lot more than they had in the past. The youth then weren't as willing as the youth in the early Sixties had been to just accept things and go along with it. They were more forceful.'

In 1974 there was evidence of this change in the clubs. In London, the old regulars at Tiles, the Flamingo and the Ram Jam moved away from soul clubs to reggae venues like the Crypt in Deptford, All Nations in Hackney, and the Four Aces. Other clubs doing good business by the end of 1974 included the Apollo in Harlesden, owned by the Palmer brothers who'd been behind the Pama label.

A key role in spreading the roots sound was played by the sound systems, tight-knit teams led by record selectors and MCs, who would set up their decks and speakers in clubs, halls and houses, often in competition with other sounds. The sound systems had played a part in entertaining the Afro-Caribbean community in Britain since the 1950s (when the selector would play Fats Domino, perhaps, or calypso), and then evolved, as reggae evolved, always hungry for the big new sounds, the pre-releases and imports. The sound systems would travel the country, but always focused first on their local community. Around 1974, some of the better known sound system operators in London included Fat Man, Count Shelly (resident at the Four Aces, and prolific producer on his own Count Shelly label), Lord Koos (another notable producer) and Count Suckle. Suckle was resident at the Q club in Paddington where he was noted for his careful selection of the best reggae, but still, in the mid-1970s, mixed with soul. The soul crowd in black clubs was being eased out a little by reggae in the mid-1970s but never went away, as the survival of The Real Thing confirms.

The Real Thing benefited when a cover version of 'Children of the Ghetto' by Philip Bailey of Earth, Wind & Fire was included in the soundtrack to Spike Lee's 1995 film *Clockers*. And a few days before I met up with Eddy in Liverpool, I heard that the queen of nu-soul herself, Mary J. Blige, was performing 'Children of the Ghetto' on her world tour. Endearingly, Eddy starts getting excited when I tell him, but then doubts my story: 'Really? Is it definitely our "Children of the Ghetto"? I'd be made up if I knew Mary J. Blige was doing it.'

Once I persuade Eddy that it's definitely their song, he reflects on how valuable the song is to The Real Thing's career: 'It's brought us a lot of success. It's never been a hit, but it's earned us a lot of money, but more importantly that song has most probably given us the credibility for me and Chris which our career with The Real Thing had never given us.'

There's something poignant about having a career that includes singalong singles that filled dancefloors, like 'You to Me Are Everything', irresistible feel-good tunes like 'Can You Feel the Force?', and classic ghetto medleys – all that idealism – but still being painfully aware of a harsher, depressing reality. Especially racism: 'I don't think things are as bad as they were in the early Seventies,' Eddy says, 'but even now if you go into the town centre of Liverpool you can actually count the number of black people who work in the town centre on your hand.'

He still finds it hard to accept the way he was cold-shouldered when the number one artists were invited down to the Albert Dock. He thinks it tells us a lot about how the black community in Liverpool is perceived. 'If that happened to us, and we've been a highly successful band, what must it be like for people who haven't had the success that we've had or haven't reached the position that we've reached? What must it be like for them if it's like that for us? To my mind, that says it all.'

Eddy has had to answer the phone a number of times during our interview, and he's given me an hour of his time, despite being a busy man, and he draws things to a close by offering me a lift to the station. Despite the forceful things he has to say about racial issues in Liverpool, he seems a very centred, sweet-natured guy. He tells me that Ray Lake from the band died a couple of years ago, reportedly the victim of a drugs overdose. As we know, Dave Smith is still in The Real Thing, as is Chris Amoo, although Chris has also carved out a parallel career as an award-winning dog breeder.

Sweet Sensation's is a sadder story. It soon began to go wrong, perhaps even before the end of 1974, as the band appeared increasingly uncomfortable and ill-suited to their position in the very middle of the pop market, the most commercial and cut-throat part of the music industry. In 1975 and 1976 they released several singles, including 'Mr Cool' and 'Sweet Regrets' but saw no chart action. By 1977 their fortunes had sunk low: their 'You're My Sweet Sensation' came eighth in a competition to decide the British entry for the Eurovision Song Contest. Having built a career performing songs by Tony Hatch and Des Parton, they weren't entitled to crucial songwriting royalties, and were thus unable to earn from their back catalogue. The band went their separate ways, but Marcel King temporarily resurrected his career in March 1984 with a brilliant single 'Reach For Love' on Factory Records, but once again he couldn't sustain a career. Just over ten years later, and after numerous attempts to get back in the music industry, Marcel King died in October 1995 following a brain haemorrhage. In a tragic coda to his story, his son Zeus was shot dead on Langport Avenue in Longsight in March 1997 during a period of murderous gang warfare in South Manchester.

Eddy Amoo is aware that growing up in Liverpool 8 could have cut down his chances in life, but he's made it. He's led a charmed life in comparison to other children of the ghetto. Looking back, he finds it hard to imagine how things might have been for him if it wasn't for that career in music. 'I really don't know; a lot of my mates ended up doing time and have come out and have got their lives together and maybe it would have been the same for me. Maybe the same thing would have happened to me. Maybe I would have got into trouble with the police, the way you do; basically, that's how it's laid out for you.'

CHAPTER SIX

'Land of a Thousand Dances' (1975)

In 1975 the Sex Pistols played their first gigs. It was a year in which business failures and industrial unrest grew, living standards fell, runaway inflation hit an historic high and unemployment reached its highest level since the Second World War. The everyday confusion caused by living in a collapsing economy was played out against a background of continuing murder and mayhem in Northern Ireland and a severe escalation in violence at football matches. In this context, when the Sex Pistols finally released their first single, 'Anarchy in the UK', twelve months after their first gig, the title was less a threat than a description.

At the beginning of 1974 the big question being posed in newspapers was 'Is Britain becoming ungovernable?' At the beginning of 1975, with Labour nominally the governing party but with the country in chaos, the question was still a reasonable one to ask, despite Wilson's initial success on taking power in February 1974, when the miners' strike was called off and the three-day week ended. The Government had then devised a Social Contract to formalise this new spirit of cooperation between the Government, the unions and big business, but even in this period of relative calm there were still unofficial strikes, including industrial action by the train drivers, led by Ray Buckton, and by hospital workers.

Following the guidelines in the Social Contract, acknowledging a need to maintain workers' living standards, wage settlements were supposed to track rises in prices, but hefty increases in the retail price index during 1974 produced wage demands in the region of 20 per cent. Extra claims were also being made by unions whose pay had fallen behind that of workers in other sectors, for wage rises that would anticipate future price rises.

In February 1975, for example, the National Union of Mineworkers pushed for, and then got an average rise of 35 per cent for their 246,000 members. The NUM increase had an immediate knock-on effect in the coal industry, with coal prices rising instantly – by 22 per cent for domestic consumers, 7 per cent for industrial users – putting pressure on the whole of manufacturing industry. By the beginning of 1975, average earnings were increasing by 25 per cent, retail prices were rocketing, and unemployment was up to 700,000 (an increase of 20 per cent in a year).

Conflict was replacing cooperation. The Social Contract was at breaking point, and optimism about the continuing troubles in Northern Ireland had been dealt heavy blows in 1974, first by the collapse of the power sharing executive, and then by the carnage of the Birmingham pub bombings on 21 November. The Birmingham pub bombs came after an eighteen-month period during which the West Midlands had been hit by dozens of explosions; a week earlier, James McDade had been killed planting a bomb in Coventry city centre. Two city centre pubs in Birmingham were targeted that November evening: the Mulberry Bush – at the foot of one of the city's landmark office buildings, the Rotunda – and the Tavern in the Town. In virtually simultaneous explosions, only five minutes after a vague telephone warning to the local paper, both pubs were devastated, twenty-one people were killed and over one hundred and fifty others injured. The city was traumatised by the loss of all those young lives, and anti-Irish feeling spread on the local streets and in local factories; an Irish family in Witton Road had their house petrol bombed. Six men were arrested on their way to the Irish ferry, and a few days later Parliament passed the Prevention of Terrorism Act. In Northern Ireland a number of church leaders, shocked by events in Birmingham, brokered an IRA ceasefire, announced in February 1975, but destined not to last.

The sense that society was fragmenting was an inescapable feature of the mid-1970s, reflected in tribalism in the youth culture of the time. As we shall see, in 1975 there were communities inhabiting different worlds almost, dancing to different tunes; the consensus was dying and the breakdown of cooperation – evident in the split in the Social Contract and the situation in Northern Ireland – was also present in the tension between militant shop stewards and their union leaders. There was increasing support for the Scottish National Party and Plaid Cymru; rising support for splinter groups and political organisations on the furthest reaches of the political spectrum; scapegoating of minority communities by the National Front; and enmity between black youth and the police.

It was also a year of heightened football rivalries, and out on the street the most visible and violent youth cult in 1975 consisted of football fans. Until the 1970s, although almost all football fans behaved impeccably, football matches had still been the focus for sporadic violence – local youths throwing bricks at coaches carrying visiting supporters had become a feature of life near all football grounds – but terrace trouble escalated in the mid-1970s, and what had involved a tiny minority turned into a massive free-for-all.

Terrace fashion experts and trend-conscious commentators have mapped how football hooligans evolved through skinheads via suedeheads to bootboys in the first half of the 1970s, but in 1975 the minutiae of tribal allegiance were hard to see. What was significant wasn't what the hooligans were wearing but how many of them there were. Football violence was a mass participation craze involving thousands of drunkards, young dudes, fat blokes, ex-mods and schoolies. You'd see crowds of skinheads, but long hairs too. They'd be wearing Crombie coats, parkas, army surplus jackets. They were everywhere, every weekend.

Attending football matches became a ritual of goading and battling with opposing fans. It was in the mid-1970s that a new language and the heady ritual of football hooliganism developed; fans gathered in firms, attacked their opponent's end. It was also in the mid-1970s that these activities began to impact on the image of Britain abroad, at least in the eyes of our European neighbours. Out went the dominating image of the blue-blooded aristocracy, or those loveable mop-tops The Beatles, and in came the hell-raising football hooligan. In 1974 Tottenham were banned from playing two European games at their home ground after their fans rioted at the UEFA Cup Final at Feyenoord. In May 1975, after trouble involving their fans in Paris, Leeds were banned from European football, and a few months earlier Derby County had been thrown out of the UEFA Cup after trouble at a match in Yugoslavia. However, not all Europeans reacted with disdain to our new national export; young lads in Germany, Italy and the Low Countries were inspired to develop their own hooligan firms.

Since the early 1980s, the behaviour of English fans has been contrasted unfavourably with the followers of the Scottish national team, but in the 1970s Scotland fans could also be destructive. In 1977, after a victory at Wembley, the Scottish fans invaded the pitch, dug up the turf and took away the goalposts. This one incident could have been written off as good natured, but a few months earlier Glasgow Rangers had visited Aston Villa for a mid-season friendly, and Rangers fans, schooled in the viciousness of sectarian

Glasgow, generated some of the worst football violence ever seen in Birmingham.

Local conflicts often contributed to outbreaks of football hooliganism, a reflection of how aggressive the rivalry in England can be between villages in the next valley, towns down the road, or suburbs of the same city. In April 1974, with Manchester United on the brink of relegation, hundreds of United fans invaded the pitch in an attempt to get their derby match versus Manchester City abandoned. In August 1974, the next season had barely kicked off when a Blackpool supporter, eighteen-year-old Kevin Olsson, was stabbed to death by a Bolton fan.

Some teams took massive away support – notably Newcastle United – and others were to emerge with a reputation for violence – Millwall, for example. But it was probably Manchester United's Red Army that did most to create a pattern, which, after just a few months of 1975, had become predictable and widespread: huge groups of fans running riot on the terraces, on trains, through town centres, outside railway stations, and in the coach parks at motorway services.

Even if Harold Wilson's Government hung on to a fanciful belief that they were in control of the country six days a week, Saturdays clearly belonged to the bootboys. In January 1975 a train carriage on a football special was completely burnt out by Chelsea fans on their way home from a match at Luton. In February there was trouble at Everton v Tottenham (Spurs keeper Pat Jennings was hit on the head with a bottle), and in March two men were stabbed at Wolves v Manchester City.

In August 1975, the new season kicked off with over two hundred arrests around the country. The worst trouble was in Wolverhampton where police arrested eighty-six people, mostly Manchester United fans, after fourteen stabbings and widespread vandalism. There was also trouble during Nottingham Forest v Plymouth Argyle (Brian Clough, in his first full season at Forest, ran onto the pitch to restrain supporters), and at Burnley v Arsenal, York v Portsmouth, and QPR v Liverpool. And after their match at Southend, Sheffield United fans ran amok in the town and on the seafront. Later in the month, six special buses carrying Spurs fans from Lime Street station to Liverpool's ground were badly damaged by missile-throwing locals. On the last Saturday of August, Liverpool supporters were involved again, this time setting fire to mail bags on a train returning from Leicester and causing £70,000 worth of damage. On the same day, thirty people were hurt in battles after a Stoke City v Manchester United game, and at Luton, Chelsea fans invaded the pitch and attacked Luton players in an attempt to get the match abandoned (Chelsea lost 3–0). The next day, *The Sunday Times* dubbed 30 August 'the day of the locusts'.

The following week, Minister of State for Sport and Recreation, Denis Howell, called for a tougher sentencing policy for football hooligans, and other voices called for harsher initiatives, including a national service corps for offenders, and even a ban on under-eighteens in football grounds unless accompanied by adults. Judge Gwyn Morris QC, faced with a dock full of QPR fans who'd trashed an underground train, said that he'd like the power to put football hooligans in medieval stocks on Saturday afternoons.

In 1975 it wasn't only the initiatives aimed at reducing hooliganism, or policies to limit wage rises which failed; Government policy in Northern Ireland fared little better. The fragile February 1975 ceasefire had fallen apart well before the end of the year. In August 1975 an IRA bomb attack on a bar on the Shankill Road killed five people, and a ten-year-old Catholic boy was killed by a rubber bullet fired by a British soldier. In September an Orange Hall was attacked by the IRA and five more Protestant civilians were killed.

The second election in 1974 having delivered such a tight result, Wilson and his Cabinet were forever looking over their shoulders, fearful of back bench rebellions and by-election reverses, making plans with their advisers. But the wider world was out of their control too. Britain was no longer master of its own destiny, but part of a world economy reeling from recession and the effects of the oil crisis, and Britain's wealth was increasingly dependent on trade with the Common Market and pegged to the fortunes of America.

It was fruitless looking to Europe or America for some good news; the real story of the Seventies was being played out worldwide. In America, President Ford and his economics adviser Allan Greenspan were presiding over the worst ravages of the recession. In 1975 the American economy went into reverse – the Gross Domestic Product fell by 1.3 per cent. At the same time unemployment rose to 8.5 per cent. The ghetto was a nightmare, but it wasn't just the poor who suffered; the average American worker was worse off in real terms at the end of 1975 than at the beginning of the decade.

America was still paying a price for questionable leadership. In January 1975 John Mitchell, H.R. Haldeman and John D. Ehrlichman were found guilty of taking part in the Watergate cover-up. And the futility of the country's adventures in the Far East was clear when South Vietnam, weakened by the withdrawal of US aid, unconditionally surrendered as North Vietnamese forces took over Saigon in April 1975 and their allies, the Communist-led Khmer Rouge, captured the Cambodian capital Pnomh Penh. Meanwhile, Bobby Fischer refused to defend his title against Anatoly Karpov, relinquishing his crown.

During the first half of 1975 police in the USA were searching for Patty Hearst, the granddaughter of newspaper magnate Randolph Hearst. In February 1974 she'd been kidnapped at gunpoint from her apartment in Berkeley, California, by two men who overpowered her fiancé, put her in the boot of a car and drove away. Patty Hearst was the heir to a fortune, and over the next few months the Hearst family was forced to distribute six million dollars' worth of food to the poor in the Bay Area in response to ransom demands from the kidnappers, the Symbionese Liberation Army. The largesse didn't win Patty Hearst her freedom, however.

What gave the story a twist and shocked America was a raid on the Hibernia Bank in San Francisco, when a gang netted $10,000 after wounding two bystanders. The incident was caught on CCTV, and the police, press and public were astonished to discover that one of the gang was Patty Hearst. The raid was followed, forty-eight hours later, by a taped communiqué from the SLA. It was a message from Patty Hearst justifying her actions by claiming that the money was required for the 'revolution'. She described the raid as a 'fund-raiser', called her parents 'pigs', claimed she'd become a part of the SLA of her own free will, defended her 'comrades' and denied being brainwashed. 'The idea is ridiculous,' she said on the tape.

Later, the media displayed a photograph Patty had sent to her parents showing her wearing camouflage clothes and a beret, holding a carbine rifle in front of the SLA flag. Another tape revealed she had taken the name of Che Guevara's girl-friend and was now to be known as 'Tania'. For middle America it was a frightening sign that they were unsafe, not just from terror groups, but from their own young. Tania, educated and from a prosperous family, was now caught up in extremes of rebellion and violence.

In Germany, after the police breakthrough in 1972, four leading Baader Meinhof members were in custody in Stannheim, but fellow gang members were engaged in various activities to try to force their release. In February 1975 a Berlin politician was kidnapped, and in April six members of the gang occupied the German Embassy in Stockholm, taking twelve hostages. The siege ended with two hostages dead and the Embassy on fire. Elsewhere in Sweden, Abba had just written 'Mamma Mia' and 'Bang-A-Boomerang'.

In Italy, the Brigate Rosse had emerged several years earlier,

one of around twenty armed groups organised on the revolutionary left in direct reaction to government repression and
fascist street violence. With a founding membership drawn
from working class Communist groups, the Brigate Rosse also
began to attract student activists. In 1975 the group issued a
manifesto claiming its goal was a 'concentrated strike against
the heart of the State, because the State is an imperialist
collection of multinational corporations'.

Although the major European countries were yet to develop
joint strategies for security and anti-terrorism, economic links,
through the Common Market, were strong, although Britain
had been late to join. In this period, two apparently contradictory pressures emerged. On the one hand, business leaders
were making strong economic arguments for Britain to be
part of a larger European structure, while on the other,
demands for devolution were being considered after increased
votes for the Scottish National Party and Plaid Cymru. The
Common Market debate had been a factor in the 1974 elections, but the issue came to a head in 1975 as a result of the
referendum on whether Britain should stay in the European
Common Market on terms renegotiated by the Labour
Government. A referendum was held in June and 67 per cent
of the votes cast were for the Yes lobby, which had been
backed by most of the media and big business. There were
splits in the Labour Party over the issue, even in the Cabinet.
When the White Paper setting out the new terms was published, it was the overwhelming support of Conservative MPs
which gave the Paper the endorsement of the Commons.

Meanwhile, the Government was getting blown off course
by the trade unions. As well as wrangles over wages and pay
policy, there was a steady increase in disputes over non-union
labour, overtime and demarcation. As Alex Patton looks back
at his own experiences over these years, he remembers relentless disruption in the workplace and an end to any lingering
belief in the idea of jobs for life. He's also of the opinion that

elements in the trade unions were playing the wrong game, resisting change or innovation, and appearing to be dogmatic and bolshy just for the sake of it; what Alex calls 'a bit bloody-minded'.

When Alex left school he went to college for a year – doing an O Level course because he'd only done CSEs at school – then, after a visit to Careers Advice on Stockton High Street, he was offered a job as a chainman on the A19 project, building thirteen miles of motorway-standard dual carriageway: 'There were hundreds of us working on it, and most of them were long hairs, all hippy types, all into rock music.'

We have seen how historian Eric Hobsbawm pinpoints 1973 as the beginning of what he calls 'the crisis decades'. For Alex, 1973 marked the beginning of a new era too: his drinking years. By the summer of 1973 he was a trainee civil engineer, happy hanging out with his long-haired, hippy-type mates in rock pubs in Stockton. 'My drinking years had started. When I started to really begin to drink, 1973, by that time there were rock pubs all over Stockton.'

For a while, that part of the North-East of England seemed to be defying the downturn. The massive ICI chemical works provided hundreds of jobs, as did the engineering firm Head Wrightsons. Locally, heavy industry was king; the River Tees was known as the Steel River. There were few job shortages for civil engineers. 'I lost my job on the A19 in the November of 1974 when the contract was finished,' says Alex. 'But within a couple of weeks I started a new job. In my game there was plenty of work, even for someone as inexperienced as me.'

Alex's father was a convener at the ammonia works at ICI, his mother was shop steward. In Stockton, Alex was brought up on Labour Party politics, delivering leaflets for the Party when he was twelve. But despite being predisposed to be supportive of trade union activity, as the oil crisis triggered economic chaos, a world recession and increased global competition, Alex began to wonder whether union power was being wielded responsibly. In 1975 there was a strike in the construction industry. 'The lads went out on strike for three months,' says Alex, 'and when we went back to work we were paid less than we were offered at the beginning.'

He remembers a classic demarcation dispute in which a group of joiners from Liverpool were on site and Alex was busying himself setting out for civil engineering work. 'I was walking down the street with a hammer in my hand and the shop steward for the joiners comes up to me and tells me I can't use a hammer, and I'm like "You're fucking kiddin' aren't you?" We had to negotiate with the joiners so I could use a hammer.'

As wage rises and prices pushed each other higher, then higher still, the Social Contract seemed to be automatically perpetuating dangerous levels of inflation, and the pressure on industry to cut costs was beginning to cause increased job losses. To restrain the economy and reduce inflation, Chancellor Denis Healey increased taxes and reduced public spending in his April budget, but six months later the voluntary guidelines in the Social Contract had failed; the Government was forced to introduce a compulsory wages policy.

Inflation peaked at 26 per cent in July 1975 – a new post-war high – and unemployment hit 938,000 (up by a massive 238,000 since the start of the year). America's experience – rising unemployment and negative growth – was replicated in Britain during 1974 and 1975. As the economy contracted, a new word – 'stagflation' – was coined to describe a situation of rising inflation and economic stagnation. During this period, several of Britain's flagship companies fell into deep trouble, including Burmah Oil, British Leyland, and the electronics giant Ferranti. All required the assistance of the Government's National Enterprise Board.

Meanwhile, as unemployment rose dramatically, there

was a search for answers (the Government launched a 'Buy British' campaign to stop the flow of imports and increase the chances of survival for British companies), and a search for scapegoats. The far right blamed immigration for increasing unemployment. The National Association for Freedom was formed, campaigning against pornography and Commu-nism, and then one of the organisation's founders, Ross McWhirter, was assassinated by the IRA. The country was being pulled in different, rival, directions, and the music scene reflected this fragmentation.

England was a land of a thousand fashions and a thousand dances, from funky disco to stoner rock. Even the long hairs had tribes of their own. Prog rock was huge in this era, and the bands and their fans placed a high value on trained musicianship, and experimental, grandiose, twenty- or thirty-minute epic songs. Audiences at Yes, Pink Floyd, Genesis or Emerson Lake and Palmer concerts would sit rather than sweat at concerts. Prog rock was big student music, and although the differences weren't always clear cut (Led Zep-pelin had their prog rock moments too, in songs like 'No Quarter'), in the tribe wars of the Seventies its greatcoat-wearing devotees sought to distance themselves from the more working class kids who tended to follow the lumpen and aggressive music of Black Sabbath and Led Zeppelin.

Black Sabbath and Led Zeppelin also didn't always have the support of the established music press, were a long way from being as cute as Marc Bolan and lived a world away from Radio Luxemburg ('Fab 208') and the Top 40. Yet uniquely, magically, they could fill every huge hall in Britain and most sports stadia in America without playing the pop game or pandering to the media; there's no present-day equivalent. They were hell raisers on tour, living off drugs and alcohol, into groupies, excess and private planes. Led Zeppelin began 1975 with some European dates and then embarked on their tenth American tour, opening in Minneapolis; they would fly into town, do the gig, heroes to hundreds of thousands of suburban rocker kids.

Led Zeppelin refused most interviews and released only LPs (in Britain at least). Without singles, they were never invited onto *Top of the Pops*, although a version of their song 'Whole Lotta Love' by Collective Consciousness Society (led by Alexis Korner) was used as the theme tune to the show from 1973 to 1981. The lack of readily retrievable TV clips of Led Zeppelin's performances has contributed to their infrequent appearances on nostalgia TV, whereas The Sweet seem to bestride the decade like giants.

In 1974 they'd established their own record label, Swan Song (with offices in London and New York, and artists including Bad Company, the Pretty Things and Maggie Bell). In 1975 Led Zeppelin released their sixth album, *Physical Graffiti*, filmed *The Song Remains the Same*, and toured extensively to huge audiences. Their scintillating London shows at Earls Court in May 1975 are now legendary. Recently, the tribute band Whole Lotta Led embarked on an obsessive project: they specifically reproduced Led Zeppelin's set from the Earls Court shows and took the show to two dozen venues, from the Brook in Southampton to the Maltings in Berwick-upon-Tweed.

The title *Physical Graffiti* captured something of the battering, visceral appeal of the band, backed up by a brilliant LP cover. Although it is currently available on CD in some high street stores for just £9.99, the packaging has none of the impact of the original, which depicted a New York tenement block; through its windows various exhibitionists cavorted, alongside Lee Harvey Oswald, King Kong, Marlene Dietrich and band members.

A sense of deterioration was common to many urban areas, from the Bronx to Birmingham, Liverpool to London, and in the depressing urban landscape graffiti thrived. The breakdown of neighbourhoods described in earlier chapters was continuing as the movement out of the city core to the suburbs gathered pace, leaving behind empty properties. And in business districts, the economic slowdown and the collapse of manufacturing industry was producing acres of derelict warehouse and factory space. Furthermore, we had the tragic scandal of recently-built estates like Hulme in Manchester falling apart, already condemned.

Cities once represented the potential of capitalism; now they represented its crisis. In addition to windswept estates and collapsing new buildings, one of the other features of the urban landscape in the 1970s was the change in the old bourgeois neighbourhoods by the accelerating flight to new properties beyond city boundaries. Leafy Cheshire drew the monied classes out of established areas like Whalley Range and Victoria Park in Manchester, and many of the big family homes left vacant were turned into single occupancy flats. The same process was happening in Notting Hill, around St Mark's Place in New York – site of the building portrayed on the front of *Physical Graffiti* – and back in Led Zeppelin's native West Midlands, where houses in the area around Woodstock Road and Ladypool Road in Birmingham saw a change of use, as families moved out and a transient population moved in. The old bourgeois homes were now bed-sits, or student house shares, or squats.

In the summer of 1975 there were around 30,000 squatters in London, living rent- and mortgage-free, often in a bid to escape the wage slave world. It was a lifestyle that made London affordable and had a network of support groups. Some of this was the remnants of counter cultural activity, and reflected a view of London portrayed so vividly by Jonathan Raban in his 1974 book *Soft City*, in which he sees London as 'scary and impersonal', peopled by strangers, rogues and angels, all pursuing a means to survive. 'The city', he writes, 'is soft, amenable to a dazzling and libidinous variety of lives, dreams, and interpretations.'

With the release of the *Physical Graffiti* LP, Led Zeppelin reached their artistic peak, all raunchy drum rolls and menacing guitar riffs, semi-mythical musings, macho posturing and occasional acoustic reveries; but the music was less about the lyrics than the rush. Powering to the top of both the American and the British charts, *Physical Graffiti* was a commercial peak for the band too. By 1975 Led Zeppelin were an example of how the alternative world of rock had become more lucrative than the mainstream it despised. Rock was being bought in bulk, and had grown from the world of *NME* and *Rolling Stone* and was now featured in broadsheet newspapers. In October 1975 *The Sunday Times* carried a two-part special on rock music in which Led Zeppelin seemed to impress but also repel the paper's correspondent. According to the journalist, 'to attend one of their concerts can arouse actual physical fear'.

In pre-punk Britain, Radio One DJ John Peel was playing Captain Beefheart, Vivian Stanshall, and the Robin Trower Band, and the pre-punk long hairs were living the good life, with more than enough music to keep them happy. A canon of classic rock had been established; speeded-up biker records like Hawkwind's 'Silver Machine' and Black Sabbath's 'Paranoid' were played in sixth form canteens and student halls right through the decade. 'Alright Now' and 'Wishing Well' by Free, 'Smoke on the Water' by Deep Purple, and 'Layla' by Derek & the Dominoes were other massive favourites, and according to Alex Patton, 'Anyone into rock has got to be into Led Zep's "Stairway to Heaven".'

Britain was neck deep in long hair. It wasn't just rock stars and footballers who let their hair grow beyond the collar. During TV coverage of the general elections of 1974, you'd see newsreaders experimenting with haircuts that tickled their shirt collars, and trade union leaders with big clumpy sideburns. Alex had long hair, almost down to his belt, and also sported a moustache: 'Everyone had moustaches, I don't know why but they were dead popular. I bought a full-length

Afghan through an advert in *Melody Maker* for something like
five quid. The winters here were bloody awful but you could
walk round with a t-shirt on and a pair of jeans, and as long
as I had my Afghan coat on I was as warm as toast.'

Then the summer came, but he still used to wear the
Afghan; it was like a tribal marker. 'I suppose we were all
posers, everyone was a poser then. When bands like Mott the
Hoople became really popular people used to walk round with
those stupid jackets Ian Hunter used to wear; I had a couple
of them. And loon pants, I mean, God almighty! Skin-tight
loon pants, bright red, bright yellow. What were we thinking?'

Alex would happily troop off to Newcastle City Hall or
Middlesbrough Town Hall to see the likes of Uriah Heep,
Wishbone Ash, and Barclay James Harvest. His bands weren't
hitmaking or even fashionable; his scene had its own heroes,
its own logic. 'I used to go and see people like UFO. The
bands that weren't popular. I'd go and see anyone who wasn't
popular.'

If you were a gig-going long hair in 1975 who wanted to
extend your social life away from rock music, in Birmingham
you might have hung out in the Arts Lab at Aston, where a
brilliant programme of experimental and arthouse films was
on offer. In Manchester there was the Squat, a semi-derelict
Victorian building next to the Students Union which was
saved from demolition after being occupied by student rebels,
and then metamorphosed into an informal venue for gigs,
rehearsal space, and, for a time, a café bar. But life in Stockton
was more circumscribed, and Alex and his mates did almost
all their socialising in the pub. 'You'd go to work, you'd finish
work and sometimes you'd go straight from work to the pub
and sometimes you'd go home and have a wash and then go
to the pub.'

There had been Janis Joplin, of course, but the groundbreaking, hard-rock all-girl band Fanny emerged in the first
three years of the Seventies, and Alex remembers how this

helped to change the rock audience. 'Even the girls were starting to get into rock: Vinegar Joe, Curved Air, Sonya Kristina. Fanny were dead popular with the girls. Round Stockton town centre you'd see girls walking round with rock t-shirts on.'

Thirty years on, he can still recall which pubs in the North-East of England had the best jukeboxes, including his favourite Stockton pub, the Talbot. They'd take trips away to Tyneside, him and his mates, hiring a coach or taking a bus to the pubs of Newcastle: the Man in the Moon – which had all the Yes covers painted on the wall – the City Tavern, and Percy's Bar. But the first place they'd usually find themselves was in the area around the Haymarket pub (the Haymarket was where he'd heard the seven-minute version of 'Riders on the Storm'). There were three pubs in a row called the Plough, the Hotspur and the Haymarket, all selling Newcastle Exhibition. 'Newcastle Exhibition was the drink of choice back then for us hippies – a nice pint; it's crap now, but then it was a nice pint.'

The Haymarket attracted a lot of students and drinking types, with a room off to the right where the old guys would sit. In 1975 Alex and his mates would make their way there for a Saturday afternoon session. The Wishbone Ash fans boozing in the Haymarket generally weren't interested in the football. 'You'd go in there and sit down and the conversation wasn't football, it was music. You'd all have your rock t-shirts on, go there and sit down and you'd talk about music. Great, brilliant pub. Seven nights a week I'd be in the pub and three nights a week I'd also be in nightclubs.'

Now bars and pubs in the big cities are often open until the early hours, whereas in the Seventies if you wanted a late night drink the only option was to go to a nightclub. Locally, Stockton had Incognito's (popular with the teenagers); Bailey's (with a slightly older crowd and occasional rock groups); the Fiesta in Norton (which used to feature a lot of acts, cabaret-type Sixties bands whose star was waning), and from 1974 some occasional rock nights in one of the rooms of the Swallow Hotel just down by the river. Mostly, though, Alex was resigned to putting his music tastes on hold for a late drink or five.

Trips to the nightclubs of Stockton also meant having to overcome the nationwide dress code of the time which required male patrons to be dressed in black shoes, always with a jacket and tie, and never in jeans. Every high street discotheque had these rules; so peace-loving hippies were excluded but a psycho in a Moss Bros suit and a wide tie was welcome. Going out in town could compromise your personal safety.

Alex had a special set of clothes, his passport to a late drink. 'You couldn't get into a nightclub wearing an Afghan, and you couldn't get in with jeans unfortunately. It was embarrassing what you had to put on to get in. Kipper ties, waistcoats, stupid trousers. We didn't have trainers then, so you'd wear boots or shoes and that wasn't really a problem.'

He never felt smart. 'You'd be in a shirt and a tie and we'd all be wearing waistcoats – we all wore waistcoats – and we used to walk round with our hands in our pockets, don't know why, like idiots.'

He wasn't having much luck with the ladies either. 'A lot of times we just went there to get pissed drunk. We didn't do too much picking up in them days, we were too bloody shy. Stockton wasn't the capital of sex, drugs and rock and roll, I'll tell you that for nothing. You'd go to a nightclub and dance a bit, but none of us could dance. I was an awful dancer.'

In the mid-1970s there was no denying the attractions of Newcastle Exhibition, Cinzano Bianco, Babycham, Blue Nun, Double Diamond, snakebite or barley wine. Boozers had some hard-drinking bands to follow too, including The Sensational Alex Harvey Band. Alex Harvey was in his forties but had a loyal following among beered-up crazies, football fans and *NME* readers, and generated even more converts with two big records in 1975, 'Delilah' and 'Tomorrow Belongs to Me'. Harvey appeared caged, deranged, and the band had the aura of a street gang. In Stoke in 1975 there was a near riot during an SAHB set. In interviews, Alex Harvey would reveal a vociferous disdain for authority, on one occasion telling Charles Shaar Murray, 'When I see these poor men, Wilson and Heath, walking about and blustering and saying, "We'll do this and we'll do that" with their silly suits on – they're a hundred years out of date. They've got nothing to do with what's going on.'

Post-glam, pre-punk was the golden era of pub rock, represented by the likes of Brinsley Schwarz, the Count Bishops, the Hamsters, the 101'ers, and Bees Make Honey. The pub rock sound was a kind of head-down, basic blues boogie best heard in a sweaty pub through a cranked-up PA; it was a reaction against the hi-fi meanderings of the progressive rock bands, and in that sense pub rock was a precursor to punk, and a number of pub rock bands, notably Eddie & the Hot Rods, featured on the bill at early punk gigs.

Foremost among the bands connected with the scene were Dr Feelgood. Formed in 1971 around Wilko Johnson's manic, ack-ack guitar playing and Lee Brilleaux's brilliant blues shouting, they tore the roof off live – thin ties, mod suits, Wilko's psychotic stare, the sweat pouring from Brilleaux – and released a couple of great pre-punk LPs, *Down By the Jetty* and *Malpractice*. Their sound – which, in truth, appeared to be fuelled as much by amphetamines as by alcohol – became influential in the relay of ideas passing between New York and London in the months before punk broke. According to Debbie Harry of Blondie, 'If there's one group that could take credit for giving direction to the New York scene, it must be Dr Feelgood.'

1975 would be an important year for a new generation in

New York, as characters like Richard Hell and Patti Smith, and bands like Blondie, The Ramones and Television piloted the city's move from a grim post-glam hangover to a pioneering punk city. Venues and bands became magnets for malcontents. Debbie Harry remembers The Stillettoes, an early incarnation of Blondie: 'We attracted the most fucked-up and interesting people and had the cruddiest equipment.'

Debbie Harry had been keeping out of the city for a few years, but by 1972 she was refreshed, back on track and back in New York. She formed The Stillettoes and met Chris Stein, a part-time guitarist and roadie for the Magic Tramps, who soon joined The Stillettoes, and became part of a generation who gave New York a new start, and rejuvenated the energies that had been flying around Warhol's Factory in the late 1960s. This new generation gigged at clubs like Max's and CBGBs; the Mercer Arts Center was now history.

CBGBs was a biker bar when Tom Verlaine and Richard Lloyd asked owner Hilly Kristal if he would host a Television gig. Television's look underlined the new spirit among New York bands: their torn shirts, baggy pants and short hair were in stark contrast to the big hair, tight pants and glitter of The New York Dolls. Television were thin, bookish and subversive. Tom Verlaine and Patti Smith were lovers; Richard Hell gave Lloyd a shirt to wear with the words 'Please Kill Me' written on it. Their attitude was uptight, their songs ramshackle.

Debbie and Chris played gigs at CBGBs with various musicians and under various names (including a few appearances as Angel and the Snake), although the line-ups barely survived a few weeks. Former MC5 guitarist Fred Smith left Debbie's band to join Television, by which time the band had just changed names again, from Blondie & the Banzai Babies to, simply, Blondie. Playing gigs at CBGBs with The Ramones, their hottest number was a cover version of 'Lady Marmalade'. Blondie's following remained somewhat strange, Debbie Harry later recalled: 'Strange', she says, 'was always good.'

Characters like Patti Smith thrived in rundown, bankrupt, bohemian New York. It wasn't a rich city financially, but hosted a community of people eager to exchange ideas and search for a cutting edge. Key to the impact and the longevity of the New York scene in particular was just how highly intelligence and creativity were prized. Later, when Patti Smith's band got a new drummer, the poor lad had to drag a load of books and armfuls of records home every night to research his role.

The bohemians in New York took an interest in poetry, photography, art and underground film-making, but more than any other city in the world at the time, New York believed in the redemptive power of rock & roll. According to Richard Hell, who wrote a piece in *Hit Parader* magazine, 'The occupation of rock and roll is so appealing now – it's an outlet for passions and ideas too radical for any other form.'

In June 1974 Patti Smith recorded her first single, 'Piss Factory', the lyrics drawing on her experiences working at a toy factory in Blackwood, New Jersey, dreaming of a way out, desperate for some choices. At the end of the song she makes herself a promise: 'And I'm gonna go, I'm gonna get out of here, I'm gonna get on the train and go to New York City, and I'm gonna be somebody . . . I'm gonna be a big star.'

Edie Sedgwick had been one inspiration to Patti Smith in her early days in New York, and Patty Hearst became another; Smith seemed to enjoy the fact that they shared the same Christian name, and also celebrated her renegade status. The other side of the record was a brilliant, in-yer-face version of 'Hey Joe', a song written by Dino Valenti and made famous via a version by Jimi Hendrix. In the new intro rapped by Patti about Patty Hearst, the heiress was asked if she had been 'gettin' it every night from a black revolutionary'.

Both with unique, striking looks, Patti Smith and Debbie Harry shared ambition and attitude, but had different takes on female assertiveness. Patti was spiky and challenging, while

Debbie was untouchable and pouty. Rock & roll remains a masculine domain and neither had obvious role models in rock. In some ways this was an advantage; they made their own way, and became, instead, role models for others. According to Victor Bockris, documenter of late 1960s and early 1970s New York, 'Without Debbie Harry there would be no Courtney Love, there would be no Madonna.'

There was no going back for Patti Smith after she'd featured in a storming two-month residency at CBGBs with Television in the spring of 1975. It was a case of the right band in the right venue in the right city, and Patti was inspired. 'It was the greatest atmosphere to perform in, it was conspiratorial. It was real physical, and that's what rock and roll's all about: sexual tension and being drunk and disorderly.'

Those gigs at CBGBs turned the group into a band. Young drummer J.D. Daugherty had joined them onstage occasionally, and once he'd read those bags of books and listened to the records, he finally joined the band permanently, having also mastered their approach to songs such as 'Land of a Thousand Dances', one of the songs in their set that gave them the opportunity to improvise and let rip.

Written in the early 1960s by Chris Kenner, 'Land of a Thousand Dances' namechecks many of the popular dance moves in those early days of rock & roll – the Pony, the Mashed Potato, the Alligator and the Watootsie – and became a minor hit in 1965 when it was reworked by an obscure beat group in LA recording under the name Cannibal & the Headhunters. But it was in 1966 when Wilson Pickett recorded the song that it became a standard, covered by dance bands and played by DJs. In Patti Smith's hands, 'Land' became fused with a breathless rock poem about a kid getting beaten up and horses breathing flames, with the names of the dances embued with an assertive erotic charge. Charles Shaar Murray was one of the journalists who saw the band during this time. He reported back to *NME* readers that their show at

CBGBs was 'Undoubtedly the most gripping performance that I've seen by a white act since the last time I saw The Who'.

In November 1975 the Patti Smith LP *Horses* was released, an experimental, eccentric, intense work which reveals, in retrospect, an important quality, taking strength from the past – there's an obvious Jim Morrison influence, for example – yet prefiguring punk, or, more accurately, post-punk in its ambitious mix of avant-garde art and angry rock & roll. The poetry of William Burroughs is in there, but the attitude and the angry crescendos of Nirvana too.

During the summer of 1975, a world away from the biker bars of New York, freaks and the police were in conflict in the English countryside over the issue of free festivals. For almost a decade every summer had witnessed a number of gatherings in various locations, among them Windsor. In 1974, the Windsor free festival had been the target for the biggest operation that Thames Police had ever mounted, but five hundred officers in cars, jeeps, vans and a helicopter hadn't deterred large crowds of hippies, drop-outs, pot smokers, White Panthers, Jesus People, and psychedelic and progressive music fans from arriving at the festival, which the event's (dis)organiser Sid Rawles dubbed a 'tribal gathering'. 'You need to live with people', he said, 'and experiment in living.'

Under intense pressure from the authorities, the 1975 festival was cancelled and the Windsor regulars instead went to Watchfield. Meanwhile, the more commercially-oriented Reading festival was attended by over 100,000 people, and the big draws were Wishbone Ash and Yes, complete with their light show and projections. Lou Reed was billed to play but didn't show. Festival-goers entertained themselves by throwing cans at each other and shouting 'Wally'. Among others appearing at Reading that year were Hawkwind, Soft Machine, Supertramp, Caravan, Babe Ruth, Dr Feelgood and Alberto Y Los Trios Paranoias. Dominating the crowd were greasers, or 'fribs' as they were known in some parts of the

Midlands – rock fans with long, unkempt hair, maybe hippies who'd hit the bottle, or Black Sabbath fans still welded to heavy metal. Not every rock band appealed to them; they wouldn't like Status Quo, for example – who lacked a touch of Satan – but they had bands galore to get into, from Bad Company to Nazareth. Lemmy left Hawkwind to form Motorhead in 1975; they became major greaser heroes.

Folk music was another thriving scene in 1975, and one of the highlights of the year was the release of the *Rising for the Moon* LP by Fairport Convention. The folk scene was big enough at the time to propel a number of acts in the direction of commercial success, including Steeleye Span and Ralph McTell (his 'Streets of London' single was in the Top 10 in January 1975). Although he included the traditional folk standard 'Spencer the Rover' on his 1975 LP *Sunday's Child*, John Martyn was taking a jazz-influenced, melancholy, experimental direction, while maintaining folk and acoustic roots; his *Solid Air* LP in 1973 was probably his finest work of the decade.

In this land of a thousand dances, what united most of the tribes – from greasers to Northern Soul fans – was hatred of the mainstream. They felt fenced in by the commercial world, and were universally dismissive of Abba, even offended by them. They had alternative views of the world and an attitude of wanting to live outside the Top 20. When journalist Tony Cummings made a visit to Tiffany's in Newcastle in 1974, one of the regulars at a Northern Soul night told him, 'We want to hear sounds we can't hear anywhere else. Something special, like.'

In 1975 Kraftwerk released their debut LP *Autobahn*. Their use of electronic instruments, the crisp and minimalist sound they created, stood out from the untidy, ramshackle music around them and reflected a modern, even futurist outlook. In contrast, the Northern Soul fans were still in awe of mid-Sixties American soul, and in the rock world there were still too many ideas stuck in the late Sixties. Elsewhere there were plenty of glances even further back in time; for a number of years, for example, Malcolm McLaren, eager to avoid hippies and looking for new excitement, had considered Teds as the authentic, original spirit of rock & roll. Also in this pre-punk era Bryan Ferry popularised the GI look and Bowie took to wearing a zoot suit. So many references to the past were a reflection that a new rush of excitement was needed. Even fashionistas starting boutiques and stalls in 1975 were specialising in retro stock.

When Alan Jones was wandering King's Road to shops like Granny Takes a Trip and buying clothes from Alkasura, he'd pop into number 430 where Malcolm McLaren and Vivienne Westwood had a shop, which underwent several changes of name and stock. After a 1974 refurbishment, out went threads for Teds, and the shop became known as Sex: 'Specialists in rubberwear, glamourwear & stagewear' according to their business card. Vivienne Westwood's designs were sleazy, early versions of what would later be the gay clone look, with maximum use of leather, bondage, and porno imagery.

Alan Jones remembers various early encounters with Malcolm McLaren and Vivienne Westwood, including badgering McLaren to sell him a Marilyn Monroe EP which was displayed in a glass cabinet in Sex. He also befriended shop assistant Jordan, an outrageous-looking young lady from Seaford in Sussex, and began to accompany her on nights out to clubs like the Masquerade. They made a right pair, provoking, posing, pushing things to the limit. Alan remembers the looks they would get, and they loved the attention. Cars used to stop at zebra crossings and he and Jordan would strut across the road and the drivers would go mad.

In New York the period was defined by the music at CBGBs; in London it was defined by Sex, provocative fashions, and the likes of Alan Jones wandering the streets in a 'Fuck Your

Mother' t-shirt. But in mid-1975 there was still no name for the underground; the 'punk' label was still a few months away. Richard Hell had provided a great slogan though, with the title of his song 'Blank Generation', written earlier in the year. In addition, the model for the new sound was being displayed by The Ramones: sheer energy chewed and spat out, songs lasting two minutes or less.

There were further exchanges of ideas between New York and London when Malcolm McLaren started hanging out with the rock fraternity in New York, and then began working with The New York Dolls, who had released a second LP, *Too Much Too Soon*, in 1974, but had struggled to improve their shambolic career. He gave them an image make-over, ditching the last vestiges of their glam look and imposing deep red politics on them. Vivienne Westwood made them new outfits, including red vinyl trousers and high-heeled Sex boots. But McLaren's intervention in their career only seemed to hasten their end; in February 1975 they played in front of a hammer and sickle backdrop, but a week or so later two of the band members left and the band broke up.

When Malcolm resurfaced, bringing together the Sex Pistols some months later, he'd clearly learned from his trips to New York, as he later admitted when discussing the beginnings of the Pistols: 'I was taking the nuances of Richard Hell, the faggy, pop side of The New York Dolls, the politics of boredom, and mashing it all to make a statement, maybe the final statement, and piss off this rock and roll scene.'

The fashions Alan was parading weren't bland; they had repercussions, as he discovered the day he bought a t-shirt depicting two cowboys. Vivienne Westwood had designed the range, sleeveless t's, printed either brown on pink or red on green. The two cowboys are facing each other, wearing their hats and boots, but neither of them wears trousers, and bang in the centre of the image their generously-sized penises are almost touching.

In Sex, words like 'anarchy' and 'subversion' and phrases like 'the politics of boredom' were being bandied about by Malcolm, Vivienne and graphic designer Jamie Reid. The characters hanging out at Sex wanted to provoke and unsettle, to act as some kind of catalyst for chaos, to shock like a Baader Meinhof action. And one sunny day Alan found out that this frisson could be created without really trying. With his Norwegian friend Mousse, he went to the shop and bought the two-cowboys t-shirt which he immediately put on and began walking down the King's Road. 'I can still remember people staring at the t-shirt and smiling,' he says.

But after walking through Sloane Square and along Piccadilly, he was stopped by police and taken to Vine Street where he was charged with gross indecency. Nicholas de Jongh, then a reporter at *The Guardian*, turned up at court and reported the story on the paper's front page. Alan pleaded guilty. 'I didn't know what else to do. Malcolm said he would do everything he could to get me off, he'd be there, and of course he wasn't. And there was a fifty-pound fine which Malcolm said he would pay and he never did.'

By the end of 1975 Alan was working in Sex, but never got the £50 Malcolm promised him, although a few years later he got paid for his appearance in the film *The Great Rock & Roll Swindle*, having made a point of collaring McLaren's accountant Sophie Richmond. 'I told Sophie I wanted to be paid and there was no way I was going to do it unless I got two hundred pounds or something for those scenes, three days standing around in a stupid bath.'

By the end of 1975 the hunt for Patty Hearst was over after she'd been arrested in the Bay Area, and her trial was set for early the following year. But a sense of threat remained; the same month Patty Hearst was captured, the Manson family came back to haunt America, when former family member Lynette 'Squeaky' Fromme was arrested for pointing a gun at President Ford. Just seventeen days later, Sara Jane Moore attempted to kill Ford in San Francisco. A revolutionary, she'd been recruited by the FBI to gain intelligence on the Symbionese Liberation Army, but after Patty Hearst's arrest, her cover was blown. The shooting of Ford was believed to be her attempt to regain credibility in the revolutionary underground.

In London, the hot summer of 1975 turned into an autumn of drizzle and football hooliganism, the Labour Government set about cutting back public expenditure, the punk movement was stirring, and the talk was of extremism and anarchy. An ILEA inquiry into the William Tyndale School in Islington, which had suffered eighteen months of teacher walkouts and unrest, heard evidence from a teacher that 'chaos and anarchy' reigned at the school. The headmaster was criticised for telling pupils, 'Literacy is of doubtful value.'

In October, Prime Minister Harold Wilson made a speech at the Labour conference attacking the 'infestation' of the Party by 'extremists', but was powerless to prevent the Party's rank-and-file members from voting the Chancellor of the Exchequer, Denis Healey, off the National Executive. Among all official political parties in the West, there was a fear of extremism flourishing outside the democratic process, as evidence of political violence multiplied in the final months of 1975. In Germany the Baader Meinhof trial was in progress; there were violent clashes in Tokyo between rival radical student groups; in Manila a member of President Marcos's Cabinet was shot dead in the Presidential Palace, and in Argentina the owner of a Mercedes factory was kidnapped.

On 28 October 1975 the front cover of *The Times* detailed eight cities that had suffered attacks by terrorist bombers in the previous twenty-four hours, including eleven blasts in New York, Washington and Chicago carried out by a group seeking independence for Puerto Rico; bombs in Spain and Portugal; a bomb at a tourist hotel in Jerusalem; and blasts in Beirut (battles in Beirut between Christian phalangists and

Muslim militiamen were claiming dozens of lives each day, and Lebanon was on the verge of collapse). Most curious of all was a petrol bomb attack in Paris on the home of a member of the committee which selected the Prix Goncourt literary prize. To *The Times*, all this illustrated 'the extent to which the terrorist bomb has developed into the standard international protest during the last decade'.

A few days later, an IRA bomb exploded at Green Park underground station, one of a variety of soft targets in London, including car bombs outside restaurants in Chelsea and Westminster. In Northern Ireland, although the police and the Army were still targeted by the IRA, the chaos and carnage were exacerbated by an internal IRA feud which claimed almost a dozen lives between October and Christmas 1975. Rival Loyalist organisations, the UVF and the UDA, were also at loggerheads, but the UVF maintained their sectarian offensive too; on one day at the beginning of October, twelve people were killed in Ulster during sectarian bomb and gun attacks, all civilians and all victims of the UVF.

In the last months of 1975 there was no let-up in the activities of football hooligans, despite the intervention of Denis Howell, who announced a ban on alcohol on football coaches. On one Saturday in October dozens of police fought running battles with Manchester United fans during a match at West Ham, which was held up for twenty minutes when supporters spilled onto the pitch. On the same day, the match between Blackpool and Bristol Rovers was also disrupted by crowd trouble, leading to the referee claiming, 'We are reaching the situation where it would be ideal to play matches in front of empty terraces.'

The violence that day set off another bout of soul-searching in the media. In previous articles *The Sunday Times* had called for a crackdown on the terraces, greater involvement in the community by clubs, and increased activities to channel the energies of young people, but had also pointed to a lack of credible leadership in public life, politics or the media. Now the newspaper was even more convinced that the roots of football hooliganism were deep in society, pointing to a stagnant education system, a sensationalist media that fanned the flames of violence, and the demoralisation of large sections of society, 'when ordinary people are continually asked to work harder for diminishing returns'.

The Sunday Times described a series of specific links between the destructive discontent of the young and Government policies: 'Last week the Government proposed cutbacks in the very areas – youth, recreation, education, community and social services – that can offer any hope of ameliorating these problems.'

On 6 November 1975 the Sex Pistols played their first gig, at St Martin's College, supporting Bazooka Joe. Bass player Stuart Goddard left Bazooka Joe the following day and formed a band called The B-Sides; after witnessing the half-hour set the Pistols had played he could sense a new chapter in music was opening, convinced by the committed energy of the Sex Pistols. And it was around this time that punk got its label. The new generation of New York bands had already been featuring in magazines like *51* and *New York Rocker*, but near the end of 1975 the first issue of *Punk*, a new comic rock mag, appeared in New York, founded by John Holmstrom and Legs McNeil. They posted signs everywhere the New York musicians hung out, proclaiming 'Punk is Coming! Punk is Coming', and it was assumed it was a band trying to hype themselves (or, as Debbie Harry later put it, 'We thought here comes another shitty group with an even shittier name').

The following year, punk broke into the public consciousness in England; the situation *The Sunday Times* was describing as the background to football hooliganism was also the breeding ground for punk. By the end of 1975 the citizenry was losing faith in its rulers, civic society was in crisis, and welfare spending was being cut. There was a growing army of kids living for the moment, not giving a damn about the future, and seeking instead the top buzz of fighting in the street, upsetting strait-laced passers-by, or getting on the television news. *The Sunday Times* taunted the Government: 'A year, another year of young violence, and less credibility than ever in all the authorities.'

In cities with – in Raban's phrase – a 'variety of lives', in the land of a thousand dances, fragmentation had replaced consensus. There were few alliances or shared beliefs, and no shared future. Onstage, Joe Strummer used to wear a boiler suit carrying the slogan 'Hate & War', not just to challenge the hippie slogan 'Peace & Love', but also because it was a reflection of the times.

In the second half of the 1970s, the sense of conflict and hate was more widespread than in the songs of a few punk bands. Punk stripped away the fake harmony of our society and locked into a basic truth: we define ourselves against others, and we're happy to allow hate to become key to our self-definition. Hate fuelled the deadly sectarianism of Northern Ireland; the Scottish identity would be severely diluted if hatred of the English was removed; censorious moralists are never happier than when they're ganging up on gays; if you support Leeds United you hate Manchester United. Hate was the glue that bound us all together on the terraces in the mid-1970s. Among the football chants from that era were: 'We hate Nottingham Forest (We hate Liverpool too)', sung to the tune of 'Land of Hope and Glory', and 'We all fuckin' hate Leeds' (to the theme tune of the film *The Dambusters*).

The perception that politicians lacked insight or even control persisted. Punk fed off this conflict, this tribalism and aggression, and took energy from it. As the blank generation reacted, they created, and this was one of the features of the 1970s, and one of the continuing glories of the alternative world – the excitement and influence that could be created by a coterie of characters emerging from secondhand clothes shops, reggae record stalls or dodgy venues. Punk wasn't the invention of the lucky few – the kids with privileges – but seemed to attract the people Debbie Harry celebrated as 'strange'; the ones she'd described as 'fucked-up and interesting'. There was no desire to be accepted or even understood. The blank generation found exhilaration in this, as John Lydon later recalled: 'We were all extremely ugly people. We were the outcasts, the unwanted.'

CHAPTER SEVEN

'Young Hearts Run Free' (1976)

Reminiscing, wrestling with personal memories, you encounter problems trying to recall how things were, how they felt, pinning things down to certain dates and then putting them in a reasonable order, and with detail. Occasionally, long unremembered memories emerge out of the darkness, but every minute of every day other recollections become vague, then slip away forever.

And we're not in control of this raw material. Memories are fallible. You may or may not remember the name of the first person you kissed; what the field looked like before they built the hospital; the gloomy shortcut by the church; the name of the young lad killed on his motorcycle who used to go to your big sister's youth club. In the deep waters of our memory, sometimes it's not so much a case of pinpointing a specific event, as trawling through murky impressions; standing on the terraces, walking through town between buses at dusk.

We have all forgotten a lot, whether by accident or design, but what's even more intriguing is the way we can shape, and even invent memories, to create a past and an identity. In recent years, for example, biographers have uncovered the truth behind the lies of Jeffrey Archer, and revealed how

Johnny Adair, the Loyalist hard man, shaped his past to create and sustain a violent, intimidating image.

Our personal histories are a ragbag of memories, secrets, well-worn tales, and distortions, all subject to myth-making, and the same is true of our collective memory. Nations create an identity by manipulating a past, choosing what to forget or to recall. Scotland's folk memory prefers to tune into heroic deeds at the Battle of Bannockburn in 1314, when Robert the Bruce led an army of bravehearts and defeated Edward II of England, rather than the occasions when English forces got the upper hand, at Flodden Field in 1513 and Culloden Moor in 1745. The French remember Jeanne d'Arc; we remember the Battle of Trafalgàr. And we're more likely to remember events that brought us together – the Blitz – than things that revealed our divisions: the General Strike, Peterloo.

Like personal memories, much of the raw material available to create a communal past is fallible. Going back to newspaper archives, for example, you're at the mercy of the news agenda, and we've all lived long enough to be wary of how events can be skewed, ignored or manipulated in the press. But there's also a choice to be made about which part of the paper matters most: the mass of news, reviews or sports results; weather forecasts, TV listings, celebrity gossip or political intrigue. Certainly during the summer of 1976, the hot weather was receiving a lot of coverage, but journalists and voters curious about the state of the political parties, or parliamentary intrigue and power shifts, also had plenty to digest. On 16 March, for example, Prime Minister Harold Wilson suddenly announced his decision to resign, for reasons which remain the subject of speculation and even a conspiracy theory or two. There was talk of scandalous private papers being stolen, and plenty of evidence that elements in the establishment and MI5, preferring an authoritarian right-wing government, had been working on a series of plots to destabilise the Labour Government.

In the wake of Wilson's resignation, the two main candidates to succeed him as Leader of the Labour Party, and thus take the office of Prime Minister, were James Callaghan (who was considered slightly right of centre) and Michael Foot (the more radical of the two). Callaghan defeated Michael Foot in the final ballot, but the contest accentuated a split in the Labour Party, already acknowledged by Harold Wilson in October 1975 with talk of 'extremists'. The radical left – a vocal majority of the membership – sniping at the centrists in the higher echelons of the Party would be a feature for a decade and a half, a disunity Tory leader Margaret Thatcher never hesitated to exploit.

Meanwhile, the third biggest supported party, the Liberals, also found a new leader in 1976 after Jeremy Thorpe resigned. Thorpe had become embroiled in a scandal involving 'male model' Norman Scott, who claimed that he'd had a homosexual relationship with Thorpe, in a statement he made in court during a case against Andrew Newton, a former airline pilot who shot Scott's dog on Bodmin Moor. Those few, bizarre, random clues were all we knew of the story in 1976, but later in the decade more rumours and accusations emerged, culminating in claims that Thorpe had subsequently been plotting to have Norman Scott murdered.

But there was still room in the newspapers for other events. In the *Manchester Evening News*, Sheila Walker, a cocktail bunny at the Manchester Playboy Club on Canal Street, appeared in the paper somewhat under-dressed. Gratuitous shots of girls in bikinis were common in many local papers at the time: a second young woman was pictured a few pages away, cooling off in a fountain. Apart from news of bikini-clad lovelies falling into fountains, stories in the *Manchester Evening News* over that Bank Holiday included the opening of *The Omen*, and the scarcely less scary announcement of an opportunity to attend a charity cricket game alongside a clutch of top Seventies celebrity guests: Mike

Yarwood, Stuart Hall, Leslie Crowther, Jimmy Ellis and Judith Chalmers.

Another news story building through the later weeks of August 1976 was the rising profile of peace rallies in Northern Ireland. Spontaneous demonstrations had taken place following the deaths of three children after a terrorist car ran out of control, and a peace movement emerged. Two women were at its forefront – Betty Williams and Mairead Corrigan – and their rallies attracted growing numbers of marchers from across the sectarian divide. On 28 August 25,000 Catholics and Protestants marched through the Loyalist Shankill area, though later a small crowd of young Catholics threw stones and bottles at the peace marchers.

Yet even close scrutiny of daily newspapers can't reveal much of the grain of the everyday life led behind or beyond the headlines – the routines, the commute to work, the walk to school – except that it's a fair bet that on most evenings of the week, whatever the year, the citizens of Britain are most likely to be found sitting in watching TV. On the Saturday of that Bank Holiday weekend in August 1976, *Match of the Day* was missable (that weekend's football results included Derby County 0, Manchester United 0; Manchester City 0, Stoke City 0; and West Ham 0, Leicester 0). Among the television treats the following day were *The High Chaparral* in the afternoon, and *Bridge On the River Kwai* in the evening. On the Monday of that weekend the citizens of Birmingham were invited to stay in all evening and watch *Carry On Up the Jungle* with Frankie Howerd and Sid James on the local station, ATV.

Seventies TV comedy had its very strong moments – *Fawlty Towers* and *Porridge*, for example – and many, many weaker ones. ITV's regional stations were strong, with a free rein to commission and make their own programmes, but there was little choice. With only three channels, however, there were big audiences for what would now be considered minority programmes. This was one of the factors in the success in the mid-1970s of the BBC's *Play for Today* slot, as well as its ability to attract great writers – Willy Russell, Dennis Potter, Malcolm Bradbury, Elaine Feinstein, Alan Bennett – many of whom took the opportunity to produce work that portrayed contemporary social themes.

It was also something of a peak year for single-part plays on television. Those broadcast that year included Mike Leigh's *Nuts in May*, Bill Bryden's *Willie Rough*, and Jane Lapotaire in Watson Gould's *The Other Woman*, as well as Jack Rosenthal's *Bar Mitzvah Boy*. In 1976 Dennis Potter's *Brimstone and Treacle* was made for the BBC, but its content was deemed too controversial and its broadcast was postponed.

Yet that hot, slow, August Bank Holiday weekend, with the nation lazing in front of the TV, was to culminate in one of the most significant events of the year: riots at the Notting Hill Carnival. There was a history of tension and conflict between the police and young blacks in particular, and a sense of containment and harassment was strong in the ethnic communities. Such was the tension, it was inevitable that situations could get out of hand quickly. According to a Metropolitan Police memorandum to the Home Affairs Select Committee, there was 'potential for conflict' present in every law enforcement situation between the police and the black community.

Police powers of stop and search, and application of the 'sus' laws, appeared to be used in a discriminatory way against black youths, as part of this policy of containment. 'Sus' effectively permitted police officers to arrest people purely on 'suspicion'; no crime had to have taken place, and therefore no victim was required. On the word of two police officers, defendants could be charged under the 1824 Vagrancy Act, which made it illegal for a 'suspected person or reputed thief to frequent or loiter in a public place with intent to commit an arrestable offence'.

In 1976 in England and Wales, 3,500 people were charged

with 'sus', leading to 2,738 convictions, but a hugely disproportionate number of those charged under the Act were black: 42 per cent, although the black community made up less than 2 per cent of the total population. There were also disparities regionally, with police forces in some areas barely using 'sus' laws, while London's Metropolitan police seemed particularly fond of the Act; 55 per cent of 'sus' cases were in London. Behind this strategy lay distorted perceptions of young black men as potential criminals, perceptions created by the police's controversial use of statistics and fed by a compliant press. The news media began to get entangled with the issue of 'mugging', for example, often with unsatisfying results.

Minority ethnic communities had become cynical about the role of the police on the streets. In June 1976, when Gurdip Singh Chaggar was taunted and then stabbed to death by a group of white youths in Southall, local Asians responded by taking to the streets; the police then brought in reinforcements and began to stop and search Asian youths. This action led, of course, to accusations that the police had their priorities wrong: containing a community angered by a racist murder instead of a vigorous pursuit of the murderers.

There was enough evidence that the police weren't neutral, and that they used powers in a racially discriminatory way. Their over-zealous defence of National Front marchers added to this perception, as did inflammatory statements from high-ranking officers. Even into the 1980s, a senior member of the Police Federation was claiming that 'nigger' was an acceptable way for officers to address members of the black community. Against this background, the Notting Hill riots could be regarded as a reaction against oppressive policing, as well as an expression of frustration and unity; rebellion as self-preservation.

These communities felt pressure, not just from flawed policing, but from gains in the polls by the racist National Front (in the Leicester by-election in the summer of 1976, the National

Front polled 18.5 per cent of the vote), and from an atmosphere in which racism was often dressed up in a suit of respectability. The concept that racists are always readily identifiable, street-fighting skinheads was undermined, for example, by the nation's judiciary, those arbiters of a nation's sense of right and wrong. In an incident in 1976, BNP leader Kingsley Read – who was arrested and charged with inciting racial hatred when he greeted the news of Gurdip Singh Chaggar's murder by announcing 'one down, one million to go' – was acquitted in court, with Judge McKinnon telling him, 'By all means propagate your views.'

The 1975 Notting Hill festival had seen tension and some violence, but in 1976 there was a conspicuous change in police tactics and a massively increased police presence, with 1,600 officers on patrol. A heavy, confrontational atmosphere built, until early on the Monday evening, the second day, police attempting to make an arrest attracted a hostile crowd and soon broken bricks, cans and bottles were flying. By the end of the evening, four hundred and fifty-six people had been injured and the police had made sixty arrests, and in the days that followed, police tactics were widely criticised. *The Evening Standard* declared, 'Scotland Yard was far too heavy-handed on Monday. The whole exercise was an error of judgement.'

There were particular problems with policing, and other race-related issues, but at Notting Hill young blacks had been joined and supported by young whites, reflecting wider disillusionment and anger. When Callaghan became Prime Minister in April 1976, unemployment was over 1.2 million, and his Chancellor, Denis Healey, had introduced cuts in public expenditure and increased interest rates to record levels in an attempt to reduce inflation. By mid-summer 1976, the number of people living on or around the official poverty line had trebled in the space of two years (the biggest rate of increase since the depression of the 1930s).

The summer of 1976 is commonly celebrated as the summer

in which punk broke, but the first stirrings were no more than flea bites in the ear of the great pop monster. In the mainstream, the Bay City Rollers were desperately trying to cling to power; from April 1974 onwards they were a hit-making machine – a bunch of lads with the right looks and simple pop hooks – but their stunning lack of creative ambition only hastened the arrival of the day their fans simply got bored, or got older, and took the posters off the wall. In 1976 that moment had come; it was the first year Showaddy-waddy had more No. 1 hits than the Bay City Rollers (that's how bad things had got for them). The first hit song of the summer of 1976 was Abba's 'Fernando'; the next was the excruciating 'Combine Harvester' single by The Wurzels.

In 1976 punk had no profile on the radio or in the charts, and during the summer there were no punks in the *Manchester Evening News* or on TV; even *New Musical Express* struggled to register its existence. The established names in rock looked impregnable – Led Zeppelin's *Presence* LP topped the American charts in May 1976 – and the big new names in rock weren't the punk rock bands; in America, the FM sound was wheeling out massive hits, like Boston's 'More Than a Feeling'.

Although rock music had a certain respectability in England – perhaps a debilitating respectability – and the likes of Led Zep and Pink Floyd were being featured in the Sunday broad-sheets, rock music was still marginalised in Eastern Europe; under Communism, music's subversive power to disturb or energise the young was acknowledged by the authorities. In March 1976, the Czech Government put nineteen musicians on trial in a clampdown on pop music.

All through the Cold War, the youth in the Eastern bloc shared some of the same heroes as the disaffected youth in the West; in the second half of the 1960s, for example, an underground hippy scene thrived, especially in Czechoslo-vakia. The reforming Government headed by Alexander Dubcek in 1968 gave encouragement to this underground, but the Soviet invasion, and the new regime that followed, began to close clubs, clamp down on bands, and control and censor the output of the media. Bravely, in the face of this official repression – but fully convinced of rock's emancipatory power – the Plastic People of the Universe formed, taking their name from a Frank Zappa song and performing at 'happenings', covering songs by the likes of The Velvet Underground, The Fugs and The Doors.

Through the 1970s, the Plastic People of the Universe developed various half-successful strategies for eluding the attentions of the police; the authorities, describing their music as 'morbid', had claimed it could have a 'negative social impact'. Significantly, these kinds of phrases sound not dissimilar to those used by Mary Whitehouse about various TV plays, or Tony Blackburn about 'Dead End Street' by The Kinks. Those supporting oppressive totalitarianism often shared common ground with those defending militaristic capitalism, not least in their fear of unhindered cultural activity, of young hearts running free.

In March 1976 the police arrested twenty-seven musicians and associates connected to the Plastic People of the Universe, and another group, DG307. Five people were eventually charged with a breach of the peace, including Vratislav Brabenec and Ivan Jirous. During the two-day trial, there were echoes of *Oz*, as prosecutors described some of the lyrics as obscene, and the band as 'an anti-social phenomenon'. All five defendants were found guilty and received jail sentences of up to eighteen months.

The West was about to hear the punk howl. Alex Patton was well used to rock pub and gig queue controversies, and he'd heard the endless T-Rex v Yes, Clapton v Hendrix and Pink Floyd v Black Sabbath debates, but the arrival of punk created an even bigger controversy. Alex has heard these arguments hundreds of times, and he soon jumps in when I suggest that the music scene needed punk. 'No way! Punk was championed by the music press who needed a new gimmick. I think The Clash were the only ones with any talent. The Stranglers weren't a punk band, they were rock and rollers, bikers. The Sex Pistols were a talentless pile of crap.'

Many others remember things differently, of course. In *England's Dreaming*, Jon Savage quotes Paul Cook talking about how boring the music scene in 1975 and 1976 was, recalling his first conversation with John Lydon. 'I remember saying to him how nothing was happening in music and how this whole youth movement needs something to get them going again.'

I pass this quote on to Alex, but he's having none of it. 'In 1975 and 1976 you had bands like Wishbone Ash, ELP, American bands like Rush, Blue Oyster Cult, bands like Barclay James Harvest, Supertramp. For me, the early 1970s going into the mid-1970s was one of the most vibrant periods of rock history and what killed it off was punk. Then they turned round with all this "rock dinosaur" bullshit.'

In the years since he first dismissed punk, Alex has had plenty of opportunity to reconsider, but nothing has changed his mind. 'No, for me, 1970 to 1976 was a marvellous period in rock music, although I do admit the fashion was abysmal, but there you go! Flared trousers; probably a mistake. Loon pants; without a doubt.'

Despite Alex's protestations to the contrary, a sizeable number of music fans were looking for new bands, new excitement. All the music that was growing in importance in 1976 – disco, punk, roots reggae – was being pushed forward in a fight against Sixties retreads and the boredom of living in someone else's culture. Graphic designer Peter Savile once recalled 1976 like this: 'So many people in 1976 saw an enormous change. With the establishment and youth culture there was a moment of paralysis.'

Life was like a bunch of nil–nil draws. After 'Fernando' and 'Combine Harvester', the *Top of the Pops* viewers in our household cheered wildly when The Real Thing knocked The

Wurzels off the top of the charts with 'You to Me Are Every-thing'; at last something with a bit of class, something half-decent to dance to at the youth club disco. But when you're fourteen years old, pleasures are fleeting; three weeks later mediocrity got its revenge and The Real Thing were toppled from the No. 1 spot by Demis Roussos.

Memories of the hot summer of 1976 are likely to involve the hosepipe ban, the sweat, the fires on heaths and moors, or maybe the England cricket team's mauling at the hands of West Indian bowler Michael Holding; but Alan, being Alan, recalls 1976 with reference to what he was wearing. His favourite look that year was another Vivienne Westwood design: a t-shirt featuring the word 'P-E-R-V' spelt out in chicken bones. 'I used to have some stage blood and I used to put fake welts down my back and I'd put the shirt on top so it looked like I'd been whipped and it was a great look.'

I was smiling when he was telling me this, him talking about taking outrageousness to the edge of ridiculousness. He spent the summer looking like that, even in Little Venice. 'Seriously,' he says, 'it was a great look, although it did smudge in the heat sometimes.'

At the Catacombs, his favourite gay bar, most of the crowd would be in leather. 'There'd be me in my plastic handcuffs, and little porno chains. I had loads of sex out of it, so maybe it was a good look for that particular time.'

Although society had become more tolerant after the 1967 Act decriminalising gay sex between consenting adults, after Stonewall, 'Lola', and the gender blurring of glam, resistance was still there. I can remember overhearing people com-plaining about the increased visibility of the gay community. 'I don't mind homosexuals,' they'd say, 'I just don't want them ramming it down my throat.'

Alan had mixed reactions to these social changes, and is still not convinced that mass acceptance of the gay scene is particularly desirable. 'Although the gay scene wasn't illegal, it was very underground and secret and there was something of a members-only thing about it. It was exciting. I've never been on any kind of Gay Lib march ever in my life, and I hate that kind of thing because I do recognise that it did take away some of the specialness of it. I'm not saying that being gay is anything remarkable, it's just that I would have preferred it to stay ghetto, that's when I felt more comfortable.'

If people were too tolerant, even unshockable, it took away the buzz. 'That's what I'm trying to say; that sense of some-thing different, staggering home to your friends wearing your leather trousers and saying, "Oh, I've just been to an orgy", getting that reaction.'

On reflection, Alan isn't sure there were many orgies in London at the time. He holds his coffee mug still for a second or two. He is trying to remember some orgies. 'I think there was one grope bar called the Gigolo on King's Road which was not much bigger than this room.'

He gets up out of his chair and tries to help me imagine the Gigolo. He stands facing a wall. 'There was a bar over here,' he points to his right, then shuffles further, until his face is pressed against the wall. 'And everyone was crushed against the wall and you could feel your way around the room.'

Now he's crushed against the wall, his back towards me, and I'm a bit clearer about what the grope bar was like – except that the lights would have been out, wouldn't they Alan, so we would have been in darkness? 'Oh yes, Dave, the lights would have been out, but, I mean, it was by no means anything very exciting!'

There were a few places to meet – clubs, basements, dives – like the Catacombs, Chararamas on Neal Street, the Mas-querade in Earls Court, the Sombrero, but most gay activity in London at the time was outdoor cruising; Earls Court was one area that became renowned, as well as Holland Park; that was another major cruising area. The weather helped, of course: long hot summers and balmy evenings.

In the early days there were some connections between punk and the gay community, and in one particular London club, Louise's on Poland Street, where the worlds collided, the gay habitués and the punk kids shared an urge to dress with attitude and get wasted.

Youthful rebellion and hedonism never goes away, nor the need for allies, like the group of mates, the so-called Bromley Contingent, who embraced a cutting-edge London existence in a reaction against suburbia and suburban values. Growing up with dissatisfied or questioning attitudes, you soon learn to look further than the mainstream in order to search for a history and lifestyle that makes sense. Specifically, Edie, Andy Warhol, Jack Kerouac, bondage, Bowie, *A Clockwork Orange* – all were loved, discovered or rediscovered in the second half of the 1970s, all available for the misfits to remix. One of the Contingent, Siouxsie Sioux, later explained their journey, literally and metaphorically, into another space: 'I hated Bromley; I thought it was small and narrow-minded.'

In the first months of punk, the Bromley Contingent played a conspicuous role, introducing the Sex Pistols to Louise's. Alan Jones was a regular there, hanging out, living the life, but was soon in trouble again when Vivienne came up with the Anarchy t-shirt featuring slogans from the 1968 student uprising in Paris, small portraits of Karl Marx, an armband emblazoned with the word 'CHAOS' and some casually placed swastikas.

The people – McLaren, Vivienne, Lydon, Siouxsie – weren't of one mind, of course, and the politics around punk at this early stage was contradictory in some senses but consistent in another: the urge to shock, provoke, and break taboos was always present. The swastika was the ultimate shocking symbol, and naturally the Anarchy t-shirt was highly controversial, but Alan remains blasé. 'I never tried to justify it, and I didn't feel I had to. I liked the look.'

Alan's position as a gay man on the punk scene was

probably less rare than his position as a disco fan on the punk scene. All through the late 1970s, in that determinedly tribal way that characterised the decade, there was no disco/punk crossover, although that's not to say that it wasn't possible to jump sides; you could be out at the local Top Rank Suite one weekend, then at the bus stop the following Friday with Doc Martens, torn trousers and a Sex Pistols badge pinned to a grubby jacket.

Alan accepts the scenes were poles apart. 'It's true, although I had feet in both camps. I loved disco and I loved the lifestyle as well; I really was out every night when I wasn't working.'

When he started going out in Earls Court in the early 1970s, he'd even danced to 'Paranoid' by Black Sabbath, but as the decade evolved, so the soundtrack in gay clubs came to be dominated by disco, although in the evolutionary process there was still lots of room for Roxy Music and David Bowie. Then, in 1975, Alan was captivated by the Tina Charles single 'You Set My Heart on Fire', jolted not just by the rhythm but the narrative (a dramatic tale of what it's like to be saved from loneliness by a lover who burns you in the flames of love). It was a significant moment for him. 'I actually think it was the first time I really realised disco was going to work.'

1976 was a big year for disco music, and the glory years for the dancefloor generation we met at Pennington's in Bradford were in full swing. Music played at discotheques had been a steady flow of funk and soul, but, meeting a rising demand for dancefloor anthems, disco now had a definable sound too: repetitive rhythms, a distillation of much that had gone before, championed by DJs in New York particularly.

DJs have always had an influence on popular music. Sometimes this has included radio DJs (the late John Peel being an obvious example), but whenever the balance of power shifts away from live music or radio, the influence of club DJs grows, particularly their ability to activate demand for songs. By 1976, dancefloor-oriented records were making their way to the charts in increasing numbers, and in recognition of their influence on the disco market, club DJs like Tom Moulton, Walter Gibbons and Larry Levan were being commissioned by record companies to deliver remixes. Many of these versions extended the original, keeping the groove alive or accentuating or repeating percussive sections, and in order to do justice to these longer versions – and to make the vinyl easier for DJs to handle and manipulate as they blended and mixed the records on twin turntables – the first wave of 12-inch singles were released on labels like Salsoul and Casablanca, and TK. The first commercially available 12-inch single is reckoned to be 'Ten Per Cent' by Double Exposure, released in June 1976.

The disco scene – with a well-established and mainly gay underground in New York, and with long semi-secret traditions in England – was about to dominate the mainstream too. Disco had already absorbed funk, soul and jazz, and was still a year or so away from *Saturday Night Fever*, yet already there was an element of cash-in. A rundown of releases that DJs could have been playing and radio producers programming in 1976 reveals a mixed bunch: the great, the good, the bad, and the ugly. 'Classical' records were given a disco treatment, and there was an explosion of songs with 'dancing' (or 'dancin'') or 'disco' in the title (even songs that aren't really disco, like 'Disco Music' by Barbara Lynn).

Disco was embraced – often with very gay abandon – by artists and managers chasing the disco dollar, but even while discotheques were filling up, wise people steered clear of the high street dancefloors. Pockets of people looking to hear dance music but unimpressed by the lack of quality control gravitated towards the smaller scenes, searching for more adventurous music and less predictable Saturday nights.

The Northern Soul scene had prided itself on being both adventurous and uncommercial, but by 1976 it was perhaps beginning to look a little jaded, although Wigan Casino had another five years of keeping the faith before it was closed.

The ritual of the all-nighter had become a bit of a cliché, and there was a noticeable drift from Northern Soul to punk among those in love with short songs, 7-inch singles and cheap speed, but who wanted a more contemporary sound-track to their lives. In the later years of the 1970s there wasn't much Mark E. Smith of The Fall didn't have some smart angle on; his 'Lie Dream of a Casino Soul' is an inspired song about a half-wired Northern Soul fan living for his Saturday all-nighter but adrift in the midweek real world.

Away from disco cash-ins and the Sixties soul sound at the Casino, DJs like Colin Curtis, Robbie Vincent, Andy Peebles, Greg Edwards, and Tommy Terrell at Sloopy's in Birmingham, and Mike Shaft in Manchester were blessed with some great dancefloor-filling records in 1975 and 1976, including 'Low Rider' by War, Parliament's groundbreaking 'Tear the Roof off the Sucker', 'Hard Work' by John Handy, 'Movin'' by Brass Construction, 'Turn the Beat Around' by Vicki Sue Robinson, and a number of records that would one day be classed as 'jazz-funk' (eg 'Rock Creek Park' by The Blackbyrds).

As the disco era began to wash away some of the more established markets, venues and acts, some soul singers couldn't or didn't want to adapt. On the other hand, this was also the era of some great female vocal performances, from Candi Staton for example. Candi Staton was born into a poor farming family in Alabama in 1940 and spent her early years picking cotton and feeding chickens. Like many of the great soul singers, she had a gospel upbringing, later moving on to the secular soul scene under the guidance of Clarence Carter, who invited her to tour with him and introduced her to the producer Rick Hall. Candi Staton was a prolific hitmaker between 1969 and 1975, with hits like 'I'd Rather Be an Old Man's Sweetheart (Than a Young One's Fool)'. But it was her work with a new producer, Dave Crawford, that delivered dance hits including 'A Little Taste of Love', 'When You Wake Up Tomorrow' and 'Young Hearts Run Free'.

The disco dancefloor could give clubbers a shot of positivity and unity in a mixed-up world, but it was also democratic and participatory. A few years ago, in a revealing online chat on the Soul Patrol website, during which she discussed various aspects of her career, Candi Staton described this key appeal of disco: 'It made regular club goers feel very important, they didn't have to look to a stage or a star to be entertained. Everybody was a star.'

During the same event, she also acknowledged that although disco couldn't solve all the problems, it did play an important role in promoting racial harmony. 'Yeah, I think it did. You saw everybody on the same dancefloor dancing to the same music, that did help bring down the walls of segregation in music in a way.'

It's also always been clear that in the 1970s many of disco's most devoted fans were women. Songs like 'Young Hearts Run Free' were part of the soundtrack to the new assertive attitudes of women in the Seventies, their greater rights and extended independence. Women out on the town weren't expected to have male company as the previous generation had. From 1970 women at work benefited from equal pay legislation, and then the Sex Discrimination Act of 1975 gave them more protection at work. The Domestic Violence and Matrimonial Proceedings Act (1976), piloted through Parliament by Jo Richardson MP, at last legislated against violent husbands and also removed some of the obstacles to divorce. The number of women filing for divorce in the first year in which the Act came into operation –100,832 – was over three times the number eight years earlier.

In an earlier chapter we saw the close connection between gay liberation and women's liberation, making waves together, taking strength from each other, and in many ways the disco scene consolidated these links. Disco had its roots in black music and seemed to have an irresistible attraction for young women, but its most devoted followers were the gay audience. Gay men could enjoy, and perhaps even identify with the female singers pouring their hearts out on records like 'You Set My Heart on Fire'. In 1976, *Blues & Soul* would occasionally print a playlist under the heading 'Valentino's Gay Guide' (which invariably featured songs like 'Young Hearts Run Free' and 'Love Hangover').

Alan Jones remembers the powerful pull of the dancefloor and the great days of disco, but finds it hard to believe the distorted view of the music now. People remember *Saturday Night Fever* and expect him to have a wardrobe full of white suits, he says. 'Who would wear that? And when you wanted to dance you'd be sweating like crazy? Don't be daft! It was the girls with their hotpants, the glitter, and they looked fabulous and it was their fantasy. Disco is still seen as the kitsch footnote that has no social relevance at all and I think it's vitally important.'

In 1976 dance music was alive and evolving, feasting on Latino, soul and gospel influences, for example, but also happy to embrace computer technology; songs on the Kraftwerk LPs *Autobahn* and *Radioactivity* were landmarks in the evolution of electronic music, but so was disco producer Giorgio Moroder's work on big Euro hits like Donna Summer's celebratory, erotic 'Love to Love You Baby'.

It's often the case, though, that when a music trend hits a moment of roaring, heady excitement, it's suddenly vulnerable to distortion, corruption and a wave of corporate cash-ins. And one of disco's most celebrated moments – the opening of Studio 54 on 26 April 1977 – was perhaps also the moment all was lost. Studio 54 had 3,000 square feet of dancefloor, and, celebrity-driven and over-hyped, it was, in many respects, a long way from the roots of disco. For unpredictable, cutting-edge creativity we'd have to look beyond the superclubs, as we would in the current era.

Within months of the release of the film *Saturday Night Fever*, and the soundtrack LP (in Britain this was early in

1978), it was again obvious that the most visible parts of the disco scene had capitulated to pop, and soon afterwards we suffered the release of Rod Stewart's disco record 'Do Ya Think I'm Sexy?'. Disco was duly blasted by a backlash. According to Simon Frith, writing at the time, 'Everybody hates it. Hippies hate it, progressives hate it, punks hate it, teds hate it, *NME* hates it.'

Even just a few miles from the uptown, white, hyped Studio 54 scene, DJs had already found a new direction for funk and dance music; at informal block parties in cheap halls and rented rooms, DJs like Kool Herc, Grand Wizard Theodore and Grandmaster Flash were laying the foundations for hip hop. Even back in 1973, South Bronx DJ Kool Herc (aka Clive Campbell) had a reputation for whipping up the crowd with their favourite funk and soul records, but he also developed innovations to give his sets a special twist. For example, he took to isolating the instrumental section of a song – a few bars of saxophone or a funky drum pattern (the bits of a record the musicians call 'breakdowns', shortened to 'breaks') – and then cutting across his two turntables from break to break, or looping the same break by using two copies of the same record. The kids who were most enthused by all this called themselves 'b-boys' or 'breakdancers'.

A landmark event in the history of hip hop took place on 2 September 1976, when Grandmaster Flash and Melle Mel played the Audubon Ballroom at 166th and Broadway. All the turntable tricks he learned at block parties and hideaway clubs like the Back Door – cutting and scratching, locking the beat – Flash showcased at the 3,000 capacity hall and per-formed with Melle Mel on the microphone, vibing up the crowd. At this point, hip hop was all about the DJs, although rappers would soon take centre stage. It was still miles away from the mainstream, but the activities surrounding hip hop already encompassed b-boys, street fashions, and widespread, flamboyant new styles of graffiti. Nelson George calls this activity the first flowerings of the 'post-soul generation'. And at the centre of it all, two turntables and a microphone.

Compared to the development of hip hop – which was slow and away from the media spotlight – the rise of punk was quicker but still far from instantaneous. Back in the first half of 1976, the Sex Pistols couldn't fill some of the smallest clubs in London. In April 1976 they played at El Paradiso, a tiny, dirty, sleazy strip club on Brewer Street, a gig disorganised by Nils Stevenson and Malcolm McLaren. Alan was there, performing his first (and only) DJ-ing gig: 'I haven't done any since and I'm not interested really. It was only because there wasn't anyone else to do it. I was just along for the ride and I'd do whatever came along as I think you do when you're that age.'

Even though it was only a small club, the Pistols fans came nowhere near to filling it. 'Nils was on the door and he was literally letting everyone in and he was at the door shouting out all these promises about girls, girls, strippers,' says Alan. 'And all these people were getting thrown in through the door; he would take any money from anybody, so the audience was a mixture of punks and this very straight raincoat brigade who thought they were there to see some hot action.'

There was no hot action, just Alan playing a confusing mixture of records – one minute 'White Punks on Dope', the next 'Thoroughly Modern Millie' (he thought it would be fun to play a Julie Andrews record). Although the Sex Pistols were beginning to attract press attention, that night at El Paradiso was evidence that London still had a long way to go to catch up with New York. In the same week The Ramones released their debut LP, a blitzkrieg of songs like 'Judy is a Punk' and 'Now I Wanna Sniff Glue'.

Alan saw the potential of the Pistols, particularly John Lydon. 'Johnny I always thought had something. He always looked grungey even though that term wasn't used then, and he had these rotten green teeth and he had this old supermarket carrier bag he'd be dragging along with all his belongings in. I used to love that.'

Alan wasn't convinced that the boys would actually get anywhere, let alone make headlines. 'It was all a bit of a shambles to begin with. We used to go to the recording studio and you'd think it was never going to work in a million years! But then, of course, it did.'

He watched the world begin to notice punk. 'The Nashville was the one I think when we knew it was going somewhere. It was when Caroline Coon asked me what the Pistols were and I told her to come and see them and I took her along; that's when I suddenly realised it was all being taken quite seriously.'

Nevertheless, there was a lot of resistance to the Sex Pistols in the music press (and outside the music press, plain indifference) – in April 1976 one *Melody Maker* review ended 'I hope we shall hear no more of them' – but a handful of journalists, including John Ingham and Caroline Coon, pushed to get coverage for the Pistols in the weekly music papers (although it would be hip young gunslingers like Tony Parsons and Julie Burchill who would become the most influential evangelists for punk). Caroline Coon had cofounded the drugs information and civil rights organisation Release in 1967, and had appeared as a defence witness in the *Oz* trial. Alan accompanied her to the Nashville. 'She turned up with this bootlace tie and she'd put safety pins all the way down it,' he remembers. 'And I thought "Er, OK!" I loved Caroline. Caroline – should I say this? – she was the last girl I had sex with.'

In the middle of 1976 there were one or two acts on the coat-tails of the Sex Pistols, notably Siouxsie & the Banshees, with a line-up that included Marco Pirroni and Sid Vicious. Sid Vicious was playing bass and had a refreshing attitude to musicmaking: 'You just pick a chord, go twang and you've got music.'

With a nucleus of Pete Shelley and Howard Devoto, the

career of the Buzzcocks was launched in July 1976, supporting the Sex Pistols at a gig at the Lesser Free Trade Hall in Manchester. In his teens, Pete Shelley had been in a band called Jets of Air playing cover versions of songs like Roxy Music's 'Editions of You' and David Bowie's 'Suffragette City', as well as some of Shelley's own material; and from the start, the Buzzcocks were blessed with short, sardonic songs like 'Nostalgia' and 'Sixteen Again' that sounded like Ray Davies singing love songs with The Ramones.

The music and the attitudes were picked up like a rumour. A few people, that's all it took, and just as they had at Sex, small scenes gathered in all kinds of places. Just down the road from Vivienne and Malcolm's shop was Acme Attractions, which had a growing clientele from 1975 onwards in the basement at Antiquarius, at 135 King's Road. Working at Acme were Don Letts and Jeanette Lee. Letts was a young Brixton lad who'd graduated from funk to roots reggae. At Acme they sold mad retro clothes and pumped out reggae all day. The music was spot-on, some of the lads took a shine to Jeanette Lee, and the shop became a regular hangout for the likes of John Lydon, Paul Simonon and Joe Strummer. Jeanette Lee would later feature in Public Image Limited and take a major role at the independent record label Rough Trade.

The punk bands that emerged through 1976 and the following year had a variety of qualities, including humour, iconoclasm and knockabout comedy, and invariably there was a strong sense of rebellion against the music establishment. Punk caught the mood of the times. By the second half of the 1970s, even tennis players – Nastase and John McEnroe – were questioning authority.

The Sex Pistols played twice at the Nashville in the first half of 1976, but the second show descended into violence, although it was not a mass brawl, as by all accounts the gig was sparsely attended. Suddenly, invariably, punk became the catalyst for violence. At first Alan Jones accepted the aggressive atmosphere: 'It was just part of it, although the whole pogo thing and the spitting did get a bit boring.'

The move from pub rock to punk was tracked by a change from beer to speed, as the fashions for drug use through the 1970s evolved. By 1976 England had reached new highs in the use and variety of drugs. Amyl nitrate was new, and LSD came in new forms (an LSD-based drug known as 'yellow' complemented the classic disco years in New York). Mushrooms, Mandrax and heroin use were rising. Cannabis was endemic in youth culture; even during the first summer of punk, the free festival spirit was alive and skinning up. A thousand hippies and freaks gathered at the Kent Free Pop Festival at Seasalter, for example, with predictable results: run-ins with the police and local landowners who objected to their presence.

The punks defined their distance from hippies or the heavy rock fraternity in various ways, including the cut of their trousers, a disdain for musicianship or lengthy guitar solos, and different drug choices. Punk and amphetamine sulphate reinforced each other: the jumpy aggression, the edge, the furious energy. Speed had been the drug of choice for the mods, so pre-dated the hippies, but the mods had used pills whereas the punks preferred using speed in its powdered form. Many punks were totally wired, including Captain Sensible of The Damned – 'We used to take sackloads of speed, as much as we could possibly get' – and John Lydon: 'I loved the stuff. I'm normally a very slow person and it made me more intense. I'm naturally paranoid and it made me feel better. But you get bored with these things, the thrill wears off.'

The spread of drug use was not a phenomenon confined to the music scene; we were living in a progressively more chemically-enhanced world. Cold War athletes were running, lifting and throwing under the influence, and tranquillisers like Mogadon and Valium, and various sleeping pills (or benzodiazepines), were being prescribed in larger numbers than ever before. There was something of an epidemic of legally sanctioned drugs; for a couple of decades, pharmacologists and doctors had been prescribing drugs for depressive illnesses, particularly to women. In the Hulme area of Manchester almost half of all families were in receipt of supplementary benefit, and due to the catastrophic condition of the newly-built flats and maisonettes, the local council was considering mass demolition of their homes. As elsewhere, poverty was contributing to poor mental health, but society seemed content to respond chemically rather than politically to desperation and depression; there were six doctors serving Hulme, and in 1977 they prescribed a quarter of a million tranquillisers and anti-depressants per month. Naturally The Fall were weighing in on the drug debate, in songs like 'Rowche Rumble' and 'No Xmas for John Quays?'.

Punk was exploding in 1976, full of anger and energy, but seemed to be flailing, its anger inarticulate and its targets indiscriminate. The group who did most to give dissent a direction were The Clash, formed by Mick Jones (formerly of the band London SS) and Joe Strummer. Strummer's first group, a pub rock act called The 101'ers, had been supported by the Sex Pistols at the second Nashville gig, and Strummer had been fired up by their confrontational and uncompromised performance. The bands threw in their lot together temporarily; The Clash's first live gig was supporting the Sex Pistols at the Black Swan in Sheffield on 4 July 1976.

In cities outside London, cells of activity were becoming apparent. In Liverpool, one of the rallying points in the late 1970s was Probe Records. The owner, Geoff Davies, had packed in his job selling carpets, and the first Probe opened at the top end of town and then on Button Street. He was a bright spark in what seemed like a dull city; in the mid-1970s Liverpool didn't have the thriving network of pubs and clubs that had been a feature in the Beatles era, and as the city's economy hit hard times, so did the music scene, which had shrivelled to nothing much more than country and western acts, old men singing sea shanties, and poorly stocked juke-boxes. Liverpool was not alone in this lack of life. In May 1977, Paul Morley had this to say about Manchester in its pre-punk phase: 'Manchester was a very boring place to be. It had no identity, no common spirit or motive. It was probably a reflection of the country at large.'

The pub rock scene of bands like the Count Bishops was much stronger in London than elsewhere. In Birmingham you could catch bands like Ricky Cool & the Icebergs and the Steve Gibbons Band at the Barrel Organ near Digbeth Station. In Liverpool you might have caught a semi-decent band at the Back of the Moon on Bold Street. In 1976 The Real Thing were hitting their commercial heights, but some of the young white bohemians of the city may have tried to make a case for Deaf School as Liverpool's best band in the pre-punk era. They were an art school group unlikely to win over a bigger audience; the group could have more than twelve or thirteen people onstage, on occasions not all of whom seemed to be playing the same song.

You could look hard in Liverpool and still not find anything inspiring. Pete Wylie and Ian McCulloch – who were both leaving school and starting to go out at the time – considered themselves freaks, their tastes in music unrepresented by any-thing in Liverpool venues at the time. But they did have somewhere to hang out; at Probe Records, Geoff Davies would entertain them for hours by playing Captain Beefheart tracks and dub reggae.

Another quirky independent shop had opened in Liverpool by the beginning of 1976; Anne Twackey's was a venture of Jayne Casey's. In her own words, Jayne became 'a right little businesswoman', selling vintage clothes. 'I just knew where to find stuff and I knew that if you got hold of weird stuff there was a market there,' she says. 'Loads of different people used to hang out there, all sorts.'

She'd sourced such great Sixties clothes – snakeskin jeans, boots – in old shops around Liverpool that she started taking them down to London. 'We sussed out where we could go down to London to the King's Road where there were shops like our shop,' Jayne remembers. 'So Paul Rutherford and I started going down and there was a place called Beaufort's Market and we'd sell these things to a girl there who was Poly Styrene and then we'd sell to Acme. Sometimes we'd get our money and we'd go to Sex and spend it all. So we got to know that scene before punk really. And they were all doing second-hand clothes as well, and alternative clothes.'

Jayne denies there was a lack of venues in Liverpool; as far as she was concerned, the problem was a lack of *good* venues, or even venues that welcomed her. 'You couldn't get into clubs. Nobody would let you in. The gay clubs used to get pissed off that the boys were bringing a woman in because at that time gays were scared – a lot of them were married – and the clubs were downstairs and it was all behind closed doors. It was like a secret they wanted to keep and they didn't like having a woman in the club.'

In the straight clubs they'd attract violence. 'Straight clubs certainly wouldn't have you. Black clubs, some were OK, but then we started to hang out with a black girl who had bleached white hair, and then the black clubs wouldn't let us in because they didn't mind us being freaks but then there was this black freak! That was too much for them.'

One day a guy arrived in Jayne's shop and told her he was opening a club on Mathew Street. 'A guy inviting us into his club was just amazing; somebody wanted us in a club! So we went to Eric's.'

Roger Eagle had founded the Twisted Wheel in Manchester, and then left to play at the Stax; he'd gone from there to play at the Magic Village, also in Manchester. Now he'd surfaced in Liverpool, and together with Pete Fulwell set about establishing Eric's, a club that would be as important for a generation of Liverpool music fans as the Cavern had once been. Opening on 1 October 1976 with a gig by The Stranglers (admission was 90p), Eric's provided a focus for young music lovers, and safety in numbers; it attracted working class school leavers, hairdressers, speed freaks and art college kids.

Jayne's visits to London continued, and she makes a point of recalling Jeanette Lee at Acme Attractions. 'At Eric's it was all laddy and there were girls who were around, but they weren't my kind of girls, girls who wanted to do stuff, who wanted to be up there with the boys. So it was exciting to meet Jeanette; it was like, wow, there are girls on this scene!'

Jayne Casey's stall was in an old building owned by Peter O'Halligan on Mathew Street, near Eric's, just around the corner from Probe. She was sitting there one day, looking pretty far out as usual – with a shaved head and eye make-up in a pyramid shape – when in walked Ken Campbell, who had cofounded the Science Fiction Theatre of Liverpool earlier in 1976 with Chris Langham. They were planning a stage adaptation of the *Illuminatus* trilogy (written by Robert Anton Wilson and Bob Shea and described by Wilson as 'the most anarchistic novel of this century'). 'Ken started freaking out and he came over and introduced himself,' remembers Jayne. 'He was looking for a venue and he'd come for a walk down Mathew Street and there and then he decided he had to put the play on in that building because I had my eyes in pyramids which was the sign of the Illuminati!'

Campbell scoured Liverpool for recruits to help stage the play. Among those who ended up working with him were a number of characters who were to go on to play leading roles in the Liverpool music scene over the next decades, including Bill Drummond and Ian Broudie. *Illuminatus!* opened in Liverpool on 23 November 1976, in the same week as 'Anarchy in the UK' was finally released.

In mid-September the 100 Club hosted a two-day punk festival which included the Pistols, Subway Sect, the Buzzcocks,

The Damned, and Siouxsie & the Banshees with Sid Vicious again on bass, by now proving to be something of a trouble-maker; he lobbed a beer glass at the stage while The Damned were playing, and glass splinters cut several people. Vicious was arrested and taken to Ashford Remand Centre where he sat reading a book about Charles Manson given to him by Vivienne Westwood.

The Sex Pistols signed to EMI on 8 October 1976. A week later *The Sun* devoted a double page spread to punk, and then a piece about punk was broadcast on BBC1's news magazine programme *Nationwide*. But it was the band's appearance on the Thames TV show *Today*, interviewed by Bill Grundy, which introduced the Sex Pistols to the nation. The live inter-view dissolved into a flurry of swearing, and within hours a moral panic about punks took root. As town councils and the press went into overdrive, Pistols gigs were cancelled, including those at Derby, Bristol and Newcastle. In Caerphilly, after two Labour councillors failed to get the gig banned the previous week, pubs and shops in the town were closed down and boarded up. Fearing the negative social impact of the band, protesters picketed the venue (the Castle Cinema), out-numbering the few dozen inside. Vivienne Westwood tried to explain, 'There is only one criterion; does it threaten the status quo?'

But in the immediate aftermath of the Grundy incident, some people got out. 'Bill Grundy was the end of it for me really,' Marco Pirroni tells Jon Savage. 'From something artis-tic and almost intellectual in weird clothes, suddenly there were fools with dog collars on and "punk" written on their shirts in biro.'

In punk's first winter, unemployment continued to rise (to 1.5 million, another post-war record), and with the British economy effectively bankrupt, the Labour Government was forced to apply for a loan from the International Monetary Fund. In November 1976, the IMF loan was secured but with stringent conditions attached; the Government was forced to agree to increasing taxation, and to drastic cuts in public expenditure, a combination guaranteed to have a detrimental effect on living standards. Britain's economic policy had been ceded to an international banking body controlled by conservative American economists.

By the middle of punk's first winter, the new music began to thrive, attracting demoralised kids looking for a buzz in an era of economic chaos, and after a year featuring 'Fernando', 'Combine Harvester' and Demis Roussos in the charts, *Carry On* films on prime time TV, an epidemic of anti-depressants, rising unemployment and riots in Notting Hill.

By the end of the year, and after seeing the Notting Hill riots, The Clash had ditched some of their early songs (like 'I've Got a Crush on You') and created a new set list soaked in social relevance, including 'I'm So Bored with the USA' – having a go at the power of the yankee dollar and the vacuity of American popular culture – and the seminal 'Career Opportunities'.

As music, and the moment, changed, realignment and reinvention became necessary. Stuart Goddard (ex-Bazooka Joe) became Adam Ant shortly after that first Sex Pistols gig. Drummer Chris Miller of The Damned was now known as Rat Scabies, while Siouxsie Sioux, Sid Vicious and Poly Styrene were all newly-minted names. Pre-1976, Howard Devoto and Pete Shelley of the Buzzcocks had been Howard Trafford and Peter McNeish. Post-punk, Jane Jackman became Jane Suck, Roger Bullen of Eater became Dee Generate, and Bill Broad gave up studying in Brighton and became Billy Idol.

Elsewhere, a fan of the Plastic People of the Universe drew on music's power to contribute to realignment and rebellion in order to campaign for social change. Playwright Vaclav Havel – who had become a personal friend of Ivan Jirous, and attended the trial in Prague – began to help gather recruits to form a human rights organisation. He believed in a strong link between unfettered creativity and democracy, and through his awareness of the Plastic People he was also introduced to some of the music that had influenced them: The Velvet Underground and Frank Zappa. The new organisation developed a Charter, a rallying cry for the political and creative communities of Czechoslovakia which pressed the Government to abide by the human rights promises made at Helsinki.

The Charter was completed during the last days of December 1976 and was published on the first day of 1977. The organisation, known as Charter 77, grew in significance over the next decade and a half, but citizens signing up to the Charter faced persecution from the authorities. Havel himself served a total of five years in prison. Later, much later, the slow burning revolution would deliver change and he would become President of the Czech Republic.

CHAPTER EIGHT

'In the City' (1977)

In graphic design, one of the most popular techniques in the 1970s was airbrush. In the hands of artists like H.R. Giger, Roger Dean and Alan Lee, airbrush art featured heavily in comic books, record sleeves and book covers, especially those with a fantasy or sci-fi theme. Airbrush artists also appeared to dominate advertising, where the technique's ability to deliver a world free of imperfection was prized; in such illustrations wet-lipped young women stood tall, and cars had an extra sheen.

The poet Simon Armitage was born in West Yorkshire in 1963, and thus spent his formative years in the 1970s. He published a novel, *Little Green Man*, in 2001 in which there's an evocative passage describing the hot trends in home improvements in the 1970s, as if they somehow reflected a desire to keep things hidden, covered-up. 'In the 1970s', he writes, 'walls were draped with woodchip, antique doors were boarded over and panelled off . . . Ceilings were clad with polystyrene tiles . . . Every inch of wood was treated and primed and slapped with coat after coat of shock-resistant, blindingly shiny gloss.'

Coverage of Watergate, and the subsequent film *All the President's Men*, revealed the machinations and tortuous lies of the affair. At Wattstax, the Rance Allen Singers had pleaded for honesty and progress with a song called 'Lying on the Truth'. Abbafication has since distorted our view of the Seventies, but during the decade itself, life was already being warped; the way the Watergate tapes were erased, and documents were being manipulated or going missing seemed part of a general attempt to withhold evidence about what was really going on.

With Abba at the top of the charts and a Valium epidemic among the poor and despairing, it was, at the very least, a confusing society in which to grow up, especially during the Queen's Silver Jubilee celebrations in June 1977, when the airbrush was wielded again. Britain was in a parlous state, yet the merchandisers churned out millions of decorated plates, special stamps and souvenir mugs. According to historian David Cannadine, the Silver Jubilee celebrations were 'an expression of national and imperial decline, an attempt to prove, by pomp and circumstance, that no such decline had taken place, or to argue that even if it had, it didn't matter'.

The spectacle of the Jubilee seemed somehow linked to the determination of the daytime Radio One DJs to fill the airwaves with the likes of The Wurzels, Slik, and Brotherhood of Man, especially considering that, in contrast, so many obstacles were put in the way of 'God Save the Queen' by the Sex Pistols.

Punk was about breaking illusions, right back to Patti Smith, who knew there was a point to what she was doing; in a world sleepwalking towards mediocrity, she was on a mission ('I knew we weren't that great at the beginning,' she said later, 'but we felt like human alarm clocks – Wake up! Wake up!'). But in 1977 it was as if the world of official civic culture was in denial, and some of the citizens were happy to fall in line. Record pressing plant workers refused to handle 'God Save the Queen' by the Sex Pistols, it was banned by almost all radio stations, and sales figures were massaged in order to prevent it from reaching No. 1 in the charts. Woolworths always listed the Top 20 on a big board every week; for the week ending 11 June 1977 the No. 2 position was blank. They were pretending the Sex Pistols didn't exist.

In 1977 the crimes of the Yorkshire Ripper became public knowledge, and the activities of the Baader Meinhof gang reached a savage crescendo. Rock Against Racism continued to promote the battle against the National Front, and in the aftermath of punk, the music agenda was blown wide open. The new energies created by punk also fed into film-making and fanzines, but musicians, writers, film-makers and artists intent on responding to the streets had many opponents. Radio One DJ Tony Blackburn, for example – who had previously slammed 'Dead End Street' by The Kinks, and The Who's film *Tommy*, but who supported Clive Dunn's 'Grandad' – once again decided to take sides, this time voicing his distaste for punk. 'I think it's disgusting the way these punks sing about violence all the time. Why can't they sing about beautiful things like trees and flowers?'

The notion that the dutiful citizen is obliged to ignore reality by hiding behind an illusion carried well beyond music and well beyond Britain. In 1976, the feverish American celebrations of two hundred years of independence looked desperate to some. Not only, in the words of Rick Moody in *The Ice Storm*, were they 'commercial madness', but there was a clear credibility gap created by the USA partying in the midst of rising unemployment, post-Vietnam trauma, and power cuts, and as New York struggled to avoid bankruptcy, the city suffered the 'Son of Sam' killings.

The killer, David Berkowitz, struck for the first time during July 1976, the month of the American bi-centenary celebrations. In the first five months of 1977 he killed four more young women with his .44-calibre handgun, and left a note at one of the murder scenes addressed to Captain Joseph Borrelli of the New York City Police Department. The letter was later published in New York's *Daily News* (the edition sold 1,116,000 copies, a sales record). Savage and rambling, and full of misspellings, it read, in part: 'I am deeply hurt by your calling me a wemon hater. I am not. But I am a monster. I am the "Son of Sam". I love to hunt. Prowling the streets looking for fair game – tasty meat. The wemon of Queens are prettyist of all. It must be the water they drink. I live for the hunt – my life . . . To the people of Queens, I love you. And I want to wish all of you a happy Easter.'

The year had started with public death and murder in the news. Convicted killer Gary Gilmore was executed by firing squad on 17 January, six months after he'd shot dead two people in Utah, and after weeks of legal wrangling and manic media interest. Punk band The Adverts marked the killing with the macabre song 'Gary Gilmore's Eyes'. The public's fascination with outlaw activity was nothing new, but seemed to be accelerating through the decade. When the system is cracking up, even brutal, then the life of those outside the system seems more attractive.

Perhaps the stories of Gary Gilmore and David Berkowitz were fascinating rather than disturbing because they were, after all, distant, on the other side of the Atlantic. But closer to home the media had uncovered the story of the so-called 'Yorkshire Ripper'. If you were in Birmingham, your memories of the Seventies are scarred by the pub bombings. In London in the mid-1970s, the tensions and battles at the annual Notting Hill Carnival dominated. In Northern England in the 1970s, Peter Sutcliffe – the Yorkshire Ripper – cast a long shadow.

Sutcliffe attacked prostitutes on three occasions in Keighley and Halifax in 1975 (although the cases were barely reported and not linked by police at the time), and the same year committed his first murder. Trawling through the red light areas of Chapeltown in Leeds in his lime green Ford Capri, Sutcliffe picked up twenty-eight-year-old prostitute Wilma

McCann, and took her to some playing fields where he battered her to death with a hammer. In June 1976 he killed another prostitute, Emily Jackson, again in Leeds. In 1977 he killed four times, first in February in Leeds, and then in April in Bradford. Sutcliffe's victims had all been prostitutes, but in June 1977 he killed a seventeen-year-old shop assistant, Jayne MacDonald, as she walked through Chapeltown after a night out in Leeds city centre. It was this murder that drew public attention to Yorkshire; it was clear there was a serial killer in the area, and Assistant Chief Constable George Oldfield was appointed to head the police hunt.

Nineteen Seventy Seven, David Peace's second novel, is set in Yorkshire and portrays a shabby world blighted by the activities of the Ripper, but also by the corrupt police hunting the killer. Peace is a relentless writer, banging our senses with prostitutes, pimps, bodies and bad news, interweaving the story with a mass of contemporary detail and fictional transcripts of phone-ins on Radio Leeds. The Silver Jubilee is barely mentioned, and it doesn't have to be; it flickers like a side issue, an irrelevance in the lives of characters mired in darkness and violence. According to one of the characters in the book, life is worse than any bad dream: 'It's when you pull back them bloody curtains. That's when it hits you.'

The twenty-five years of the Queen's reign had coincided with a sense of national decline, and the painful, untidy break-up of the British Empire. In Rhodesia, for example, elections were held in 1977, but of the country's six million blacks, a mere 7,000 were eligible to vote, and in the sixty-six-seat Parliament, fifty seats were reserved for whites only. It was the first stage of a plan, however, to phase out minority white rule over the next two years.

A few weeks later, in South Africa, leading black activist Steve Biko died in police custody. At first the South African Government claimed that he'd died as a result of a hunger strike, and an unrepentant Minister of Police, Jimmy Kruger, was quoted as saying, 'Biko's death leaves me cold.' However, it soon became clear that the death had come after Biko had been interrogated by members of the security police. An official post-mortem revealed he had sustained extensive injuries to the brain 'caused by the application of force to the head', as well as a scalp wound, a cut inside his upper lip, and bruised ribs.

Biko was a founder member of the South African Students Organisation, and was one of a number of black activists attempting to take on apartheid at a time when an older generation of black African leaders from the African National Congress – among them Nelson Mandela and Walter Sisulu – were in jail. Biko was subject to various banning orders to deter him from organising or attending meetings or demonstrations, and pressure on activists from the authorities increased in a crackdown that followed riots in Soweto in June 1976 when hundreds of young black Africans were killed by the military. Finally, on 18 August 1977, Biko was arrested under section 6 of the Terrorism Act, and his ill-treatment began. In police cell 619 he was starved and beaten. During the inquest it was admitted by police that Biko was unconscious on his cell floor for some time before he was handcuffed naked, shackled, and driven seven hundred miles to hospital on the floor of a car. The three-week inquest, however, was ended by a cursory three-minute ruling by the chief magistrate of Pretoria, who declared that there was no evidence that the death was anything other than accidental.

It was an astounding example of an official cover-up, but Biko's death brought the injustices of the apartheid system further into disrepute. In Britain, ex-Genesis star Peter Gabriel was inspired to write one of his finest works, 'Biko'. In Manchester, the Students' Union building was renamed the Steve Biko Building.

In South Africa, though, the Government was unbending, and Kruger and Prime Minister Vorster continued to arrest black leaders and outlaw black consciousness organisations. International calls for an arms embargo and economic sanctions against the apartheid regime were supported by US President Jimmy Carter, but not by all political figures. The Foreign Secretary in the Labour Government, David Owen, was hardly the most enthusiastic supporter of sanctions, as the business community's desire to retain economic links and protect British investment appeared to scare politicians from taking effective action.

In the second half of the Seventies, Conservative Party leader Margaret Thatcher consistently denounced Mandela as 'a Communist and a terrorist', and opposed international calls for sanctions and sporting boycotts, happy to give succour to South Africa's apartheid regime. Columnist Hugo Young, writing in *The Sunday Times* in October 1977, picked up on this: 'Since the death of Steve Biko, which now looks very clearly like political murder, there has been no word from the Tory Party. Secretly, and not so secretly, some of them admire Mr Vorster as an exponent of order, authority and anti-Communism.'

Margaret Thatcher continued to dismiss Mandela and the ANC almost until the day of his release in February 1990. In 1987 she said that anyone who considered the ANC fit to govern was living in 'cloud cuckoo land'. The apparent support for South Africa's apartheid regime in the higher reaches of British politics fuelled the anger of those opposed to racism, including the rioters at Notting Hill in 1976; as the police approached, the crowd began to chant, 'Soweto, Soweto'.

Joe Strummer of The Clash had been inspired to overhaul the band's set list after witnessing the Notting Hill riots. Among the songs that he wrote in the weeks that followed were 'Two Sevens Clash', 'Sten Guns in Knightsbridge' and 'White Riot'. Strummer was encouraging the white youth to rise up with the same ferocity he'd witnessed in the black youth at Notting Hill. However, 'White Riot' was picked up by the far right as some kind of racial call to arms. Punk could be like that – an ambiguous rebel yell. Acts like Sham 69 seemed unable to extricate themselves from a following that included a proportion of racists. Other bands, claiming to be the 'true spirit' of punk, became part of a movement known as 'Oi'. More London-oriented than most other music genres, early Oi bands, including the Angelic Upstarts and the Cockney Rejects, claimed to come from the anti-racist political left and made much of their working class roots, their love for football teams like West Ham United, and their disdain for middle class students, liberals, governments, and fancy-pants post-punk groups. However, National Front and far-right influence grew among many bands that came to be associated with Oi, most notably in the case of bands like Skrewdriver and Brutal Attack.

Rock Against Racism plugged into punk's sense of a new start, but was determined to intervene with an unambiguous, more positive message. Formed in August 1976, RAR was a direct response to the way leading figures in the music industry seemed to be abetting the rise of racism. David Bowie had been flirting with fascist imagery and ideas, claiming that Britain could benefit from a dictatorship and that Adolf Hitler was 'the first superstar'. There was also a furore over comments supporting Enoch Powell made by guitarist Eric Clapton, initially during a concert in Birmingham, but subsequently repeated.

Bowie later acknowledged his misjudgement and claimed drug use had led to him losing the plot, but it was bizarre that two decades later, when Melvyn Bragg interviewed Clapton during an hour-long documentary on his career, Clapton was not asked to explain or retract what he was saying in 1976 in interviews with magazines like *Melody Maker*: 'Powell is the only bloke who's telling the truth, for the good of the country.'

Rock Against Racism was launched after photographer Red Saunders and six friends wrote to the music press criticising

Eric Clapton, pointing out his debts to black music ('Own up,' said the letter, 'you're rock music's biggest colonist'), and laying down their intentions to organise a movement against racism. The first Rock Against Racism gig was in November 1976 at the Princess Alice in Forest Gate, followed by a show featuring Matumbi and Carol Grimes at the Royal College of Art, then a conference at North London Polytechnic in January 1977.

Throughout 1977, Rock Against Racism developed into an influential force, articulating political ideas and a love of music, and giving the post-punk generation a motivation and a structure for action and activity. In some sense, Rock Against Racism was a renewed expression of the kind of political engagement that elements of the Sixties counter culture had championed. Although it was getting support from *NME* and other music papers, Rock Against Racism also published *Temporary Hoarding*, which demonstrated this Sixties influence, fusing the scissors and paste energy of punk fanzines with the political edge of the underground press.

RAR was also part of a long history of shifting attitudes on the political left. Traditional leftism could be very hidebound and wary of popular culture (could be, in fact, intolerant, puritan, anti-Presley and anti-disco), but RAR tried to reassert the radical potential of popular culture. The letter to the music press which launched Rock Against Racism was full of excitement and promise: 'Rock was and still can be a real progressive culture, not a packaged mail-order stick-on nightmare of mediocre garbage. Keep the faith, black and white unite and fight.'

Ex-*Oz* journalist David Widgery was one of the organisation's prime movers and articulated the aims and ideas of Rock Against Racism brilliantly. In *Temporary Hoarding* he made clear the links between racism on the streets and in the institutions of power, between paki bashing and the judiciary. 'The problem is not just the new fascists from the old slime a master race whose idea of heroism is ambushing single blacks in darkened streets. These private attacks whose intention, to cow and brutalise, won't work if the community they seek to terrorise instead organises itself. But when the state backs up racialism it's different.'

RAR raised its profile in concert halls and in print, but direct action against the National Front also continued, organising activists in order to create a presence on the streets. There was a sizeable RAR contingent in the multi-racial crowd that counter-demonstrated against the National Front at Lewisham in April 1977, for example; while an official counter-demo led by local councillors, Communists and clergy took place over a mile away, around 5,000 people confronted the NF directly. Pitched battles ensued, and the NF march, despite police protection, ended in disarray under a hail of bricks and bottles.

But after Lewisham, Rock Against Racism activists – who were mostly Socialist Worker Party members – helped to set up a broader based pressure group, the Anti-Nazi League (ANL), which attracted musicians, actors, writers, MPs and comedians, and also reached out to establish local groups nationwide. In this era, the RAR and ANL badges became part of the post-punk look. The Rock Against Racism logo was displayed wherever gigs took place, as RAR supporters throughout the country expressed their anti-Nazi beliefs. In 1977 it was a way of taking sides.

During 1977 some of the punk innovators would develop their careers on a stage, with debut LPs by the Sex Pistols and The Clash, but the established 'dinosaur' groups didn't seem unduly perturbed; members of Pink Floyd were dismissive, and many others ploughed on regardless, some as rock & roll as ever. In January 1977 Keith Richards of The Rolling Stones was found guilty of possessing cocaine and fined £1,000, and just over a month later, in Toronto, he was charged with possession of heroin. Meanwhile, Led Zeppelin toured America, playing to massive crowds; their gig in Pontiac in April attracted more than 75,000 people and broke the record for a single act concert. A distinctly old wave Peter Frampton, ex-Humble Pie, was still seeing chart action with the 1976 LP *Frampton Comes Alive* (after eighteen months it had sold sixteen million copies). In 1977, Bob Dylan released his film *Renaldo & Clara*, and The Eagles flew high with the hit singles 'Hotel California' and 'New Kid in Town'. The *Rumours* LP by Fleetwood Mac was massive in 1977; Fleetwood Mac were deep into a cocaine and private-plane rock-star lifestyle, but there was a great deal of personal confusion and hurt in the band, and the album had an unsettling edge to it.

The Sex Pistols line-up now included Sid Vicious on bass, who had replaced Glen Matlock in February 1977. In March the band signed to A&M and scheduled the release of 'God Save the Queen' (Managing Director Derek Green said, 'The Sex Pistols becoming available presented us with a unique business opportunity to be linked with a new force in rock music which is spearheaded by this group'), but a week later they were asked to quit the label.

American rock critic Greil Marcus spent some time in England during the summer of 1977, and wrote a piece for *Rolling Stone* in October, ambitiously linking the publication of Margaret Drabble's novel *The Ice Age* to the release of the Sex Pistols single 'God Save the Queen', as a way of trying to understand the state of the country at the time. In the novel, Margaret Drabble portrays a very Seventies London – shabby streets, resentment and confusion in what passes for civil society, communities frozen into despair and inactivity. Others shared this sense; in May 1977 the Art Attacks re-corded a song about London called 'Rat City', describing days of unease, boredom, going on the tube to work, eating fish fingers for tea, and watching (and hating) TV. 'Rat City,' the chorus proclaims, 'It's so shitty.'

The Soft City had become the Rat City. 'Society seems to have come to a dead end,' says Marcus, and points to Jamie Reid's sleeve design for the Sex Pistols single 'Pretty Vacant', which features two single decker buses with their destinations emblazoned on the front: one says BOREDOM; the other, apparently, is going NOWHERE.

Given the state of society, the despair is easy to understand, but what is equally significant is the way punk and Rock Against Racism both demonstrated that a determination to answer back was also present. A way out of the dead end was being mapped out, and punk was making this possible. 'God Save the Queen' was an absolute antidote to the delusionary pomp of official civic culture, a perfect reminder of how music can meet the time and place head on.

Punk rewrote the agenda and gave a voice to the unheard, the mad, and the malcontented. Some of what was produced was cartoonish, some was earnest, some nothing more than a corporate cash-in, but politics, anger, novelty and stupidity all had a place. Like all revolutions, the punk movement was about opening doors; free expression as revolution.

Marco Pirroni had written off punk soon after the Pistols had sworn at Bill Grundy. Disillusion came quickly to many others who had been close to the original moment in London in 1976, with the fanzine *Sniffin' Glue* announcing the end of punk in January 1977, and *NME* looking back in 1978 and declaring that punk had died soon after it had begun. 'The euphoria was being polluted by the spring of 1977,' it claimed, blaming joint action by big business ('who want to make money from rebellious youth') and the authoritarian establishment ('who want to give rebellious youth a palliative').

But the story of punk in 1977 was more about evolution than disillusion. Certainly the small groups of people who felt they owned punk were no longer in control. They'd opened doors but didn't like the look of the people coming through them. But throughout 1977 and 1978, and even beyond, punk attitudes, and the inspiration of the Sex Pistols and The Clash, brought some brilliant bands together. Once let loose, the music moved on and a generation was empowered. Paul Gilroy left Brighton and moved to Birmingham in 1978: 'That view that it was all over with the mainstreaming of it is very London-centred in a way. When I got to Birmingham, there were kids there who were just getting it.'

In 1977, apart from 'God Save the Queen', the Sex Pistols also released 'Pretty Vacant' and 'Holidays in the Sun', as well as the *Never Mind the Bollocks* LP, but by the end of the year they looked burnt out; they didn't have longevity, but they left a legacy. From Penetration in County Durham to The Pop Group in Bristol, bands were being formed by anyone who knew a couple of chords and had something to say. It was healthy that punk became so many other things so quickly; became, for example, the shouty political engagement and punk reggae of The Clash, and the giddy pop-art of X-Ray Spex.

A second generation of bands emerged with a more concili-atory label, 'new wave', which had the three-minute thrash but with controlled, diluted emotion. In the post-punk era there were novelty songs, and deeply banal thump-thump-thumping songs, as well as some great adventures using dub influences, computers, and the influence of Kraftwerk. Out-side London, punk took on new shapes. Just as the look moved on from the King's Road or the Bromley Contingent to Oxfam and Army & Navy surplus stores, and bondage trousers became a cliché, so bands inspired by the Sex Pistols had no desire to sound like them. For post-punk groups away from London – the likes of Joy Division and Cabaret Voltaire – David Bowie's *Low* LP, and Iggy Pop and The Stooges, were among the preferred inspirations musically, opening up terri-tory a long way from the two-chord thrash of punk.

In addition, the energised politics of RAR also provided more than the bondage-trousered cliché. In short, that purist view, that it was all over quickly, misses out the value of what happened next. A generation was given the opportunity to change their names, change their lives, and change their spaces.

Beggar's Banquet released *Streets*, a compilation of lo-fi punk tracks on under-capitalised UK indy labels. The sleeve notes describe the year: '1977 was the year that the music came out of the concert halls and onto the streets; when independent labels sprang out of the woodwork to feed new tastes; when rock music once again became about energy and fun; when the majors' boardrooms lost control. Suddenly we could do anything.'

The Buzzcocks had emerged in the first months of punk, and were at the forefront of Manchester's response to punk and among those who gave value to its DIY ethic. In January 1977 they released an EP on their own New Hormones label, having recorded and mixed the four songs – including the classic 'Boredom' – in just over five hours, with producer Martin Hannett (then known as Martin Zero).

A number of independent record labels began to win themselves a reputation over the next year or two. A profile in the weekly rock papers and on the John Peel show could send sales towards 10,000 and beyond. The post-punk era witnessed some genuinely strange records ('Violence Grows' by the Fatal Microbes), and some mad novelty songs ('I Touched Iggy Pop's Jacket' by Those Naughty Lumps). Among the important labels that emerged between the middle of 1977 and the end of 1978 were Fast Product (based in Edinburgh and founded by Bob Last), and Rough Trade (founded by record shop owner Geoff Travis), which had some gems among its first few releases, including songs by Metal Urbain, Subway Sect, and Swell Maps. And there would soon be others: Postcard, Factory, and Mute (formed in October 1978 by Daniel Miller to release his own 'Warm Leatherette' single under the moniker The Normal).

Punk had been a catalyst and encouraged a DIY spirit. There were few barriers to entry. Pink Floyd premiered their new quadraphonic live sound with walls of speakers and lights surrounding the audience at a concert in Portland, Oregon, in May 1977, but the punk generation were causing a stir with what Blondie's Debbie Harry admitted was the 'cruddiest equipment'.

Progressive rock bands might write songs about runes, or topographical oceans, and wouldn't release a single but might release an opus; punk reacted against this, offering a new start. It wasn't exactly a Year Zero, though. Punk tapped into the raw energy and the music of many of the underground or unheralded bands mentioned in the first chapters of our story, including The Stooges and the MC5, as well as British acts like Hawkwind and Dr Feelgood. The Clash listened to Captain Beefheart, and the Sex Pistols incorporated a cover version of 'Substitute' by The Who in their early sets.

The Jam had even more obvious debts to The Who. Cover versions in their live sets in early 1977 included The Who's 'So Sad About Us', and 1960s soul classics like 'In the Midnight Hour'. In the fervid London scene, their Woking roots threatened their credibility, but Paul Weller was an abrasive and powerful songwriter, and the band flaunted a visually distinct mod-influenced look: thin ties, mohair suits, and not a safety pin to be found.

After a few years on the dark side of the moon, punk was bringing music back down to earth, in London, Liverpool, Manchester, New York, on the street corners, down in the tube station at midnight. Another group at the time, The Slits, were formed by Ari Up and Palmolive, two teenage girls who met at a Patti Smith gig and who persuaded each other to form a band. They got themselves on The Clash's 'White Riot' tour in 1977, and recorded a John Peel session in September 1977; a bunch of sharp, discordant songs about hanging around, including the classics 'Shoplifting' (all one minute and twenty-nine seconds of it) and 'Newtown'.

In Stockton-on-Tees, Alex Patton might have been riled by punk, but another of our eye witnesses, Mark Reeder, understood its appeal. He was born in 1958 and grew up in Denton, on the outskirts of Manchester, where Mick Hucknall was one of his schoolfriends. Leaving school aged sixteen, he went to college to study graphic design and worked part-time in the Manchester branch of Virgin Records. Mark remembers how punk seemed to liberate people. At first, he understood it as a music revolution. 'It was the feeling of people wanting to have something different. Young people not being able to relate to stadium rock bands like Yes.'

But after a couple of years, what had been underground and marginal began to filter out. 'People started to feel the energy and feel the release that finally they'd discovered something that was going to give them a way to express themselves. People stopped being despondent.'

The sense of inertia was being challenged. 'Everyone was going, "There's no future, there's no future", but at the same time by indulging in punk rock and everything surrounding it, they were creating a future for themselves.'

In 1977 this is a significant development in the story of our cities. During the brutal and botched urban regeneration of the 1960s and early 1970s, we'd lost much, and gained only crumbling high rises, Spaghetti Junction, and half a dozen Arndale shopping centres in return. The slow death of the manufacturing industry had brought economic uncertainty, unemployment, and Government policies intent on public expenditure cuts; cities were being written off, they appeared blitzed, wounded, derelict. But against these considerable odds, this grim environment was being reclaimed, repopulated.

It wasn't just the sight of gaggles of cheaply-dressed youths throwing themselves around basement venues, or knocking on the doors of half-derelict warehouses looking for places to rehearse; there were other signs that a new generation was out there reclaiming our cities. There were many short-lived Seventies crazes, like clackers and soap-on-a-rope, but one craze which lasted was skateboarding, which enjoyed its first *annus mirabilis* in 1977. Concrete, pavements, ramps and steel girders became a playground; in 1977 there was concern at the dozens of young kids gathering underneath a concourse by the Royal Festival Hall, and the craze was so quick to grow that by the end of the year, the inaugural meeting of the Pro-Am Skateboarding Association of Great Britain had taken place at the Hammersmith Assembly Rooms.

The Jam's 'In the City', written in 1976 – their first single and the title track of their first LP – was far from being the noisiest, heaviest punk record ever made, but it did capture something of the rush and the passion of punk, and the pull of London's bright lights. It was a neat summation of the way the kids in the suburbs venerated the big city. The appeal of punk had spread well beyond its original small cells of activity, and now, in its 'new wave' guise, it was also the sound of the suburbs. According to Paul Weller, talking about 'In the City', 'Loads of punk songs were about boredom, and it was like, well, you should come and live in the suburbs where there's literally nothing going on except drinking and fighting. London seemed so exciting, and it was that feeling we were trying to capture.'

It's probably no coincidence that punk and hip hop both emerged in 1976 and 1977, reflecting the cacophony and collisions of urban life. The texture of music was changing as a new generation moved even further away from the sounds favoured by the Sixties generation. By the late 1970s it was as if music itself was speeding up, getting noisier, crashing down hard on the mellifluous California sound of The Eagles, and drowning out contemplative, languid, rural records like Mike Oldfield's *Tubular Bells* LP. Many rock musicians had been inspired by dreams of arcadia, blue skies, and the urge to see for miles. Bands had fled the cities to get their heads together in the country, and fans had gathered in parks and fields at the Isle of Wight, Windsor and Watchfield. But by the late Seventies, music was very urban-oriented, a reflection of steel, grey concrete, noise, confusion and pace.

By the middle of 1977, the idea of dropping out into a rural life was reversed. Cities were becoming the star attractions. The Bromley Contingent felt at home on Wardour Street; for young Paul Weller from Woking, London was full of promise; and Patti Smith's escape from the New Jersey factory to NYC described in 'Piss Factory' had become one of the iconic experiences of the decade.

Not everyone embraced or celebrated city life with the fervour of Paul Weller, but both punk and hip hop were a way of dealing with the urban experience, taking possession of it. For hip hop crews, it was about breakdancing in the parks and shopping precincts, and marking their new territory with graffiti. The first hip hop fans even took possession of the air around them, their portable cassette players – ghetto blasters and boom boxes – filling the city streets with sound.

Like punk, there were few barriers to involvement in hip hop. Now hip hop and rap have become big business worldwide, but back in the mid-1970s it was a neighbourhood phenomenon, and the neighbourhood was the Bronx, rundown and written-off. It was an unknown scene that had grown organically, around DJs, graffiti artists and breakdancers. One of the breakdancers back then was a guy called Crazy Legs, who later looked back on those days in the Bronx like this: 'It was our outlet and our way of expressing ourselves, and showing our individuality, our strength and our attitude.'

Post-punk, many cities – including Liverpool, Manchester and Sheffield – were sites of high excitement, if you knew which dark corner to explore. Punk gatherings in this era invariably featured someone spinning Iggy Pop's 'The Passenger', a thrilling song, Iggy surfing the danger and the delights of the city at night.

In Liverpool, a tentative physical and psychological switch was occurring, a repopulation and reinvention of the city's spaces. Back in New Brighton in 1971, Jayne had danced to T-Rex at the Chelsea Reach and dreamed of meeting boys in mascara. Five, six years later, she was not just an Eric's regular, she was one of the club's defining characters. 'Roger was very kind and he let us rule the roost. In Eric's we were fulfilling a dream.'

In amongst the post-industrial debris, deserted streets and rundown shops, Eric's was a great community of like-minded kids, but it wasn't the most glamorous place. Jayne: 'It was a right mess. Mathew Street has always had trouble with the sewers and the place would flood and the rats would come out.'

The DIY element in punk was so strong that consuming soon turned into producing, and it was only a matter of time before Jayne was in a band, Big in Japan, the bare bones of which had been formed during the first run of *Illuminatus!* After various manoeuvrings, Big in Japan settled on a line-up including Bill Drummond, Ian Broudie, Holly Johnson and Jayne, and a drummer called Phil Allen whose brother was in Deaf School. Phil was then replaced by Budgie; Budgie would one day depart to London and join Siouxsie & the Banshees, but he'd grown up in St Helens and in 1977 was at art college in Liverpool.

Many of the most celebrated female singers in the mid-1970s were from American singer-songwriter traditions, or were working in England's folk scene – people like the talented Sandy Denny (singer with Fairport Convention) – but punk's female singers were intent on making a contribution to a very different, jarring, urban sound. Patti Smith, Nico and Marianne Faithfull were possible role models, but Pauline Murray from Penetration and Poly Styrene from X-Ray Spex had to find their own voice. Jayne Casey, meanwhile, says she couldn't sing, but she could still perform. For her, the stage was the place to be: 'It was the best thing ever, do you know what I mean? From where I had come from! The best thing ever!'

She'd play gigs at Eric's with a shaved head, shrieking, wearing a nappy; it was madness. But it was enjoyed – or at least tolerated – by the Eric's regulars. Roger Eagle and his partner, Pete Fulwell, introduced under-eighteen alcohol-free matinee shows at Eric's, and most Saturdays the headline act would also do an afternoon show. There'd be eleven-, twelve-year-olds there, enjoying The Clash, The Stranglers, and, invariably, the unsettling pleasures of Big in Japan. Jayne laughs: 'We were the heroes to the matinee kids.'

In May 1977 The Clash played at Eric's, and among the crowd that night were Pete Wylie, Julian Cope, Ian McCulloch and Pete Burns. McCulloch was out celebrating his birthday. Wylie was wearing cowboy boots and a dodgy parka, and Pete Burns was dressed head to foot in PVC, his hair in a quiff that looked like it was made out of molten vinyl. But they all went on to be in groups, with each other and without, as Eric's became a hotbed of bands forming, bands splitting up, rivalries growing, egos careering out of control. Within weeks of The Clash show, The Mystery Girls played their first gig, with a line-up including Pete Burns, Julian Cope and Pete Wylie. This time Wylie was wearing red satin girl's trousers from Bus Stop, a pair of Doc Martens, his mother's white polyester blouse (with green and gold flowers and gold buttons), a white mac, and a toilet seat, although there is some disagreement about the details; some eye witnesses claim he wore the toilet seat round his neck, while he usually maintains he wore it dangling from his waist, looped through the belt of his trousers.

Bands needed somewhere to play, somewhere low rent. In 1977 London had venues that could be hired for a pittance, and despite punk's reputation, a number of clubs opened featuring punk bands, including the Roxy (on Neal Street), opened by Andy Czeczowski, which was a hot venue in the first four months of 1977, and the Vortex on Wardour Street, which opened soon after the Roxy closed. Not all cities were so blessed, but in Birmingham the usual stop on the new wave gig circuit was Barbarella's on Cumberland Street.

Birmingham was a pissed-off place in 1977, enlivened by bitter humour, and a small number of new bands, including The Prefects. The Prefects brought together the bass-rolling repetition of The Velvets, with a quick-fire quirkiness that usually left reviewers namechecking Captain Beefheart. They were outsiders, and never became big in Birmingham like the Buzzcocks did in Manchester. Their songs, uncompromised and bordering on the idiosyncratic, embraced the mundane and the confrontational, including 'The Bristol Road Leads to Dachau'. One early music press mention is hilarious: 'Suspicious and arrogant, they have no friends, want none, and despite creating an evolving sound, their potential for recognition is limited.'

Among other bands in Birmingham at the time were the Dum Dum Boys, Spizz Oil, and The Killjoys, who were fronted by a young lad from Oldbury, Kevin Rowland. Two of The Killjoys – Kevin Rowland and Kevin Archer – went on to form Dexy's Midnight Runners in July 1978. Dexy's had some success with 'Dance Stance', and some chart action with 'Geno', before releasing their classic debut LP *Searching For The Young Soul Rebels* in 1980. They remained pissed-off and suspicious; other bands would try to engage them in conversation and Dexy's would ignore them, if they were lucky. Kevin Rowland talked about this some years later: 'I used to insist on the members of the group not speaking to other groups ... I had someone come up to me at *Top of the Pops* and say they thought our records were excellent. "Yeah," I replied, "I think yours are fucking shit." It was awful really.

It wasn't nice. I'm not proud of it today. It's how we were, can't change it.'

The new Birmingham bands could struggle to find places to play; pubs like the Fighting Cocks and the Barrel Organ, clubs like Rebecca's and Bogart's, upstairs rooms like the Star Club on Essex Street. Maybe they'd cadge support slots at bigger venues like Barbarella's, the Mayfair Suite and the Cedar Club. The young punks would be looking for somewhere to go, something to do, congregating on a Saturday afternoon behind New Street Station.

Jayne Casey remembers her trips from Liverpool to Birmingham with Big in Japan. 'I used to love Barbarella's. That was the best laid out club, all the dark corners. But Birmingham at that time was a scary place. People were angry, and the punks got that, didn't they? I remember the Birmingham pub bombings and I always remember we used to go and play Barbarella's, and in Birmingham punks couldn't get into pubs. All the lads would go out after the soundcheck or whatever and me and Holly just used to sit in the dressing room every time we played Barbarella's. Nobody would let you in anywhere because the whole place was security conscious and paranoid and for some reason the punks were seen as part of that threat.'

This was the Birmingham depicted in the TV series *Gangsters*, set in the city's criminal underworld. And it was a Birmingham where it was all too easy to be bewildered by the reality gap, as the Jubilee celebrations took place, the decorated mugs and plates went on sale, and the street parties were planned. Bunting was everywhere, like it was a rerun of VE Day.

It's hard to tell whether there was only limited anti-monarchist activity or whether it was a case that anti-monarchist voices had limited exposure. Some disruption to the official celebrations did occur, however; when Her Majesty went to visit Aberdeen the Internationale was played

by a group of residents as the cavalcade drove by, and on the
day itself the Communist Party of Great Britain held an event
at Alexandra Palace. Elsewhere, 'Stuff the Jubilee' slogans
were painted on walls, and *Socialist Worker* included a highly
critical eight-page supplement to mark the Jubilee.

In June 1977, unemployment in Britain stood at 1.5 million. In London, at the Grunwick film processing factory, striking staff – many of them low-paid female Asian workers –
were deep into a year-long dispute which erupted in violent
clashes between police and pickets. Just before the Queen was
due to parade in London, *Time Out* predicted 'barracking from
people, angry that the year of a worsening economic crisis
should be seen as a time for celebration'.

Although many people were happy to take advantage of
the extra day's holiday and longer pub opening hours granted
in honour of the Jubilee, perhaps apathy was a more widespread reaction than hostility or enthusiasm. In Denton, on
the day itself, Mark Reeder was being a proper sulky teenager,
alone in his bedroom with a Sex Pistols poster taken from
work up on his wall. 'I put the record player on auto-repeat
and opened the windows and put loudspeakers facing out
of the windows and played "God Save the Queen", but
the neighbours complained and my parents were disgraced
because everyone else was indulging in a party with bunting
and all that.'

Paul Gilroy also avoided the street parties, but he can
remember being in a 'seedy Graham Greene-style' pub in
Brighton where he and his friends would often meet up, rub-
bing shoulders with East End criminals fencing antiques. The
pub was always friendly and hospitable, and he was pleased
to discover that the Jubilee wasn't being marked there. 'We
spent the day buried in the pub. We liked it there because it
was like someone's front room, with a budgerigar in a cage
and furniture falling apart.'

Alan Jones, who'd worked with Malcolm and Vivienne,

seen the Sex Pistols come together, and invited Sid and Nancy
over to stay in his flat, was losing patience and passion. Heavy
drugs and random violence were taking their toll. 'I think
those of us who were in at the beginning did get tired of being
on the front line when anything happened,' Alan says. 'And
people were starting to threaten us with violence, and I just
didn't feel comfortable anymore.'

At first Alan says he felt immune from the violence, but
among those targeted was John Lydon, who was beaten
up by a gang of men wielding knives and razors outside a
pub in Finsbury Park in the week of the Jubilee (the *Daily
Mirror* said a backlash had begun). Gaye Advert and TV Smith
were beaten up by Teddy boys in Hammersmith. Hospital
staff were unsympathetic when Gaye Advert was admitted.
'What do you expect if you go round dressed like that?' she
was told.

For Alan, the turning point was when the Sex Pistols played
live on a boat trip along the River Thames to mark the Jubilee
and to celebrate the success of their single, pursued by the
press and the police. Alan went along, taking Steve Strange
with him. He says Vivienne got drunk and was pissing over
the side of the boat. He remembers walking away that
evening, leaving it all behind. 'It was those events afterwards
when the police surrounded us and we got off and people
were being molested and beaten up by the police, that's when
I thought this was not really any fun anymore. Nils said to
me afterwards, I knew when you walked away from it all, it
was then, and that was true.'

By then he wasn't working in Vivienne and Malcolm's
shop; he'd moved on and was involved in the early days of
video and trying to get a career going writing about films. A
Star Wars preview took place in July 1977, and that was one
of the screenings he went to that year, dressed in his favourite
outlandish gear. He hadn't lost the art of making an impression. 'To this day', he says, 'people remember me. ''Oh, you

were that guy who turned up to *Star Wars* with that ensemble, all those chains!" '

Alan stopped enjoying wearing Vivienne's clothes – 'they became too frou-frou,' he explains – and removed himself from the punk in-crowd, as well as taking steps forward in his writing career. And, in terms of music, he dropped punk and went to disco. 'Absolutely,' he says. 'Totally. I went totally disco!'

For the next three years or so, disco was going mainstream and predictable, but Alan was still looking for unusual pleasures, enjoying the gay scene's burst of activity in London as nightclubs began to host regular gay nights like 'Bang' at the Astoria; trips to Scandals and Glades were common-place. 'Then I suppose my fashion sense transformed into being more gay clone,' he says. 'And I even tried to grow a moustache.'

Punk was also part of the continuing war on pop, on the commercial mainstream, on accepting that everything is as it should be. For good or ill, punk was about saying the unsay-able. Punk's assault left pop looking hollow (in 1977 Boney M, who'd had hits with 'Daddy Cool' and 'Ma Baker', made a belated and surreal attempt to gain gravitas with a single called 'Belfast'). Mark Reeder was on the front line of the music wars, working at the Manchester branch of Virgin Records. People would be buying Abba and Boney M records, much to his exasperation. 'I used to be thinking, do I really have to sell this stuff?'

Some days were better than others. In March 1978, the Buzzcocks played live in Virgin and Mark Reeder remembers someone walking off with one of the loudspeakers. When Mark confronted him, the guy said, 'Oh, sorry mate', and carried it back into the shop.

The direction the punk bands chose often seemed to change from town to town. In Brighton dozens of bands formed in the wake of punk. There would be people formation dancing at the Top Rank Suite one weekend, then deciding to ditch disco; they'd be in a punk band by the following Friday, with a gig at the Vault a week later. Brighton bands in particular seemed to favour jokey, stupid band names, and satirical, mocking songs like 'Lord Lucan is Missing' by The Dodgems, and 'I Don't Want My Body' by The Piranhas. One band, Joby & the Hooligans, had a song called 'Looking Through Gary Glitter's Eyes', which takes on a more sinister connotation in the light of what we now know about Gary Glitter.

Joby & the Hooligans were fronted by Joby – who wore a safety pin through his nose – and included Helen Hooligan on bass. At one point Paul Gilroy was asked to join as an extra guitar player and attended some rehearsals before bowing out gracefully. Helen later joined The Chefs and achieved a degree of cult status under her new name, Helen McCookery-book.

In Sheffield, a more intense, confrontational sound predominated. Sheffield had been one of the great steel manufacturing cities of the world, but by the mid-1970s the industry had collapsed. Just as the textile factories in Denton had closed and the mills of Bradford were derelict, now knife blades were being made in Korea and Singapore, and the workshops and steelworks of Sheffield were disappearing. But the post-punk era spawned bands like Cabaret Voltaire and the Human League; maverick bands, rebelling against punk and heavy rock stereotypes, their releases tended to be experimental and uncommercial soundscapes. Even the titles screamed craziness: 'Nag Nag Nag', 'Baader Meinhof' and 'Do the Mussolini (Headkick)' by Cabaret Voltaire; 'Being Boiled' by the Human League.

There's no way of proving this hunch, but from Brighton to Birmingham, Liverpool to London, there were probably more bands formed in 1977 than in any other year since records began. In Leeds, singer Jon King, guitarist Andy Gill and drummer Hugo Burnham had all studied art at Leeds

University, and formed a band in spring 1977. They had arrived in Leeds as students, and stayed on, having found in the city pockets of people with short haircuts and straight leg trousers, and a fondness for punk, reggae and left-wing politics, into listening to John Peel and forming bands. Generally in 1977, Leeds was a hardnut city torn apart by the Ripper, home to some of the country's most troublesome football fans and a team not known for its friendly football. Worlds would collide and pissed-up racists would trash student pubs. Activity during the first few months of punk was slight, then John Keenan promoted a night called the 'F' Club at various venues. The first three band members were joined by bass player Dave Allen, who had moved to Leeds from Kendal, and the Gang of Four played their first gig in May 1977 in the basement of the Leeds Corn Exchange.

In these unprepossessing, bleak, rundown cities, bands acting outside the mainstream, forming in the wake of punk, were providing a potent soundtrack to the last years of the 1970s, propelled by a burgeoning network of small independent labels. Close to the Gang of Four in Leeds, The Mekons were self-deprecating and idealistic; by the end of 1977 both Leeds-based bands found themselves working with Bob Last at his independent label Fast Product, in Edinburgh, who first released 'Never Been in a Riot' by The Mekons, and then agreed to release an EP by the Gang of Four.

Mark E. Smith and The Fall had a determination to avoid standard rock & roll lyrics, and with V-neck jumpers and a casual stage presence, created unique, biting music. The Pop Group's 'We Are All Prostitutes' was a brilliant single on Rough Trade. Essential Logic formed by Laura Logic, the saxophone player in X-Ray Spex, echoed Patti Smith on her blaring track 'Wake Up'. The Gang of Four wrote a song about alienation you could dance to called 'At Home He's a Tourist'. Songs like 'Typical Girls' by The Slits and 'It's Obvious' by The Au Pairs contributed to increasingly intense debates about gender politics. The Tom Robinson Band's contribution to all this was 'Glad to be Gay'.

Paul Gilroy recalls some of the tensions in Rock Against Racism, and he tells me about an RAR event in Brighton around this time. The line-up included Southall's Misty in Roots, alongside the Fabulous Poodles, fronted by a former college friend of Paul's, Tony DeMeur. 'Tony is a funny man, a comedian,' says Paul. 'I never liked the music that much, but anyway, they had this song called "Tit Photographer Blues", which had a chorus "I've got the tit tit tit tit, tit photographer blues" or something like that, something sardonic, music hall-style, very Brighton actually.'

The sardonic comedy of the song wasn't appreciated by feminists in the audience. 'They stormed the stage and tried to get the band off. It was a horrible event, and in my mind it did expose the cracks in RAR. You were trying to hold this combination of things that in some ways didn't belong together. Sometimes their coming together releases good energy, but a lot of the time it just messes things up.'

Like most RAR gigs, this one in Brighton had been organised not by head office, but by enthusiastic supporters. This unstructured informality in RAR generally made for unpredictability; but when it worked, it worked well. Another RAR show, on 21 August 1977 at Hackney Town Hall, featured Generation X and The Cimarons, and ended with both groups onstage leading the crowd in a chant of 'Black and white, black and white'. Within weeks of the Hackney Town Hall show, The Cimarons had released a tribute to the movement called simply 'Rock Against Racism'.

At the end of 1977, another RAR show at the Royal College featured punk band 999 and Misty in Roots, and was opened by the Art Attacks, who delighted the audience with a rendition of 'Rat City'. The students at the college had access to film equipment and projectors, and displayed slides of street fighting, the American Deep South, and a photograph of Steve

Biko which was projected onto a wall and overlaid by a hand-written scrawl: 'He will be revenged'.

On 1 October 1977 the Yorkshire Ripper struck for the first time outside Yorkshire, killing Jean Jordan in Manchester. She lived on Lingbeck Crescent in Moss Side with her husband and their two children, and worked in the local red light area. Sutcliffe picked her up and killed her on some allotments near Southern Cemetery. He killed three more victims before the end of May 1978: Helen Rytka in Huddersfield, Yvonne Pearson in Bradford, and Vera Millward in the car park at Manchester Royal Infirmary.

On the last day of July 1977, David Berkowitz killed Stacy Moskowitz, but his car, blocking access to a fire hydrant, received a parking ticket, and police eventually made the connections, traced the owner of the Ford Galaxie (licence plate 561 XLB), and on 10 August 1977 arrested Berkowitz for the 'Son of Sam' killings.

In Germany, five members of the Baader Meinhof group were being held in the high-security wing of Stammheim Prison while lawyers argued their cases in court. Meanwhile, other group members and Red Army Faction (RAF) sympathisers were continuing their attempts to force the release of the prisoners, and to destabilise the German state. On 7 April 1977, three people, including a Federal Prosecutor, were killed in Karlsruhe. Later in the month, after a trial lasting nearly two years, Andreas Baader, Gudrun Ensslin and Jan-Carl Raspe were found guilty of three murder charges and over thirty counts of attempted murder, and all received life sentences. But outside Stammheim the killings continued; on 30 July Baader Meinhof's ability to penetrate deep into the heart of the German establishment was in evidence again when Jurgen Ponto, the chairman of the Dresdner Bank, was shot and killed in his home.

On 5 September, Hanns-Martin Schleyer – board member at Daimler-Benz, and President of the German equivalent of the CBI – was kidnapped; his chauffeur and all three police officers assigned to protect him were killed in the raid. For four weeks, Schleyer was kept hidden in Erfstadt-Liblar, but hundreds of telephones were tapped as the police tried to intercept communications between RAF members. In Stammheim, meanwhile, the prisoners were denied all contact, although they had smuggled a lot of items into the high-security jail, including modified radios via which they were able to communicate.

On 13 October the episode entered a major new phase when four Palestinian terrorists hi-jacked a Lufthansa Boeing 737 and flew the plane and passengers – mostly German tourists – to Dubai. It became clear that the terrorists considered the Red Army Faction to be allies. One of the hi-jackers, the self-styled 'Martyr Mohammed', told air traffic control that 'the group I represent demands the release of our comrades in German prisons. We are fighting against the imperialist organisations of the world.'

A few days later the plane went on to Aden where the pilot was shot and killed by the hi-jackers, and then on to Mogadishu in Somalia. The hi-jackers demanded that all imprisoned RAF members should be flown immediately to Mogadishu or the plane would be blown up, but the situation developed quickly; that same evening, a commando unit from the German Army stormed the plane, killing or wounding all four hi-jackers while avoiding serious injury to any of the hostages.

It was in contrast to the botched operation to free the Israeli athletes back in 1972, and a major blow to the RAF prisoners in Stammheim. Within hours of the raid on the plane, three of the prisoners – Gudrun Ensslin, Andreas Baader and Jan-Carl Raspe – killed themselves in a suicide pact, using two hidden guns, and the raids and the suicides were swiftly followed by the execution of Hanns-Martin Schleyer. 'His death is of no significance in our pain and rage at the slaughter of Mogadishu and Stammheim,' announced the Red Army Faction.

At the end of October 1977, Andreas Baader, Gudrun Ensslin and Jan-Carl Raspe were buried in Stuttgart's Wald-friedhof Cemetery in the presence of several thousand mourners, and the coffins were sealed with a two-ton lead cover to prevent grave tampering. In 1976 Ulrike Meinhof had hanged herself in prison.

In 1978 Mark Reeder moved abroad, ostensibly as a roving representative of Factory Records, and ended up living in Berlin. In 'Holidays in the Sun', the Sex Pistols had sung about the city, particularly the paranoia and claustrophobia. When Mark got to Berlin he realised it wasn't so different to Man-chester: gloomy streets, collapsing old buildings.

Bands with associations with Eric's who went on to make a career for themselves in music include Wah Heat, Echo and the Bunnymen, Teardrop Explodes, Dead or Alive, and The Lightning Seeds. In 1979 the Gang of Four signed to EMI; over fifteen years later, despite never having had a Top 40 hit, they're namechecked as influences by groups including the Red Hot Chili Peppers, Franz Ferdinand, Radio 4, and Spoon.

Having adjusted their line-up several times, the Human League went on to have two massive-selling singles in 1981 ('Love Action' and 'Don't You Want Me?'), but in their earlier incarnation they were a weird electronic band. In 1980 they were dropped from a support slot on a Talking Heads tour when it was revealed that the band would be presenting thirty minutes of slides, short films and pre-recorded music while the band sat in the audience. At the time it was brilliant, funny even, that a Sheffield band could out-art New York like that. Richard Hell & the Voidoids did the tour instead.

CHAPTER NINE

'Handsworth Revolution'
(1978)

The second half of the 1970s was a boom time, perhaps the best time, for reggae. Central to this was the genius of Bob Marley, but there were other performers who lit up the decade, Burning Spear and Augustus Pablo among them. In many English cities, black youths made use of red, gold and green (the national colours of Ethiopia), wore their hair in dreadlocks, and the attitudes, language and music of Rasta-farianism became identifiable and influential.

We have already seen the beginnings of a homegrown reggae scene in 1972 and 1974 – The Cimarons and Matumbi, for example – but there were other homegrown acts in the Caribbean community in Britain in the second half of the 1970s, including Steel Pulse, Aswad, Merger, Black Slate, X-O-Dus, Cornerstone, and Misty in Roots. In August 1978, dub poet Linton Kwesi Johnson released an effective and widely-praised debut LP, *Dread Beat & Blood*, produced by Dennis Bovell.

Dennis Bovell was a key character in British reggae in the 1970s, not only via Matumbi but in his production work too. He ran Sufferers Hi-Fi, one of the most popular sound systems in the London area in the mid-1970s. In 1974, however, his career was jeopardised after a raid during his DJ set at the

Carib Continental Club in Cricklewood in North London, when one hundred and forty policemen went there to quell a disturbance after police had arrested a man. In autumn 1975, after an eighty-two-day trial, nine men were acquitted of 'incitement to cause an affray' and no decision was reached with regard to the other three, including Dennis Bovell.

In the second half of the 1970s, reggae also made a powerful impact on the wider community, influencing bands like The Clash and The Slits; giving a musical and ideological strength to Rock Against Racism, and laying the groundwork for the ska explosion in 1979 and the rise of Soul II Soul in the 1980s.

We have already seen a shift, as roots reggae – with a new sound and a new agenda – made a direct appeal to black youth in English cities. No longer could reggae be mistaken for an offshoot of the novelty pop market; now it was about dub, roots and consciousness. As Lloyd Bradley puts it in his book *Bass Culture*, 'The way these kids looked at reggae music was through a window very different from the previous generations; within the first couple of years of the 1970s the whole idea of roots and culture gained enormous currency in Britain's inner cities.'

Those early years of roots reggae inspired David Hinds and Basil Gabbidon, the backbone of Steel Pulse. The band had formed in Handsworth, Birmingham; one of those areas of the country, like Toxteth and Moss Side, that had a sizeable Afro-Caribbean community that found itself on the front line of the race issue throughout the 1970s and beyond.

Even before Enoch Powell had stirred controversy with his 'rivers of blood' speech, Birmingham and the West Midlands had more than its share of far-right activity, discrimination and racist abuse. Smethwick was the site of the controversial 'nigger neighbour' campaign by the Conservatives in 1964. Then, in 1965, there was a flurry of local activity by the white supremacist organisation Ku Klux Klan; the KKK began harassing the newly-established Commission for Racial

Equality, and there were dozens of reports of letters posted by
the Klan threatening the West Indian community, especially
black men living with white women. In June 1965 *The Sunday
Times* reported on the inaugural meeting of a KKK branch
in Birmingham. A few weeks earlier, the local ATV station
reported that a burning cross had been hung on the front door
of a black family's home on Albert Road in Handsworth. In
the late 1960s Birmingham's housing chiefs attempted to
implement dispersal programmes in the allocation of council
housing, hoping to reduce the build-up of racial ghettos, but
it wasn't always a popular initiative. In Birmingham, white
tenants in a block of maisonettes in the Ladywood area of the
city had threatened a rent strike against the Council's attempts
to house a second black family in the block.

Sometimes the activities of the racists gained a disproportionate amount of media coverage; a close reading of the
newspaper reports of that KKK meeting in 1965 reveals that
only seventeen people attended (and yet it was featured across
the media, including coverage on ABC Television in America).
Of course it wasn't just in Birmingham that racist intimidation could strike – around the same time, a burning cross,
doused with petrol, was nailed to the door of a Pakistani-
owned shop in Plaistow – but race relations in the area were
often problematic.

In 1973, in neighbouring West Bromwich, National Front
leader Martin Webster became the Party's first candidate to
retain an electoral deposit when he obtained 16.3 per cent
of the vote (with 5,000 votes in all) in the West Bromwich
by-election, and in 1977, during a by-election in the Ladywood constituency which includes parts of Handsworth,
the National Front mobilised again. A few days before the
Ladywood by-election, and three days after the clashes
at Lewisham, demonstrators gathered outside a school on
Boulton Road in Handsworth where a meeting of the National
Front, addressed by John Tyndall, was due to take place.

By 7.30pm there were around a hundred NF supporters inside the hall, and six hundred protesters outside who were already engaged in clashes with the police. After a number of arrests had been made, the crowd laid siege to Thornhill Road police station, and later, looting and burning occurred on Soho Road. The racial tensions in the area were such that a local academic, John Brown, published a report on Handsworth soon after this incident entitled 'Shades of Grey' that was almost apocalyptic in tone, warning of great civil unrest and encouraging Birmingham's *Evening Mail* newspaper to describe Handsworth as a 'powder-keg'.

Throughout the 1970s, and even beyond, local politicians from the Tory Party had a reputation for not straying far from a Powellite line. In May 1980 the Home Office Committee of the House of Commons recommended that the 'sus' laws should be repealed, arguing that 'sus' had become a major obstacle to improving relations between the police and the black community, and describing it as 'a piece of law which is contrary to the freedom and liberty of the individual'. Only one member of the Committee opposed this recommendation: Jill Knight, MP for Edgbaston, Birmingham.

In 1966 Basil Gabbidon had started at Handsworth Wood Boys' School, also the alma mater of drummer Carl Palmer who played with the Crazy World of Arthur Brown before becoming a founder member of Emerson Lake and Palmer. By the late 1960s, Basil's guitar hero was Jimi Hendrix, and he also loved The Rolling Stones. Then he got into Mandrill and The Isley Brothers. Basil began to teach himself how to play the guitar. 'It's not like today,' he later recalled, 'we made things happen ourselves.'

In the sixth form, one of his friends was David Hinds, and with both of them having Saturday jobs at the Co-op supermarket in Winson Green, they saw a lot of each other outside school hours. After leaving Handsworth Wood, they both went on to Bournville College of Art, where the student hall hosted one of South Birmingham's most popular dance nights. By this time they had begun jamming and rehearsing relentlessly, with Basil taking lead guitar and Hinds playing rhythm guitar as well as providing lead vocals. With Ronnie 'Stepper' McQueen on bass, they recruited others to the line-up, including vocalist Mykaell Riley and keyboard player Selwyn Brown.

At first the band rehearsed at the Gabbidon family home on Headingley Road, Handsworth, then in Ronnie McQueen's attic bedroom on Sandwell Road. Eventually they met regularly at the Hinds household at 16 Linwood Road. Like every young band, the early months were about grabbing rehearsal space and helping each other to learn their chosen instruments. They covered songs by their favourite groups, but wrote their own music too. Selwyn Brown later recalled, 'We basically taught each other how to play, so there was no ego thing. We just wanted to play and enjoy music and inspire people and write something conscious.'

As we've already seen, reggae had a chequered reputation. Not only did the biggest hits tend to be novelty songs, but to many in the black community, reggae also had too many skinhead connections. The skinheads who'd frequented reggae clubs weren't antagonistic, of course, but others in the tribe could be. But from the first years of the 1970s, perceptions changed, and no longer was reggae about songs like 'Skinhead Train' by The Charmers. The skinheads had begun to drift away from reggae, perhaps moving on to Slade and Bowie by 1972. One black music specialist confirmed this shift in 1974, describing how 'the white working class kids in bovver boots and hedgehog haircuts have disappeared'.

For the Afro-Caribbean community there was a desire for retrenchment and realignment, and sometimes this meant a move towards separation from the majority community. Many sections of society in the 1970s were engaged in a search for enlightenment. Feminists were intent on consciousness-raising, while Steve Biko had explored and celebrated black consciousness. A similar aim lay behind the 'conscious' lyrics of the roots reggae stars: to share new definitions of their history, reality and identity, developed from within their community, not imposed by the mainstream.

Although reggae was closely, and rightly, identified as a Jamaican sound, it also had a close relationship to the American civil rights struggle. Reggae songs like Ken Boothe's 'Something is Holding Me Back (Is it Because I'm Black?)', and Jimmy Cliff's 'You Can Get It If You Really Want' were part of the same struggle for empowerment as James Brown's 'I Don't Want Nobody to Give Me Nothing (Open Up the Door I'll Get it Myself)'. There's always hidden history, and David Hinds, from the early days of Steel Pulse, was inspired to tap into ideas still alive under the surface, after reading about Angela Davis, for example. 'From the age of thirteen or fourteen we learned about political issues in the States,' he later recalled, namechecking George Jackson, Angela Davis and Jonathan Jackson. Roots reggae was a new way of saying the same thing as civil rights era soul music, but took its vocabulary from Rastafarianism.

Young black British lads like David Hinds and Basil Gabbidon knew their parents had travelled to England looking for work and for their own version of the promised land, but it looked as if the dream had been unfulfilled. The local economy was suffering; this was the Birmingham of Black Sabbath, the Dum Dum Boys, and The Killjoys, and the Birmingham of car plant closures and rising unemployment. In addition, the local black population was facing hostility from the far right, and an unequal share of job losses; a Commission for Racial Equality report found that between November 1973 and November 1977, while national unemployment figures doubled, unemployment among ethnic minorities quadrupled. In 1978, UK-born whites were suffering unemployment levels of 5.3 per cent, but the figure for UK-born blacks was 21 per cent. It's no surprise that Rastafarianism held an attraction for the Steel Pulse generation.

The Rasta movement began in Jamaica in the first quarter of the twentieth century, influenced by the iconic Marcus Garvey whose Universal Negro Improvement Association (UNIA) was decked in red, gold and green and preached black pride. 'The world has made being black a crime,' Marcus Garvey wrote. 'I hope to make it a virtue.'

Based on his reading of the Bible – specifically the Book of Revelation – Marcus Garvey also predicted the arrival of a great new black emperor in Africa, and when the emergence of Ras Tafari Makonnen as Emperor of Ethiopia in 1930 appeared to fulfil the prophecy, the formal creation of the Rastafarian movement was triggered. Ras T. Makonnen took the name Haile Selassie; to Rastas he was the Messiah, the King of Kings, the conquering Lion of the tribe of Judah.

In the nineteenth century Africa had been carved up by colonial powers – Britain, France and Belgium – and Marcus Garvey, motivated by his strong anti-colonialist beliefs, advocated a new black state in Africa, free from white rule. The UNIA also arranged the financing of the Black Star Line steamship company, which became a potent symbol of the Rasta dream of returning to the African motherland after four hundred years of exile.

A central concept in Rastafarianism is the notion of Babylon: four hundred years of oppression, from the days of slavery to contemporary exploitation, and hostility. The Rasta desire is an escape from Babylon, a return to roots; this means Africa, sometimes literally, or if not, symbolically. Africa is the homeland, the pre-slavery site of ethnic unity. Peter Tosh expressed it like this in his 1977 song 'African': 'Don't care where you come from, as long as you're a black man, you're an African.'

Garvey died in London in 1940, and in the decades that followed, the Rasta community was marginalised, even despised in Jamaica, living up in the hills and subject to police harassment. Even after the formal end of colonialism in the region, when Jamaica gained independence from Britain in 1962, Rastafarianism remained controversial. Rasta took most of its support from the Jamaican poor, and was therefore seen as a threat by the authorities in the newly-independent state. Nevertheless, Rastafarianism continued to win converts, mostly among the dispossessed, but also among the urban middle classes.

Just as rap would some ten years later, reggae lyrics covered diverse subjects, from sexual innuendo to political revolution, but social concerns were never far from the surface. Increasingly, reggae music was debating Rasta ideas of exile, exodus, and the movement of the people, in songs like Bob Andy's 'Going Home', and Desmond Dekker's 'Israelites' (both from 1969), the latter marking reggae's ability to clothe a complicated and potentially controversial subject in the sweetest, most swinging music.

Some of the more established reggae DJs/producers, like Duke Reid, resisted the Rasta influence on reggae. Others embraced it, notably Lee 'Scratch' Perry at his Black Ark studio which attracted a Rasta crowd, as did Coxsone Dodd's Studio One. Even into 1973, though, dreadlocks weren't a part of reggae; at that time, Big Youth was one of the only artists happy to go onstage with dreadlocks. There are few locks in *The Harder they Come*, and, at the time of *Catch A Fire*, Marley himself was only just getting into locksing. As the 1970s evolved, labels with a strong Rasta image gained strength, like Augustus Pablo and his Rockers International label (home to the likes of Jacob Miller, Junior Delgado, and Paul Blackman).

The roots movement was purposeful, and a leading figure in the early days was Winston Rodney, who had taken the name Burning Spear in 1969. He expounded Rastafarianism and Marcus Garvey's messages of black liberation with such evangelical zeal and brilliantly uplifting reggae that David

Hinds once paid him this tribute: 'I would say Burning Spear was responsible for the birth of Rastafari in England.'

In the first half of the 1970s, through careful and successful marketing, Island Records had built a growing, cross-cultural following for Bob Marley and The Wailers. The 1973 tour included college- and university-based venues, and an appearance on *The Old Grey Whistle Test*, and then in June 1974 Peter Tosh left The Wailers, giving Marley greater prominence. In November 1974, the *Natty Dread* LP was released, which brought into the music a trio of female backing singers, the I Threes (Rita Marley, Judy Mowatt and Marcia Griffiths), and a softer production style which undeniably gave the LP accessibility. *Natty Dread* was released with a portrait of Marley on the front cover, all short dreads and sultry expression, and *Catch A Fire* was subsequently repackaged, with the original cover replaced by a large photograph of Marley smoking a spliff. By the end of 1975, Marley's was the most prominent Rasta image in the world.

Clover had grown up in Moss Side in Manchester with her brothers and sisters in a house decorated with pop star posters pulled out of *Jackie*. By the time she left school, aged sixteen, in 1976, she, and the times, had changed. She'd already realised it was time for her to move beyond *Top of the Pops*, Alvin Stardust, the Bay City Rollers and Gary Glitter. 'Once I'd left school, it was a case of what now? There didn't seem to be much going on, just the same pictures in *Jackie* and stuff, so I was growing up a bit and I moved on, and my sisters did as well.'

Reggae had never connected much with Paul Gilroy in North London, while Clover – a young black teenager in the mid-1970s – had heard reggae on the radio and sat through the occasional hit on *Top of the Pops*, but also hadn't found the music attractive. 'I couldn't identify with it at all, it seemed boring. Not interested, definitely not.'

But throughout British inner cities, roots reggae and the Rastafarian movement began to speak to the young black

British, creating a sense of discovery, history, unity and identity. In Birmingham, Steel Pulse were beginning to make headway, and found a network of venues to play. Their debut gig took place at the Crompton Arms in Lozells in July 1975, and over the next eighteen months they played locally – at Barbarella's, the Santa Rosa, and the Tower Ballroom – but also further afield, including venues in Huddersfield, Bristol, Bradford and London.

In Manchester, the social and spiritual appeal of Rastafarianism came before Clover's enjoyment of reggae music. 'I didn't really know which way to go. I left school with no qualifications and I went right into this way of life. At the time it was great, it was so sheltered and safe. And that was when I was introduced to the music, through that.'

The ideals, the structure and activities of the local Rastafarian culture appealed. 'Being a Rasta for me became like a family, it had that unity type of thing. It felt like it was a cushion, something that would guide a little girl growing up and going out into the big world on your own. It felt safe for me, a family atmosphere that was easy to slot into, and all this "one love" thing.'

It was about a lot more than clothes and music for Clover, who became a member of what was called the Twelve Tribes. 'If you were interested you stuck with it and you became a member, which I was. And a lot of the guys there were older and a lot of sisters were older and that was quite an attraction, being with older people, because I didn't want to be running about in glitter jumpers anymore.'

There were specific texts to study, and unique words and phrases which had been developed to describe the Rasta way of seeing the world. Some of it was religious language, but it was used in everyday contexts too. 'Absolutely,' says Clover, 'I got into that. If you saw someone out it would be "irie", and things were "ital" – that was the ultimate. "Greetings" you'd say if you met somebody.'

Although Rastafarianism has its roots in the Bible, Christianity is rejected by Rastafarianism, along with Christian interpretations of the Bible. During her involvement in Rastafarianism, Clover occasionally struggled with some of its ideology. 'When you went to the meetings – and you had to pay your dues at these meetings – you'd have your Bible to hand and you'd sit down and reason. My understanding from going to Sunday school when I read the Bible there – when I was brought up with Christianity – it was so different; it was the same Bible but with a totally different slant to it! It was confusing to begin with.'

Rasta considered that the orthodox Christian religion had distracted the black community from the reality of their deprived, exploited, everyday state in the here-and-now, with promises of salvation in the afterlife. In 'Get Up, Stand Up', Bob Marley described Christianity as a 'game'. The message of 'Get Up, Stand Up' was for black people to take control of their own destinies. Salvation was possible, soon. 'You will look for yours on earth,' says Marley.

The hard-headed political radicalism fed by black power and the spiritual beliefs inspired by the Bible didn't always mesh well. To some people it was a political movement, to others it was a religion; in the magazine *Race Today*, Linton Kwesi Johnson called it a 'cult'.

Clover hesitates at the use of the word 'cult'. 'It was almost like a cult, I suppose, offering a different way of life, and a family; we called ourselves "sisters" and "brothers". We'd have meetings and you would sit down and "reason", as they called it, with the sisters or the brothers, although not so much the brothers because it was quite segregated; the men were with the men, and the women were with the women, and the sisters would reason together.'

At sixteen years old, Clover was trying to work out the world, and the Rasta lifestyle and the music made sense. 'And the dress sense as well, and the humbleness.'

Teenagers new to the Twelve Tribes received guidance. 'We had what were called your elders, who would talk to you about things, stuff that you didn't learn at home, and it was a relaxed and a very humble way of life. The dress code was simple, you wrapped your hair and you didn't wear make-up and you wore your militant, khaki-type clothes and sandals and you didn't deal in vanity.'

In the mid-1970s every male Rasta had dreadlocks; now, of course, not every dread is a Rasta. Similarly to an afro in the early 1970s, in the mid-1970s dreadlocks were a symbol of militant black power. Cutting, straightening or washing hair suggested an attempt to be accepted in Babylon, but the idea of dreadlocks was also related to the Rasta aim of living a natural life, a life of ital food, humbleness and simplicity. Once again, Rastas took guidance from their reading of the Old Testament. 'All the days of the vow of separation, no razor shall pass over his head. Until the day be fulfilled of his conse-cration to the Lord, he shall be holy and shall let the hair of his head grow.'

The Rasta brethren often withdrew from the company of the white community, although Rasta teaching on the issue of separation was never clear cut. To this extent, the range of attitudes to white people were similar to those held by the black population in America during the civil rights era. It was clear that Bob Marley, for example, wasn't always comfortable as a figurehead for black separation, and his personal circum-stances – his (largely absent) white father – presumably played a part in this.

Clover tries to analyse the Rasta perspective on race from her own experience. 'There were white sisters there, although I don't remember any white brothers. There are some white sisters who still have links to it now. I don't know, it wasn't a racial thing, there wasn't any exclusion.'

I tell her that it was during that era that, as a white person living in a multi-racial city, the visibility of the Rastafarians made me aware of a new generation in the black community, a generation that appeared to have a clear identity, and not an identity given to it, but an identity of its own. The older generation tended to dress formally, and conformity was prized, but for the younger generation, just the look was enough to mark a difference and have an impact. She agrees, but she also reminds me not to generalise. 'It was definitely so, but I know that there were plenty of people in the black community who didn't like it, a lot of the older people didn't like it.'

There was a great deal of conflict between the generations in the Afro-Caribbean community in Britain in the 1970s. Often from Christian Pentecostal backgrounds, parents had appreciated some of the benefits of coming to England. But the Seventies generation was being dragged down by unemployment and discrimination, and were more likely to reject, or at least question society.

Clover had some personal experience of this when her parents rejected her Rasta way of life. 'My parents really didn't like it, that's why I left home; I was so convinced it was the right thing to do. And they never changed their views, my parents, they never warmed to it. It was the same with a lot of people; I think that at that time the Rasta thing was very powerful, growing, and they felt it was threatening maybe, to them. In a way it must have been the same for parents when their kids became hippies or whatever, and it was the same thing too; they didn't wash their hair, lazy, that kind of thing. It's funny, rebellion; to comb your hair or not comb your hair!'

And of course the punks were around too, shocking their parents. 'That's right, it's the same as anything else,' says Clover. 'Things were changing and the older people were wondering, what's going on here?'

Clover's mother reacted strongly against her daughter's involvement with the Rastafarians. 'My mother, she just thought they were bad people. Back home in Jamaica they're up the hills you see, and nobody bothers with them. She found them quite scary looking, and she hated the thought of it. My boyfriend had massive locks and she just didn't like the idea of it.'

Clover left home, unable to find common ground with her mother. 'She said they don't work, they have no ambition, they're dirty, don't wash their hair, smoke weed. She didn't like them smoking ganja. She'd been brought up in a Christian way of life and it was just too rebellious.'

Resistance to Rastafarianism was also present in the established Afro-Caribbean community in Birmingham. Steel Pulse had a network of good gigs, but still found some Afro-Caribbean clubs hostile. The ever-closer relationship between reggae and Rastafarianism scared some of the club owners. 'There was a stigma went out there with the reggae music. They thought it promoted ganja smoking,' David Hinds recalled some years later. 'They thought it promoted the philosophy of Rastafari, which was against the system of Babylon, against police officers, against anything the British administration was trying to throw on the black community. So club owners got scared, saying, "Hey, look, we don't want you doing this kind of music at our clubs because you're gonna be closing our clubs down".'

Bob Marley's big hit in 1976 was 'No Woman No Cry', but the beautiful ballad didn't threaten to burn down Babylon, and this obviously helped to give it wider appeal, and perhaps granted Marley himself even more acceptability. Doors were opening for Steel Pulse too; in 1976 the small independent Dip label released their first single. 'Kibudu, Mansetta and Abuku' made a conscious link between the plight of black youth in urban ghettos and the dream of a spiritual African homeland. In 1977 they won a competition at the Santa Rosa club in Birmingham which earned them studio time with Dennis Bovell. He produced their second single, 'Nyah Luv', released on the Anchor label in September 1977.

Bovell, more than any other British producer, understood the power and dynamics of dub. An adjunct to the roots sound, dub stripped reggae down and carved out spacey, instrumental, bass-heavy echoes; experimentation was prized, and the effect was unique and other-worldly (one of the finest releases in the genre was when the producer King Tubby collaborated with Augustus Pablo on the brilliant *King Tubby Meets Rockers Uptown* LP). The golden age of the dub sound lasted from 1975 until about 1978, book-ended by records like Keith Hudson's *Pick a Dub* (1975), and The Mighty Two's *African Dub Chapter Three* (1978).

Dub filled a room, made floors and walls bounce, and was ideal sound system material; with the vocals taken out of most of the records, dub encouraged toasting or chatting. In a sound system, the selector played the records and the DJ got on the microphone, barking out phrases, boasts and a humorous running commentary. It was a good time to be going to reggae dances, and Clover found herself moving away from the puritanical orthodoxy of reasoning and study, spending more time listening to music, at house parties and the local blues. 'I went off with the more exciting scene, people who felt they'd got the basic concept and then wanted to do something of their own, not without the basic concepts but in a different direction.'

Rastafarianism had started small, purist, but had become bigger and fractured, including a shift towards less orthodox lifestyles. Clover was hanging out with the guys who were organising their own sound systems, but still wearing the dreads. 'They were a bit of a problem for the orthodox regime, who thought they were giving them a bad name.'

Clover was in a relationship with one of the guys who had a sound system in Moss Side at the time; Shortee Downbeat he was called. It was very territorial on the sound system scene, and devotees were loyal to a certain team and followed them wherever they played. For a while, Shortee had a spot

at Jilly's on a Thursday. In Manchester you could also hear
the likes of Baron Hi-Fi, Lord Cas, Rocket and Count Daddy.
'They were the main Manchester ones, from Moss Side,'
remembers Clover. 'And they would play sounds from
Birmingham or London, and they'd come and jam in a big
session or amongst themselves.'

Lord Cas used to play in the Old Edinburgh on Alec Road
when there were clubs there. There were dances in the hall
at Birley High School, and at the Hideaway youth club. Pubs
and other clubs would regularly host sounds, and then there
were bigger venues in Manchester too, occasional trips to the
Mayflower, to Belle Vue at the Banqueting Suite, the Carib
in Cheetham Hill, Ravens in Longsight, and in the 1980s there
was the International.

There were few live groups on the reggae circuit, although
acts like Aswad would occasionally appear at the Russell Club
in Hulme. But that was one of the biggest appeals of the sound
systems – not just the sense of community around them, but
also because the music was so special: dub-plates, versions,
imports, pre-releases, heavy stuff you couldn't hear anywhere
else. There was hardly any reggae on the radio, and if you
were waiting for the bands to come and play, you'd never
go out.

'A sound system was something self-made, a do it yourself
thing,' says Clover. 'It was also good because any grievances
were settled with the decks. Baron Hi-Fi might think they had
the latest cut of this record – and the DJ would be like "Hear
this!" – or both sounds would play different versions of the
same record and really turn it up with no-one backing down.
Then you'd have all the followers cheering them on. It was a
great atmosphere, and they'd have dancing competitions and
who could do the best skank.'

The sound systems were a valuable outlet for competitiveness too, says Clover, who looks at the situation today,
when competitiveness between crews, and hyped-up and

distorted notions of respect can too easily result in someone pulling a gun. 'I feel maybe now there's nothing like that, something to channel all that gang thing. These sounds, they'd made them themselves, the decks, the huge boxes – the "double joys" we called them – they were all hand-made; that's where everyone's energies were going.'

For Clover it was a buzz. 'I travelled all the way to Leeds in the back of a van with double joy boxes because I wouldn't want to miss this dance that was going on in Chapeltown. Everybody would go, you'd go no matter what; you'd get the train over there if you had to. We would go to these big cellars in big old houses in Chapeltown and one sound would have one room and one sound would have the other.'

Her trips over to Leeds took place during the era portrayed in the novels of David Peace, and in Chapeltown she felt the pressure of the world of *Nineteen Seventy Seven*. 'To be honest, I found Leeds a bit scary, very hilly, gruesome, and not as friendly to me, as a stranger there at that time. I haven't been over there for years, but that's how it seemed to me at the time.'

Everybody would travel around with Shortee, even if it meant getting back across the Pennines to Victoria train station at 7 o'clock in the morning. 'This would be 1978. We went over to Leeds a number of times. And we went to Birmingham, Huddersfield, London; wherever. It was a case of the Manchester crew being there and you were on their territory and you were there to prove yourself and they had their own following. Again, you knew you weren't in your town. You took your support with you but you'd be out-numbered.'

By this time Clover was living with Shortee on the ground floor of Maladale Close, a block of black and white maisonettes between Princess Parkway and the infamous Hulme Crescents, not far from the Russell Club. This was the era in which 'Factory' nights were to become an irregular fixture there, but mostly it was a reggae club. There would be events in pubs, clubs, various school and concert halls, but also informal and semi-legal gatherings. 'We used to have a blues in my house, Friday, Saturday, Sunday. You'd have the sound set up, although they weren't big rooms in the flat I lived in, so we'd pile all the furniture into one room.'

Clover saw very few live acts in these years; reggae had poor coverage on the radio, and sound systems dominated the social life of the young black community. For the same reasons, Steel Pulse were finding it hard to build momentum, or even to get gigs, although they had some luck supporting bigger acts on tour, and opened for Burning Spear, one of their earliest influences, at the Rainbow Theatre in London in October 1977. Fellow British reggae pioneers Aswad were also on the same bill, and Burning Spear later released a live album from the gig on Island Records. The tour also visited Bristol and Birmingham. Steel Pulse made an impression with these gigs, and soon afterwards signed to Chris Blackwell's Island Records (home to Bob Marley, Black Uhuru, Third World and Aswad).

Steel Pulse's unique take on reggae was most obvious when they played live, decking themselves out in a variety of symbolic stage costumes; 'Stepper' McQueen would often wear a top hat and tails, representing the English aristocracy; Mykaell Riley would dress like a preacher with a wide-brimmed Quaker hat; Phonso Martin dressed like a Regency footman; Basil wore African robes; and David wore a convict's uniform.

In the second half of the Seventies, reggae forged something of an alliance with punk, and this was to have an important effect on Steel Pulse's career. It was an alliance built informally in various parts of the country. There was Don Letts DJ-ing at the Roxy in London, playing Big Youth, Augustus Pablo and King Tubby, and at Eric's Roger Eagle's DJ playlist would include bounteous amounts of reggae, all much appreciated by Jayne Casey's friends from Liverpool 8. At

Barbarella's in Birmingham, Ranking Roger would sit on a ledge near the decks toasting, while a dub version of Tapper Zukie's 'MPLA' burst out of the speakers. When John Lydon was invited to play some favourite records on Capital Radio, he chose Dr Alimantado's 'Born For a Purpose'.

After the initial surge of two-chord garage thrash, some bands formed in the years of punk looked to reggae for influence, like The Slits, The Clash, and Ruts. The first Ruts gig was at Southall Community Centre with Misty, and their first single was the straight-ahead 'In a Rut' (1978); then they incorporated reggae rhythms into their angry sound on singles like 'Babylon's Burning' and 'Jah War'. Their career was impressive, but tragically cut short when singer Malcolm Owen was found dead in July 1980, the victim of a heroin overdose.

Steel Pulse had an important part to play in creating and extending the links between punk and reggae, with dozens of appearances sharing a stage with punk and new wave acts; the first was a gig with Generation X at the Vortex in London, and the band went on to support the likes of The Clash, The Stranglers, XTC, The Slits, and Ian Dury and the Blockheads at venues including the Roxy and Dingwalls in London. 'We shared common goals,' Hinds says of their collaboration with the punk and new wave bands of the time. 'The punks were adopting anything the system was rejecting, including reggae.'

Steel Pulse's first release of 1978 was the single 'Ku Klux Klan', which was already one of their live favourites. One of the most striking visual images in music in 1978 was the costumes chosen by Steel Pulse for 'Ku Klux Klan'; they would be along the front of the stage in white Ku Klux Klan hoods. 'The punks went absolutely ape-shit,' Hinds recalled later. 'It was mayhem. It was immediate mayhem.'

The KKK hoods conjured up a startling image of racism, and took the debate wider than the limited image of racists as skinheads could, but in 1978 this portrayal of the KKK dramatised real fear too. The activities of the organisation back in the mid-1960s were part of the folk memory in Handsworth, but the social problems and the rising racial tensions of the 1970s had encouraged the KKK and a variety of other racist groups to come out of the woodwork, including Column 88 (established in 1970), and the League of St George (formed in 1974). Furthermore, 1978 had dawned with a call to arms to the white racists in Britain from the KKK in America. 'Britain is ready for us,' said Bill Wilkinson, a leading Klan member. 'I reckon your political climate is about right.'

Despite the economic chaos, rising unemployment and racial tension, in the Handsworth area there was one positive development: the rising profile of a group of talented black players at the nearby football club, West Bromwich Albion. At a time when football matches were said to be fertile recruiting grounds for the National Front, WBA were the first team in the top division to field three black players in the same side: Laurie Cunningham, Brendan Batson and Cyrille Regis. They played together with great success from the beginning of 1978, although their presence on the pitch often triggered racist abuse from opposition terraces. Outside West Brom's ground, however, there was never any National Front literature.

Out in the wider world, though, there was little evidence that racism was being rolled back. In the 1978 local council elections, in some urban areas there were six or seven times the usual number of NF candidates. Again, establishment voices were stoking the fires. In January 1978 Mrs Thatcher was interviewed by Granada TV. 'I think people are really rather afraid that this country might be rather swamped by people with a different culture,' she said. 'People are going to be really rather hostile to those coming in.'

The hostility Mrs Thatcher seemed to be justifying was increasingly aggressive. On 4 May 1978, clothing machinist Altab Ali was stabbed to death near Brick Lane, and the next month Ishtaque Ali was killed. Especially in the Asian community there was a great deal of fear that racists were being allowed the upper hand, as the scale of the provocation increased. Prejudice and violence was mixed with incomprehension. Margaret Thatcher's confusion was confirmed when she met a black mother on the streets of South London. 'What part of Africa do you come from?' she asked the woman. 'Tooting,' was the reply.

The immigrant communities and the anti-racists found ways to strike back. At Altab Ali's funeral, placards bearing slogans like 'Self Defence is No Offence' were displayed, and within ten days of his murder a march was organised, which began with 7,000 protesters massing in Whitechapel. In July 1978 workers mainly from the Asian community held a day's industrial action protesting at the brutality.

Rock Against Racism and the Anti-Nazi League moved up a gear; in March 1978, members of The Clash and Steel Pulse led a joint protest outside the National Front HQ, and a few weeks later, the Anti-Nazi League hosted a rally at Trafalgar Square, followed by a march to Victoria Park, where 80,000 people attended a massive gig featuring X-Ray Spex, Steel Pulse, the Tom Robinson Band, and The Clash. The next day The Clash played at Barbarella's, still on a high, and reworked the lyrics of one of their songs into 'Birmingham's Burning'.

That Sunday in Victoria Park was the largest anti-racist march in London for nearly fifty years, and on the left there was much joy that it had all come together. For many of the Seventies generation, RAR had become their cause. Red Saunders was meant to be compèring the show, and ran onto the stage shouting, 'This ain't no fucking Woodstock . . . This is the Carnival Against the Fucking Nazis!'

Victoria Park was followed by a Carnival of the North three months later in Alexandra Park in Moss Side, featuring the Buzzcocks, The Fall, Steel Pulse, China Street and John Cooper Clarke. On the poster, Steel Pulse's Selwyn Brown offered this definition of Rock Against Racism: 'First rock, meaning rock music, rock music against racism. Second, rock like you're rockin', like dancing against racism. Then it's like a rock, like stone, hard like a pebble. Put it in the water and nothing can wash it away.'

Timed perfectly between their first successful single and the scheduled release of the LP in the autumn, Steel Pulse supported Bob Marley and The Wailers in June and July through Europe (including New Bingley Hall in Stafford and gigs in Paris, Stockholm, Oslo, Amsterdam and Brussels). Burning Spear inspired Steel Pulse, Matumbi guided them, and punk widened their audience, but the seal of approval from Bob Marley virtually guaranteed commercial success for the first LP, *Handsworth Revolution*, which eventually achieved sales of over a quarter of a million, boosted by the release of two other singles from the album, 'Prodigal Son' and 'Prediction'. They also inspired other bands, notably Cornerstone, another Handsworth reggae act who rehearsed at 37 Linwood Road, literally over the road from Steel Pulse.

In the last few months of 1978 Steel Pulse enjoyed widespread media coverage; from the cover of *Melody Maker* to live television. Basil Gabbidon later discussed the reasons for their success: 'We were talking about truth and rights. Our early black audience wanted to hear cover versions of Ken Boothe and stuff like that, but we were different. Once the music press picked us up with the punk connection, the white interest increased. We had both a black and a white following, not necessarily in the same way as Bob Marley did – as Bob attracted everyone – but we drew more students and conscious black people. They had to love the lyrics, the honesty within the lyrics, the story, the consciousness.'

Rock Against Racism followed Victoria Park with Carnival Two in South London in September 1978, which attracted 100,000 people to see Misty, Aswad and Elvis Costello and the Attractions. And, in an effort to break away from the formula of big London events, this was followed by an RAR national tour featuring the likes of the Ruts, the Gang of

Four, The Specials, and Stiff Little Fingers, which ended at
Alexandra Palace on Easter Sunday 1979.

In the period between Carnival Two and Alexandra Palace,
what was dubbed the 'Winter of Discontent' unfolded, with
all its cold chaos, and a general election was called by Prime
Minister James Callaghan. Law and order became a hot issue,
and tensions grew during the election campaign. On 23 April
1979, Anti-Nazi League demonstrators in Southall, attempting
to disrupt a National Front rally, faced harder police action
than any anti-NF demonstrators had ever witnessed before.
Members of the Metropolitan Police's Special Patrol Group
were present in numbers, and hospitalised Misty's Clarence
Baker and, tragically, beat anti-Nazi demonstrator Blair Peach
to death. According to an eye witness writing in *Temporary
Hoarding*, 'The police were off the leash and on the hunt . . .'

When the 1979 election came around, however, the
National Front fared badly; in Wolverhampton, for example,
their share of the vote fell from 11 per cent to 3 per cent. A
number of factors explained these results. Partly, the black
experience had reached closer to the British mainstream (via
football perhaps, or songs like 'No Woman No Cry', or simply
through increased social mixing); this perception was reinforced by the introduction of a soap opera, *Empire Road*,
which focused on life in a black family, and was launched
on BBC2 in October 1978 with a theme tune performed by
Matumbi. As part of this process of diluting tensions and
embracing multi-culturalism, Rock Against Racism had played
an effective role. Martin Webster later confessed that the Anti-
Nazi League had outsmarted the National Front, made it
impossible to get NF members onto the street, and had won
the propaganda war, cutting away at support for the NF,
especially among the young.

But, less encouragingly, the fall in the National Front vote
could also be attributed to the appeal of the Tory Party under
Margaret Thatcher, attracting voters with an antipathy to

liberal causes who may have previously considered the National Front to have been the only party that represented their views. To give one example of this political shift, tennis player and Wimbledon regular Buster Mottram was an avowed supporter of the National Front in the late 1970s, and then switched to the Tories, applying to be the Conservatives' parliamentary candidate in Basildon.

As times changed, Clover drifted away from Rastafarianism, finding it hard to reconcile it with what she wanted from life. 'This cultural thing, back to the promised land, a lot of that, the way they saw things – it was the heavier, more intense stuff – and, for me, the concept was good, but I couldn't get into the reality of it. I'd been here since I was two years old and I felt this is where I belonged. I didn't know what I was going to do if I did get out there to Africa!'

She also acknowledges a degree of personal disillusionment. 'The guy that I was with, he had seven children apart from my children, but that was considered quite OK, all his relationships. That one love thing; it was being taken to an extreme!'

Clover was seeing things differently. 'It was getting a bit distorted for me and not making much sense once I started thinking for myself. It's the same as anything, I saw people working to their own agenda. I wasn't getting anything out of it anymore, it was time to move on. That unity and that one love and that family thing dispersed to an extent. It was like a holiday period was over.'

The insularity of the Rasta movement was a strength, but could also be a weakness, buckling as the pressure to separate from mainstream society and the Rasta demand to have no dealings with Babylon broke down. 'It had to break down because we'd had blinkers on, but then came Mrs Thatcher's Eighties and we had to open our eyes; this was reality. You were in a cocoon, not really part of what was going on. The Eighties were a bit of a wake-up call.'

The spiritual and moral Rasta codes began to be less relevant for her, and eventually so did roots music too. Clover continued to hang out with the sound systems almost to the end of the Seventies, but then life got 'a little bit harder', she says. 'I really had to grow up and take life by the hand and that was the end of that era for me. I moved on to other things musically.'

By the end of the Seventies, Clover had already drifted away from heavier sounds to the likes of Gregory Isaacs, Alton Ellis and Dennis Brown, leaving the sound systems behind. 'Some people stayed, but people I'd known for years started cutting their dreads and some of the girls had moved on and I wanted to look more feminine and wear make-up and have my hair done, and then I moved on to a different scene again, the soul scene, the Reno and places like that.'

As the Seventies became the Eighties, the change in Clover's music tastes was widely shared. There were plenty of examples of this shift in London: Joey Jay had been organising the Tribulation sound system, a favourite at Notting Hill Carnival and at dances throughout North London, but when his younger brother Norman began to share record spinning duties with him, the sound was renamed Good Times, in honour of the 1979 single by Chic, one of those tracks all the early hip hop DJs had been cutting up.

By 1980, soul and hip hop were the premier party sounds in the black community, although reggae and sound systems all over the country continued to survive and prosper, including those of Jah Shaka, Taurus and Saxon. Dub also inspired some great music, including artists on the On-U Sound label, as well as PIL, Smith & Mighty, and Massive Attack.

Paul Gilroy moved from Brighton to Birmingham in 1978 to study for a Ph.D at the Centre for Contemporary Cultural Studies at Birmingham University, founded by Richard Hoggart in 1964 but headed from 1969 to 1979 by the inspirational, Jamaican-born academic Stuart Hall. Paul had been wearing his hair in locks for some time, and absorbing and enjoying the music around Birmingham, including Steel Pulse and The Au Pairs. He also remembers walking into a record shop and Chic's 'Le Freak' was playing. 'It's one of those records; there are certain records that you always remember where you were when you first heard them. That was like that. Chic did one tour when they came to England, and I was going out with my partner now – it was one of our earliest dates – and they were at Birmingham Odeon. I have to say it was one of the greatest nights of music you can imagine, just sublime.'

Reggae continued to evolve once the roots sound fell from favour, and Dennis Bovell was once again a driving force; his production work on Janet Kay's 1979 hit 'Silly Games' marked the beginning of what came to be called 'Lovers' Rock'. But at the end of the decade an old strain of reggae also reasserted itself: ska. Ska and bluebeat had been the first forms of reggae, favoured by the 1960s mods, and the backbone of the Trojan label. In the intervening years, ska had stayed separate, untainted, minority music. But in 1979 came a major ska revival, with standard bearers The Specials.

Formed in Coventry and originally called The Automatics, The Specials were a mix of intriguing characters and black and white, including keyboard player Jerry Dammers, guitarist Lynval Golding, Neville Staples who had run a sound system in Coventry, and Terry Hall, whose parents worked in the local car industry. Although I once heard a TV interviewer discussing those early days with Terry Hall, expressing astonishment that The Specials had emerged from Coventry 'of all places', it all made glorious sense. Away from music hot spots like London and Manchester, they were able to create a distinctive sound, rooted in their down-to-earth attitudes; their particular perspective – a multi-racial one rooted in one of England's less glamorous towns – gave the music a defiant freshness, but also reflected a reality that their audience found it easy to identify with.

The Specials persuaded Clash manager Bernie Rhodes to give them a support slot on The Clash's 'Out on Parole' tour, and a few months later their first single 'Gangsters', financed on borrowed money, was released on their own 2-Tone label and distributed by Rough Trade. It was all very low level to begin with, the band attracting small crowds at venues like the Hope & Anchor, but soon the punk energy they brought to ska, and their canny, sometimes funny social awareness won them converts. In the second half of 1979, ska was the big sound and the look The Specials had created – the 2-Tone logo, button badges, thin ties, rude boy fashions – went nationwide. At the same time there was also a sudden mod revival, given much energy by the growing influence of The Jam and the release of the film *Quadrophenia*, a tale set among the mods and rockers battles of the mid-1960s. This had the effect of creating a heady mix of tribes at gigs by The Specials: skinheads, mods and ex-punks.

By the beginning of 1979, Steel Pulse had undergone some personnel changes – Mykaell Riley had left, citing musical differences – but the writing and recording of their second LP progressed. The LP, *Tribute to the Martyrs*, containing an increased African spiritual awareness and songs with a strong political message, was released in 1979. As well as playing more Rock Against Racism shows, in June and July 1979 they supported Peter Tosh on a European tour, including dates in Holland, Sweden, Denmark, Italy and Switzerland.

In 1980 they released their third and last album for Island Records, *Caught You* (entitled *Reggae Fever* in the US), and began a tour of North America in October 1980. They were in Toronto when news was broadcast of the death of Bob Marley on 11 May 1981, a moment which perhaps signalled the end of the glory days of roots reggae. Not only was Marley much missed, but there was also unease about some of the bands that were beginning to emerge, including some that appeared to wrench the political charge from reggae. For example, given the traditional enmity between young blacks and Her Majesty's constabulary, there was consternation when a trio of blond men called themselves The Police and produced watered-down reggae tracks like 'Walking on the Moon'. UB40 at least had the merit of a multi-cultural line-up; they represented another side of Birmingham, based in the Balsall Heath district, where Irish and black families in particular had shared space and mixed, one step beyond race hate and intolerance.

The National Front never recovered from their failure at the polls in 1979, and Martin Webster and John Tyndall split the Party in 1980, Tyndall later founding the British National Party who are now the dominant force in far-right politics. In some recent elections, groups like the British National Party have been attracting 10 or 15 per cent of the vote in specific areas of Oldham, Burnley and Bradford, and Anti-Nazi League posters are back on the streets in renewed attempts to mobilise against racism.

To a significant number of the Seventies generation, RAR functioned as a political education at a time when politics wasn't working. One of Rock Against Racism's messages was particularly valuable: that politics and culture could be reclaimed, and connections made. That you might start off by being into Pete Shelley of the Buzzcocks, and then discover Shelley the poet (or vice versa, of course). This was in contrast to the other England, the one which denies connections and narrows options. Paul Gilroy agrees: 'There was literacy there, an alternative cultural literacy that was really profound.'

If nothing else, RAR brought some much-needed pleasure to left-wing politics by marrying political resistance to punk passion. A lifestyle – urban, mixed, music-loving, modern and creative – had survived, despite being under direct threat from the NF. Rock Against Racism helped a generation to articulate

a belief that multi-racialism can be defended and celebrated, rather than feared or eradicated. Also, tolerance was
spreading, and though in the hands of a minority racial
antagonism could be brutal, it was also perhaps becoming
rarer.

The Specials were signed to Chrysalis in May 1979 and were
given free rein to run 2-Tone. It would be a year of mad live
gigs for the band – stage invasions and mayhem – but also
commercial success; during the last months of 1979, 2-Tone
enjoyed hits with tracks like 'The Prince' and 'One Step
Beyond' by Madness, 'On My Radio' by The Selecter, and
'Tears of a Clown' by The Beat.

The Beat, Steel Pulse and UB40, together, were a sign that
more progressive attitudes could be nurtured in the West
Midlands, despite the influence of Powellite politics and apocalyptic race war warnings. Nationally, 2-Tone was a major
cultural force. Two months after the death of Bob Marley,
RAR hosted an open-air show in Chapeltown in Leeds featuring The Specials, Misty, The Au Pairs, and Barry Forde. Neville
Staples of The Specials was ecstatic when he saw the crowd
from the stage: 'It's like a zebra crossing, black and white,
black and white, as far as you can see.'

The song 'Last Gang in Town' by The Clash, from the 1978
LP *Give 'Em Enough Rope*, reflects deep dismay at the way the
tribalism of the punks, soul rebels, Rastas, skinheads, stiffs
and quiffs often turned violent. Gigs by The Specials could be
intimidating or celebratory (perhaps both, all in one night),
but like watching Cyrille Regis crashing in goals for WBA's
talented, mixed team, they also provided us with a glimpse,
occasionally, temporarily, of what could be achievable.

Now Birmingham is represented by R&B star Jamelia
and Mike Skinner of The Streets. As elsewhere in urban
Britain – in the era of Radio 1xtra, Eminem, Dizzee Rascal,
inter-racial marriage and inter-racial music – there's a conver-
gence of black and white youth in many areas. It's often

uncontrived and unself-conscious, but it can also be problematic, yet it's just what the best days of Rock Against Racism had promised.

'Everybody's Happy Nowadays'
(1979)

At the end of the old year and into 1979, The Clash played a series of sell-out shows at the Lyceum, supported by The Slits. Footage of two songs from the show on 3 January later appeared in the film *Rude Boy*: 'English Civil War' and 'I Fought the Law' (at the time, *I Fought the Law* was the working title of the film). Outside the Lyceum, London was cold and grim, the country in the midst of the winter of discontent. Three weeks later, a day of action was called, the biggest mass stoppage since the General Strike in 1926. Four major public service unions – one and a half million people – were involved, including NHS ancillary workers, water workers, school caretakers, airport staff, social workers and rubbish collectors. Within days, scenes were broadcast on TV of piles of rotting rubbish all over the nation's capital.

Despite the industrial unrest, rising unemployment and the renewed threat of oil shortages, Prime Minister Callaghan was doggedly upbeat. Six months earlier he'd dismissed advice to go to the polls before the end of 1978, but by January 1979 there was no escaping the looming election, and Callaghan was looking increasingly out of touch. The Prime Minister delivered a New Year message claiming that over the previous twelve months Britain had 'enjoyed a well-earned taste of success'.

In the first weeks of 1979, regime change was imminent in Iran, where the Shah's military government was clinging to power despite widespread violence. The Shah had always relied on the repression of his opponents – and, crucially, the support of America – to maintain his power, but as opposition grew, the Shah was contemplating leaving the country, and his principal religious opponent, Ayatollah Khomeini, was in exile in Paris, biding his time, ready to take over. It took another twenty-five years or so before the significance of this moment – the first time a Western-sponsored regime had been overthrown by a radical Islamist revolution – was clear, but even before the Shah's flight into exile there was a taste of how events in that part of the Middle East could impact internationally; drawn into the political chaos, the state-owned oil company had ceased production, and British Petroleum faced a cut of around 35 per cent of their oil supplies.

The weather was at its worst and public transport was in chaos. Denis Howell, Minister of State at the Department of the Environment, had been called in to implement measures to alleviate the drought during the long hot summer of 1976, and miraculously, within days of his appointment, it had rained. This time his magical powers seemed to desert him as the weather deteriorated. Sporting events were hit: only three out of forty-eight Football League fixtures scheduled for New Year's Day were completed. In the top division, West Brom, on an ice-bound pitch, skated to a 2–1 victory against Bristol City, to go level on points with Liverpool at the top of the League. In the warmth of the Australian summer on the other side of the world, the England cricket team were on the brink of losing the third Test.

Later on New Year's Day, and then overnight, cold air from Siberia dropped heavy snow on Britain causing even more disruption. Postal and milk deliveries were abandoned. Manchester suffered the heaviest overnight blizzard since 1917. Throughout the North of England, ice, snow and freezing fog took hold, and motorists were advised to take a shovel and a flask of tea on all journeys. Roads in North Wales were covered by four inches of hard-packed snow and ice, and dozens of cars were abandoned on the motorways in Lancashire. With gritters implementing an overtime ban, work didn't start on gritting roads and clearing overnight snow until 8am. Facing harsh criticism, local union leader Alan Fisher defended the workers: 'The roads are in the disgraceful state they are now not because of the men but because of the penny-pinching employers.'

Away from newspaper front pages, the long, drawn out hunt for the Yorkshire Ripper was continuing. In May 1978 Sutcliffe had murdered Vera Millward in Manchester, and Assistant Chief Constable George Oldfield, leading the inquiry – with a large squad of officers and increased resources – was desperate for an end to the manhunt before he struck again. The atmosphere was tense in many areas of the North of England, women felt a huge anxiety when out at night, and a number of vigilante groups were patrolling the streets. On a few occasions, men bearing a resemblance to the photo-fit of the Ripper were beaten up.

The decade that had started with 'Lola' and Bowie in a dress, and was blessed with some groundbreaking female writing – Kate Millett, Beatrix Campbell, Marilyn French, Germaine Greer, Adrienne Rich, Caryl Churchill – ended with the activities of the Yorkshire Ripper disturbing and disrupting life. In one part of Leeds, young women on the university campus instituted the first of a number of Reclaim the Night marches, but across town, across a gulf of incomprehension, Leeds United's football fans openly celebrated the inability of the police to catch the Ripper, chanting, 'You'll never catch the Ripper' and 'There's only one Yorkshire Ripper'. Blake Morrison, writing about the Ripper, said the case 'exposed the depths of our culture's misogyny'.

Throughout the 1970s, gender roles had been the subject

of intense debate. The decade had witnessed equal pay and sex discrimination legislation, feminism, shifting attitudes to marriage and the family, and an acceleration in the rate of entry of women into the workforce. This has continued: in 1971 56 per cent of women of working age were in paid jobs; now the figure is just over 75 per cent. Yet progress for women since the 1970s hasn't been as positive as might have been hoped. The 1976 Domestic Violence and Matrimonial Proceedings Act provided women with the use of injunctions and restraining orders against violent partners, but today it's reckoned that an average of two women a week die at the hands of violent partners in our country.

On New Year's Day 1979 the ITV station Yorkshire TV failed to broadcast for the fourteenth day after a dispute between the company's management and technical and production staff belonging to the ACCT union. Channel Four would begin broadcasting in November 1982; in 1979 ITV was one of only three channels, alongside BBC1 and BBC2. Meanwhile, the Radio One schedule at the beginning of 1979 followed an established pattern: Peter Powell, Paul Burnett and Mike Read presented shows during the day, followed by David 'Kid' Jensen, and from 10pm John Peel. Over the next few years, the pre-Peel evening line-up would remain strong, featuring ex-Eric's regular Janice Long, and Andy Kershaw. On New Year's Eve, Peel had completed his rundown of the Festive 50, an annual poll of listeners who had submitted a top three of their favourite tracks, which Peel then meticulously compiled into a list and broadcast in reverse order over several nights. At the end of 1978 the Festive 50 contained a few classics from the pre-punk era, including 'Stairway to Heaven', 'Freebird', 'Layla' and 'Heroes'. The higher positions were taken up by the likes of the Sex Pistols and The Clash, but the act with the most songs on the list was Siouxsie & the Banshees (six, including 'Helter Skelter' and 'Jigsaw Feeling'); Susan Ballion from Bromley had come a long way.

While The Clash were packing in the crowds at the Lyceum, Sid Vicious was in jail pending his trial for the murder of Nancy Spungen in October 1978. The Pistols had fallen apart following Johnny Rotten's departure in January 1978 after a gig in San Francisco, and Vicious had fallen deeper into a heroin habit. At one point after his arrest for Nancy's murder he'd been bailed, but was returned to prison within days after assaulting Patti Smith's brother, Todd; he smashed a glass in his face at the New York club Max's Kansas City.

In Manchester on the first day of 1979, the city's premier punk band, the Buzzcocks, were making their way through the terrible weather en route to Strawberry Studios in Stockport to begin work with producer Martin Rushent on their projected next single. Strawberry was owned by members of 10cc, who had enjoyed a hit-filled 1970s. The Buzzcocks, however, were in a lower earnings league, although since those chaotic instore appearances at various Virgin shops in March 1978 they'd played dozens of gigs, including the Rock Against Racism event in Alexandra Park with Steel Pulse, and a short tour of Europe supporting Blondie. They'd also released a bunch of great singles, including 'Love You More', which was released in July 1978, and then a few months later, 'Ever Fallen In Love With Someone (You Shouldn't've)?'.

Plugging their second LP, *Love Bites*, the Buzzcocks had completed a seven-week British tour in the autumn of 1978, but singer Pete Shelley appeared to be in a fragile physical and mental state, worn out by touring and the demands of the publicity schedules. His unhappiness had even led to occasional attempts to leave the band. The gigs were full, but a number of shows were marred by violence. In Brighton a riot developed at the end of their performance, fans invaded the stage and some of the band's equipment was smashed or stolen. Gigs in the Seventies could be like that: punks, skinheads, mods and more, battling it out, ten tribes going to war.

In the bumper Christmas issue of *NME*, 'Ever Fallen In Love . . . ?' was voted Single of the Year, and the band had three songs in John Peel's Festive 50, yet their future was in doubt. Shelley was unhappy and had a side project called the Tiller Boys, while drummer John Maher was taking time away from the band to work with Patrik Fitzgerald. In Tony Jasper's music column in the *Manchester Evening News* at the beginning of January, 'Buzzcocks stay together' was one of his seven New Year wishes.

In the aftermath of punk, Manchester was blessed with small colonies of energised and influential groups of musicians, designers, music fans and accidental entrepreneurs; a number of scruffy rehearsal rooms and cheap recording studios in old warehouses; and one or two semi-established independent record labels. There were echoes of New York a couple of years earlier, the city suffering an economic malaise, yet home to some determined and creative musicmakers. In addition, the better post-punk bands locally were benefiting from the advocacy of several music journalists with connections in Manchester, notably Paul Morley, and later Jon Savage and Mick Middles. On the *NME*, as well as journalist Paul Morley, locally-based cartoonist Ray Lowry and photographer Kevin Cummins were powerful presences.

Local television wasn't so hot, especially once the plug had been pulled on Tony Wilson's *So it Goes* programme on Granada TV after Iggy Pop had used the word 'fuck' on air in December 1977. Wilson returned to the calmer waters of presenting the news show *Granada Reports*, but during 1978 he had been introduced to the idea of promoting gigs by Alan Erasmus (on 'Factory' nights at the Russell Club), and from there to starting the Factory record label. The first Factory release, on 24 December 1978, was a compilation featuring tracks by Cabaret Voltaire, John Dowie, Joy Division, and The Durutti Column (managed by Wilson). Factory Records would go on to launch the careers of acts like New Order and Happy

Mondays, and to host the Hacienda club, but at the beginning of 1979 no-one from the label was sure what would happen next. There had been discussions with Pete Shelley about a Tiller Boys release. Morley reported for *NME*: 'Future Factory Records projects remain endearingly vague.'

Between the initial session at Strawberry Studios and the final recording of the next Buzzcocks single, January was joyless, an almost perfect distillation of the chaos of the 1970s. The oil shortage was exacerbated by a strike by tanker drivers, who had just refused a 15 per cent pay offer. A majority of schools had oil-fired heating and were unable to open after the Christmas holidays, and buses were running a skeleton service during rush hours. Deliveries to supermarkets were threatened by the escalating lorry drivers' strikes, which in turn triggered panic buying in the shops. The train drivers union ASLEF was once again taking industrial action.

As January progressed, and the day of action took place, even industries not directly affected were forced to lay off workers. Tens of thousands were laid off in engineering and textile trades because factories weren't able to receive or deliver goods. In addition, there were temporary job losses as the retail trade was hit by the poor weather and the disruption to public transport. Long-term damage was also being done; one of the largest firms in Stockport, Mirrlees Blackstone, announced that 20 per cent of its workforce would be axed (nearly five hundred jobs in all) after the company's long battle against falling orders for their heavy-duty diesel engines was dealt a blow by the events of January 1979.

During 1978–79, the Government attempted to set a 5 per cent wage rise limit, but the TUC were adamant this figure was too low, and the Government's own assessment of what defined financial hardship would seem to lend weight to this view; the basic social security level for a family with two children was set at £55, yet around one in four local authority manual workers – bus drivers, gardeners, binmen and school caretakers, for example – were earning less than this figure. Many of these lower paid workers, despite working a forty-hour week, were forced to draw Family Income Supplement, others were doing massive amounts of overtime, and some were taking two jobs (binmen had devised ways of starting at the break of dawn and finishing their route early, in order for some of them to be able to take a part-time job in the evening).

Real disposable income, one of the best ways of measuring living standards, doubled between 1950 and 1974, but then actually went into reverse until the back end of 1978. So for four years workers had been pedalling fast, but wages were still falling behind inflation. In many families the pressure of poverty also demanded that both parents go out to work, and with one or both often required to do overtime, the quality of family life was threatened.

In those first few months of 1979, economic chaos was once again matched by chaos surrounding football matches. Liverpool fans rioted in Ipswich and over a hundred people were arrested at Norwich v Derby. Football-related violence had spread into the furthest reaches of the country; on 12 March, forty-three Swansea fans were held at Ludlow on their way to Wrexham. Twelve days later, a Birmingham City fan was found guilty of manslaughter following an incident at a match earlier in the season when a twenty-year-old Chelsea fan died under the wheels of a bus.

Eventually all the preparations were complete for the recording of a new Buzzcocks single, so the band returned to Strawberry Studios on the last weekend of January. England was suffering factory closures, rising unemployment, shortages in the supermarkets, strikes, freezing weather, and continuing street, football and race violence. The hunt for the Ripper was continuing (his last victim had been killed less than four miles from Strawberry Studios), the band was about to break up and we were into the first month of the last year of a crisis decade. And the name of this catchy, frenetic and grimly sardonic song? 'Everybody's Happy Nowadays'.

A couple of days after the recording came news of the death of Sid Vicious in an apartment in Greenwich Village. He'd just been released on bail again and had attended a party at the home of his new girlfriend Michelle Robinson. The autopsy confirmed that Vicious had died from an accumulation of fluid on the lungs, a common result of heroin addiction.

Although it was all over for the Sex Pistols by 1979, we've already seen how the inspiration of punk had kickstarted a boom in musicmaking. In 1979 The Slits released *Cut*, their debut LP, although drummer Palmolive had left the band and joined The Raincoats alongside guitarist Ana Da Silva, bassist Gina Birch, and violinist/guitarist Vicky Aspinall. The Raincoats created ramshackle, melodic, emotional music; their set in 1979 included 'Fairytale in the Supermarket' and a cover version of 'Lola'. The band's use of a rasping violin and their avowedly feminist politics gave 'Lola' a different, curious twist.

Meanwhile, John Lydon's post-Pistols project, Public Image Limited, released their second LP, the brilliant *Metal Box*. Lydon had always brought a passion to his music, now there was brittle paranoia too. The songs had the eerie, stripped-down quality of dub reggae, and featured memorable, hypnotic bass playing from Jah Wobble, and Keith Levine's cut-throat guitar. Songs like 'Poptones', 'Careering' and 'Death Disco' got rid of the albatross of the Sex Pistols, that punk straitjacket, and instead shared common ground with groups like The Pop Group (their *Y* LP was another highlight of 1979).

In 1979 The Clash embarked on their first major tour of America. Instead of being bored with the USA, The Clash were finding common cause with the rebel rockers; the mash of influences that went into their *London Calling* LP included Elvis Presley, Staggerlee, Montgomery Clift and Gene Vincent, as well as reggae, Captain Beefheart, *Homage to Catalonia*, and MC5.

In the 1980s, the global reach of the powerful American companies strengthened, but we weren't only being dominated by American brands, but American bands too. In the Sixties and Seventies, British bands – The Beatles, The Stones and Led Zep – had won over big audiences in America; and in the first years of the 1980s a new wave of British heavy metal (including Judas Priest, Motorhead, Iron Maiden and Def Leppard) made a big impact in the States. But from the mid-1980s onwards, although college radio and some underground clubs in the big cities provided an alternative, mainstream America seemed uninterested in the rest of the world.

As the 1980s began, one particular issue dominated international concerns: the nuclear threat. Despite a Strategic Arms Limitation Treaty signed by President Jimmy Carter and Soviet President Leonid Brezhnev, the planners in Moscow and Washington had clearly decided that Europe was to be the theatre of war. NATO's decision to deploy five hundred and seventy-two Cruise and Pershing ground-launched nuclear missiles in Western Europe in 1979 increased the urgency of a renewed campaign against the nuclear arms race, and the Campaign for Nuclear Disarmament (CND) took up the challenge. Active in Britain since 1958, CND's profile had dropped, but not only did the momentum of the nuclear arms race demand a response, but the perceived failure of party politics had led to the rise of special interest groups (Rock Against Racism and Greenpeace were other examples). As always, though, CND and others opposing militarism found it hard to make much headway; the major powers seemed to be addicted to war.

Related to this were the safety issues connected with nuclear power stations. Britain's Atomic Energy Authority had been created back in the mid-1950s, but the secrecy of its activities had always created suspicion among anti-nuclear protesters. An accident on the morning of 28 March 1979 at the nuclear power plant at Three Mile Island outside Harrisburg in Pennsylvania highlighted the potential risks, and more concerns over safety and secrecy were raised by the film *The China Syndrome* starring Jane Fonda, released in the same month as Harrisburg and which drew on various nuclear accidents going back to 1970.

In March 1979 we were still in the last days of the Callaghan era, with the Labour Government and the unions firmly identified in the public mind as bed-fellows; albeit bed-fellows badly in need of some marriage guidance. Despite their demonisation in many parts of the media, union members in 1979 were not a small cabal of marginalised Marxists, they were a large proportion of mainstream Britain – including nurses, farm workers, doctors, printers, teachers and train drivers – and total trade union membership increased from approximately ten million people at the beginning of 1970 to 13.3 million by the end of 1979. This was one of the paradoxes of the decade; throughout the 1970s more people joined unions, yet they became increasingly unpopular and mistrusted. Clive Jenkins of the ATSTMS said at the time, 'Nobody is in favour of somebody else's strike, but they're always in favour of their own.'

Another paradox was that although the public perception was that the unions were too strong, it could also be argued that the Seventies exposed their weaknesses; despite their strength, their history, their increased membership and a high public profile, they couldn't dam the tide of rising unemployment. Individual unions were acting in the interests of their members, but not necessarily other workers, and negative perceptions were confirmed by emotive and distorted media coverage. It didn't look good: rubbish piling up on the streets, the dead lying unburied in morgues with the gravediggers on strike.

The Buzzcocks stumbled on, with increasing tensions in

the band. On 2 March, 'Everybody's Happy Nowadays' was released, just as the band started a European tour (supported by the Gang of Four). It was non-stop; before the release in July of the 'Harmony in My Head' single, there was a tour of Britain and then a trip to America, before the release of their third LP, *A Different Kind of Tension*.

At the end of January 1979, the same weekend as the Buzzcocks were recording 'Everybody's Happy Nowadays' at Strawberry, Joy Division were recording four tracks for their first Peel session, including 'Transmission' and 'She's Lost Control'. Over the next six months Joy Division's work evolved and their profile rose. Their debut LP, *Unknown Pleasures* (released in June), and their gigs were attracting great reviews, and Joy Division were soon at the centre of a thriving post-punk network. In August they made their third appearance of the year at Eric's, complete with a matinee show, and a few weeks later John Keenan promoted his first Futurama festival at the Queen's Hall in Leeds and Joy Division shared the bill with the likes of PIL, The Fall, Cabaret Voltaire and Hawkwind. By the end of 1979, Joy Division had recorded a second John Peel session, which included '24 Hours' and 'Love Will Tear Us Apart'.

The story of The Specials had been similarly spectacular, with an amazing commercial breakthrough for the band and their 2-Tone label, including that rush of hits for the likes of Madness and The Beat. The turning point for The Specials had been a gig on 3 May 1979 when they played at the Moonlight Club in Hampstead, after which they signed to Chrysalis Records. In a twist of fate, 3 May 1979 was also election night, with the opinion polls predicting a close result. At the Moonlight Club, The Specials opened their set with the song 'Dawning of a New Era' as usual. It was indeed a new era, but not quite the one they'd been trying to believe would come to pass; instead, Mrs Thatcher was taking power.

Callaghan, on his return from a trip to Guadeloupe, had

been asked about the crisis and denied there was one. This relentless Everybody's Happy Nowadays message just made the Prime Minister look out of touch. Mark Reeder remembers the last days of the Labour Government: 'Thatcher's style of politics didn't appeal to me. I didn't like the way she talked, and I remember feeling sorry for Callaghan, he'd got himself in a mess, it was a dire situation, and it was obvious she was going to take over.'

Life was getting harder, despite one of the most conspicuous changes during the Seventies: a massive increase in the ownership of consumer durables like televisions and washing machines. But Labour weren't saved from electoral disaster by labour-saving devices. Labour had been bending to the IMF, putting the squeeze on public expenditure for a number of years, and this had hit their working class supporters. Unemployment and economic uncertainty were both increasing.

The Tory strategy set the tone for future elections; it was less a political campaign than a marketing campaign. Advisers like Gordon Reece encouraged Mrs Thatcher to change her clothes and hair, moderate her voice and make herself available for photo-opportunities. With widespread support in the media and total support in the City of London, the Conservatives promised to lower taxes, come down hard on the unions, and boost law and order.

Labour's obvious weakness contrasted unfavourably with Thatcher's promise of a new start, stability, a safe pair of hands, and strong leadership. In the last years of the Seventies, disillusion had set in with both the Democrats in the USA and Labour in the UK – Carter and Callaghan. Both were drifting, and neither appeared to be in control of events. In comparison, Thatcher and Reagan offered certainties and identified scapegoats (trade unions, minorities, socialists, peaceniks). The voters seemed flattered too that Mrs Thatcher was promising to put the 'Great' back into Great Britain, but – after the mess men had made of the world – they were also in the mood to give a woman a chance. It was an era in which female politicians of all parties – including Shirley Williams and Barbara Castle – were hugely popular.

The Conservative manifesto was all about reassuring the voters, and, if anything, looked unambitious. Soon, though, a radical change in the values guiding society became clear; in the Thatcher era, the liberal laws of the Sixties were regretted, market forces and individualism were prized, notions of equality binned, and a competitive ethic encouraged. As one of Mrs Thatcher's favoured Tories Keith Joseph put it, 'Self-interest is a prime motive in human behaviour . . . Conservatism, like selfishness, is inherent in the human condition.'

On 3 May, election day, Labour took 37 per cent of the vote, the Tories 44 per cent, and the Liberals 14 per cent. It was as though the radical left had been sleepwalking. A few people had already sensed what a Thatcher victory would mean, notably Stuart Hall of the Centre for Contemporary Cultural Studies. But Paul Gilroy admits that he'd misjudged the situation: 'My instincts were that Callaghan, Thatcher, it's all the same. I wasn't paying enough attention to the arguments that Stuart was making about what was going to be different in this next phase. The awfulness of it all he'd predicted and understood as a revolution.'

In June 1979, the first budget of the new Tory Government made cuts in public expenditure and a significant change in the way pensions were calculated (all increases would be in line with prices rather than average earnings). We were entering an era of full-on monetarism guided by economics guru Milton Friedman, which the next budget, in November 1979, consolidated; interest rates were set at record levels to curb the amount of money in circulation, put a squeeze on the economy and keep inflation in check. Monetarism put control of inflation before any other economic goals, and if the squeeze produced an increase in unemployment (which it inevitably would), then, in the phrase much used at the time, this was 'the price to pay'.

Austerity was demanded, and Government intervention to aid ailing companies was to be avoided; market forces now ruled. At the beginning of 1979 unemployment stood at approximately 1.25 million (5.4 per cent of the workforce); within just eighteen months of the Conservative Government and its new economic strategy, it had risen to 2.1 million.

In the second half of 1979 the Ripper inquiry took a grim turn. In April 1979 Sutcliffe had struck for the first time in nearly a year, killing Josephine Whittaker in Halifax, and all police leave for officers on the case was cancelled. But a few weeks later, Assistant Chief Constable Oldfield made a tragic error. He'd received a number of handwritten notes posted in the Sunderland area by someone calling himself Jack the Ripper, claiming to be the killer and taunting Oldfield for failing to catch him. In June 1979 the man sent the police a tape in which he continued to goad the police and also mentioned details of the killings which convinced Oldfield that the man was the genuine murderer. A part of the tape and an example of the handwriting was made public, but it later became clear that the tape and the letters were a hoax (although the perpetrator has never been identified).

Tragically, investigating officers were instructed to discount suspects who didn't have the same distinctive Wearside accent as the letter writer, so when Peter Sutcliffe, the real Ripper, was interviewed by two detectives in July 1979, because his accent and handwriting didn't fit, he remained free. In September he killed Barbara Leach in Bradford.

Throughout the second half of the year the photo-fit was displayed on posters all around the country, but the police were relying exclusively on the tape. TV and radio stations broadcast the voice, and in case you wanted to acquaint yourself further, Oldfield set up a Dial-the-Ripper phoneline so the public could listen in to the voice of the man dubbed

'Wearside Jack'. There were some classic records released that year – 'Everybody's Happy Nowadays', 'Gangsters', 'Rapper's Delight' – but undoubtedly the most chilling sound of 1979 was the soft, creepy voice of Wearside Jack.

Finally, in January 1981 the Ripper was caught, somewhat fortuitously, after two policemen found him in the red-light area of Sheffield with a prostitute in a car which had false number plates. But although the Ripper case was soon closed, throughout the 1970s, Fred and Rose West had been committing horrendous violence and murder in Gloucester. The first death at the Wests' home on Midland Road is thought to have occurred during 1971, a year before they moved to 25 Cromwell Street. Through the rest of the decade at least eight young women were killed at the Cromwell Street address, their bodies concealed beneath the floor of the cellar or in the garden. These nightmarish Seventies secrets weren't revealed until February 1994.

As the 1970s drew to a close, there was no cessation of Irish Republican violence. The Irish National Liberation Army claimed responsibility for the murder of the Tory Shadow Northern Ireland Secretary Airey Neave, killed by a car bomb as he left the House of Commons car park in March 1979; and Lord Mountbatten, the Queen's cousin, was killed when an IRA bomb exploded on his boat in Donegal Bay in August 1979. In the first years of the 1980s, IRA prisoners at the Maze prison, campaigning for recognition as 'political prisoners', embarked on a series of hunger strikes. In March 1991, the six Irishmen jailed for the Birmingham pub bombings in 1974 were released, their convictions quashed. The real bombers have never been found.

Despite the rapidly rising unemployment, the Labour Party wasn't in a position to take advantage of any anti-Government feeling; after the Party had received its lowest share of a general election vote for forty years, it was tearing itself apart. Key members of the Party clashed on a range of fundamental issues; Michael Foot and Tony Benn were both Eurosceptic and pro unilateral disarmament, while others, like Denis Healey and Shirley Williams, took the opposite view on both these issues. The far left meanwhile – 'extremists', Wilson had called them back in 1975 – were gaining strength among the rank-and-file Party membership, and by the end of 1979 there was also talk of a new grouping of those who considered themselves moderates, including the former Deputy Leader Roy Jenkins. In a lecture in November 1979 he proposed a 'radical centre', and then, at the beginning of 1981, along with three other senior Labour figures – Shirley Williams, Bill Rodgers and David Owen – launched the Social Democrat Party. Within weeks an electoral alliance between the Liberals and the SDP won by-election victories at Crosby, Croydon and Hillhead. In addition to the failure of the left to steer a successful course through the 1970s, the subsequent splits in the Labour Party made a significant contribution to ensuring seventeen years of Tory government.

Politically, the move to the right was underlined by the election of President Ronald Reagan in America in November 1980. Other events took place in 1979 which also set the agenda for the 1980s, including the election of the Marxist Sandinistas in Nicaragua, and the Soviet invasion of Afghanistan in support of the PDPA's attempts to prevent an Iranian-style Islamist revolution occurring in Afghanistan.

In Iran itself, after the flight of the Shah, an overwhelming number of people voted for the country to become an Islamic Republic, and anti-American demonstrations by huge crowds high on radical Islamist fervour were soon a feature in the country's capital, Tehran. In November 1979, dozens of hostages were taken at the American Embassy, and although a number were soon released, a group of just over fifty remained captive. The hostage crisis dragged on – in April 1980 a rescue mission failed – and eventually it lasted over four hundred days, weakening President Jimmy Carter's position and contributing to his defeat at the hands of Reagan.

Over the next decades we'd witness amazing transformations in many countries in Eastern Europe and Southern Africa, but elsewhere, the conflicts between the Israeli and Palestinian peoples continued to be unresolved. In the wake of the Cold War, the competing values in global conflicts appear to be driven more by religion than politics, and the Embassy siege was one of the first demonstrations of this. The hostages were eventually released on Reagan's inauguration day in January 1981, but the rise of radical Islam continued. In 1979, the *Guardian* suggested that this phenomenon had 'momentum built on disillusion'.

In 1979 it was already clear that an era of high unemployment lay ahead, as jobs were being sacrificed in the monetarist drive to tame inflation. By the end of the year, for example, British Steel was serving notice that 60,000 jobs would be likely to go, cutting the workforce by a quarter. Steel towns like Corby in Northamptonshire that had once attracted workers from all over the country began to suffer as the jobs disappeared. A pattern was being set for a decade or more.

Under the leadership of Thatcher and Reagan some people prospered through the 1980s, notably property and currency speculators and arms manufacturers, but also home-owners in parts of the country not directly reliant on manufacturing industry; for them the chance to escape the chaos of the Seventies was welcome. Bankers and other pedlars of financial 'services' were given a major boost by one of the Tory Government's first actions – the de-regulation of the City of London. This encouraged investment in the big financial institutions at the expense of other areas of the economy, signalled a shift in priorities from the manufacturing to the service sector, and cleared the ground for two decades of de-nationalisation, and windfalls for the City of London.

There was a growing sense of disconnection in many urban areas especially, and soon those who weren't prospering

turned to destructive measures. In the first two years of
Thatcher's premiership there were riots in Bristol, Toxteth,
Brixton and Moss Side. The Government denied the role that
poverty or desperation may have played in the riots, labelling
them 'pure criminality', but to other observers the events
were not hard to predict, given the continuing rise in unemployment (in April 1981, at the time of the riots, around
55 per cent of young black men in the Brixton area were
unemployed), a rage against the authorities, and the catastrophic state of the built environment. Eddy Amoo wasn't
surprised when the Toxteth riots erupted in 1981: 'It was
always leading up to that. We were able to step out of that
and make a life for ourselves, but a lot of people can't, you
know.'

In Coventry, on 20 June 1981, The Specials headlined a
benefit gig for a young Asian man stabbed to death in the city
centre. It was one of the last gigs the band would play. In the
flurry of success for 2-Tone at the end of 1979 they'd reached
No. 1 with 'A Message to You Rudy', and had followed that
with two hit albums. But in October 1981, after a short tour
of America, Terry Hall, Neville Staples and Lynval Golding left
the band to form the Fun Boy Three. Before it all fell apart,
however, The Specials enjoyed their greatest moment yet: the
release of the dramatic, evocative 'Ghost Town' in June 1981.

When Toxteth erupted in violence in July 1981, it was said
that 60 per cent of all the rioters were white, but those leading
the crowd were black, and the profile of the rioters was similar
in Brixton and Moss Side. In inner city areas, the gulf between
the police and the populace had seldom been greater. Following the controversies over the 'sus' laws and the activities of
the SPG, cynicism about the role of the police had grown. In
the early 1980s we were in an era when senior police chiefs
felt emboldened to enter the political fray, almost always from
the right. Police Chief Constable of Greater Manchester, James
Anderton, made several speeches calling for tougher laws

against picketing. In Liverpool, Chief Constable Kenneth Oxford was authoritarian, alarmist – he announced that an 'army of occupation' could be drafted in to Liverpool to control the streets – and contentious; at one point Oxford remarked that black Liverpudlians were 'the product of liaisons between white prostitutes and black sailors'.

The political will to assuage this cynicism wasn't apparent among the Tory Cabinet. After the Brixton riots, Lord Scarman made recommendations in an attempt to heal the rift between the police and inner city communities, including advocating that police officers should be dismissed for racially prejudiced behaviour, but the Home Secretary William Whitelaw rejected the suggestion.

James Anderton also became renowned for his harshly homophobic views. In the early 1980s a generation of gay men, who had enjoyed ten years of increasing tolerance and huge gains in their personal freedom, were devastated by the AIDS virus (awareness of the disease reached the pages of *Gay News* in the later months of 1981). For Chief Constable James Anderton it was an opportunity to ride the backlash against the social changes of the Sixties and Seventies, and to accuse the gay community of inhabiting a 'swirling human cesspit'.

In the 1980s collective ideals were chased away and the social fabric left to fray (solidarity was only encouraged when it was in Poland), while the emphasis was on self-reliance and individual advancement. Thatcher's golden age appeared to be the 1950s, where we started our story, before progress in the struggle for sexual or racial equality, before the motives and machinations of the authorities were questioned and social hierarchies challenged. It was a bitter irony for feminists, the most powerful woman in the country proclaiming, 'I owe nothing to women's lib.' This was Margaret Thatcher's view in March 1982: 'We are reaping what was sown in the Sixties . . . fashionable theories and permissive claptrap set the scene for a society in which old values of discipline and restraint were denigrated.'

Although the conformist, putting-up-and-shutting-up 1950s had great appeal for her, Margaret Thatcher also called for a return to 'Victorian values', but appeared to have chosen a very selective version of the nineteenth century. It was the world of 'Grandad', penny farthings on the street, contented families and social stability. After recent events in Iraq, and his country's role in arming regimes in the Middle East, writer Gore Vidal dubbed the USA the 'United States of Amnesia'. It's as if the powerful enjoy, perhaps even need their own version of Abbafication, an erasing or editing of the past to justify their power and remove unhelpful events. Mrs Thatcher had a habit of encouraging collective amnesia; her version of 'Victorian values' conveniently forgot nineteenth-century child labour, massive health and wealth inequalities, the brutalities involved in building and maintaining an Empire, and such a sorry life for the urban poor that in many Victorian cities in England average life expectancy was seventeen years.

As part of her vision of putting the 'Great' back into Great Britain, Thatcher's Government took a secret decision to augment NATO's weaponry and update the country's independent nuclear deterrent, replacing Polaris with Trident at a cost of five billion pounds. The swing to the right was unmistakable at the beginning of the 1980s. In October 1981, the Fun Boy Three's first single was entitled 'The Lunatics Have Taken Over the Asylum'. Early in 1982, one of the first great rap records, 'The Message' by Grandmaster Flash & the Furious Five, updated the word from the ghetto and reflected the self-destruction and despair of the urban projects.

It's a fallacy that the most significant trends are the most obvious ones, the ones clearly visible on the high street. We've seen how many uncommercial acts tap into deeper channels, picking up ideas that surface froth never gets near. Looking back to the Seventies, it's clear that the music that has made the most enduring and influential impact since is rap, soul, heavy rock and punk; not the mainstream music but the music out in the margins. Punk is still influencing bands: disco loops slip into house hits; PJ Harvey sounds like Patti Smith; No Doubt and the Black Eyed Peas namecheck The Specials and The Beat; The Hives have obviously listened to The Stooges; the Kings of Leon are straight out of the 1970s; Franz Ferdinand and the Red Hot Chili Peppers reference the Gang of Four; London club night 'Nag Nag Nag' takes its name from a Cabaret Voltaire single, and demonstrates its impeccable post-punk credentials with a series of flyers that have included the image of the two cowboys which led to Alan Jones being arrested, a photo of Siouxsie Sioux at Louise's, and another of Poly Styrene.

As well as discovering and memorialising some of the music of the decade, we've also been following social changes in the Seventies, among them the impact of the loss of manufacturing industries that created and sustained so many of our cities. This change in our economy – from one based on making and selling to one based on borrowing and buying – is the root of the biggest differences between where we were then and where we are now.

The move to the right initiated by Margaret Thatcher has been permanent. Market forces are now the organising principle of our society; we're competitors or consumers. One development reflecting the power of consumer culture has been the use of hundreds of records from the Seventies in TV commercials, including some surprising examples. Over the last few years we've had 'The Passenger' selling Fiat cars; 'Lola' selling Weetabix; 'Love Will Tear Us Apart' by Joy Division selling Heineken; 'Blank Expression' by The Specials selling Ford Fiestas; and 'What Do I Get?' by the Buzzcocks selling Red Mountain coffee.

The Buzzcocks split up in 1981 but have since reformed with various line-ups and are now back recording and gigging regularly. A three-bedroom house in Chorlton of the kind agents Frank Dawson were selling in 1970 for £2,750 is now worth nearly £300,000. Eric's in Liverpool closed in March 1980 after a police raid. Joy Division suffered the suicide of singer Ian Curtis in May 1980 but regrouped as New Order. Patty Hearst was released from prison on 1 February 1979 after her sentence was commuted by Jimmy Carter. In May 1978 David 'Son of Sam' Berkowitz pleaded guilty to murder and was sentenced to three hundred and sixty-five years in prison. Just over a year later his throat was slashed in Attica prison, but he survived with fifty-six stitches.

Angela Davis is now a professor at the University of California, Santa Cruz. In 1981, around the time of the hunger strikes, gunmen attempted to kill Bernadette Devlin and her husband Michael McAliskey, with what appeared to be the collusion of the SAS. In February 2003, Ms McAliskey was deported from the USA on her way from Dublin to Chicago on the grounds that she posed a 'serious threat to national security'.

Some of our eye witnesses who came of age during the Seventies have travelled further than others. Alex Patton, who started work on the A19 over thirty years ago, is a civil engineer, and his drinking years, which started just as the crisis decades began, continue.

In Germany, Mark Reeder's barely formal role for Factory Records involved him in the promotion of Joy Division's show at Kantkino in Berlin in January 1980. After the show he hitched a ride to Manchester in the band's mini-van and had a week's holiday back home. It was Joy Division's last gig abroad.

In the early 1980s, Mark made frequent visits to East Germany and began to smuggle punk cassettes to the other side – 'the kids were desperate for something,' he says – and in the late 1980s became involved in techno and trance as the dance music scene blossomed after the fall of the Berlin Wall in November 1989. His MFS record label launched the career of DJ Paul van Dyk, and more recently he's been working with Corvin Dalek. Mark says he'd rather not talk about Thatcher's Britain. 'I went to Berlin, I exiled myself from Britain and Thatcher and those values; I'd step over your dead body to get my Porsche,' he says.

Clover lives in Withington, Manchester. Paul Gilroy is Professor of Sociology and African American Studies at Yale University. Bob Dickinson has worked for Granada TV and the BBC (he's spent the early years of the twenty-first century writing a graphic novel based on Seventies life in Congleton). Alan Jones still lives in the same flat in which he hosted visits by Sid and Nancy; he now writes expertly on various subjects, from disco music to Italian horror movies.

Jayne Casey fronted various groups, watched her friend Holly Johnson have international success with Frankie Goes to Hollywood, worked in arts administration in the 1980s, then took a PR job at Liverpool's 'Cream' nightclub, and is now involved in the Liverpool Biennial and other arts projects as Chief Executive of the afoundation. When I met Jayne recently, we talked about what happened next: Liverpool in the Thatcher era, factory closures, downsizing at Cammell Laird shipyards, redundancies at Dunlop, Militant Tendency, and the tragedy at the Hillsborough football stadium. It wasn't a great decade for Liverpool, and it wasn't a great decade in her personal life either, but once again questions were raised about our choices of what to remember.

Just as the reality of the Seventies isn't reflected in any Abba-dominated image of the decade, so the 1980s are also frequently misrepresented. Watching some editions of *Top of the Pops* from the early 1980s is like watching the world's cheeriest non-stop party, and in the face of the world of conspicuous consumption, under-dressed girls and sun-kissed yachts depicted in Duran Duran videos, alternative world views struggled to be heard.

In the 1980s we had 'Don't Believe the Hype' and 'How Soon is Now'; *Meantime* and *High Hopes*. It wasn't a loadsamoney decade for most of Britain; millions were unemployed, 100,000 people rallied in Hyde Park in support of CND, Broadwater Farm rioted, and the Greenham Common protesters camped outside an American airbase. In the riot-torn, unemployment-ravaged summer of 1981, 'Ghost Town' was No. 1 in the charts in the week Prince Charles married Diana Spencer. Dr Robert Runcie, Archbishop of Canterbury, gave an address at the Royal Wedding, describing the marriage as 'the stuff of which fairy tales are made', although he wasn't alone in his propensity to be hypnotised by hype and glory.

Identifying the 1980s as a prosperous and carefree decade soundtracked by Duran Duran and Wham! erases the memory of conflict and hurt, the struggles and despair of mass unemployment forgotten. Perhaps, too, a disturbing notion remains unacknowledged: that thousands of jobs in the manufacturing industries (mainly in the North of England and the Midlands) had to be sacrificed in order to create the conditions for a boom in the City of London and the service sector economy in the South.

At the time of the Brixton riots, Margaret Thatcher's Conservative Government was 12.5 per cent behind Labour in the polls, and the direction of some of her policies was even opposed by members of her own Cabinet, characters she called 'the wets'. But in 1982 the Falklands War created a new reality, as Anthony Sampson recognises in his book *The Changing Anatomy of Britain*, in which he describes how the war provided an opportunity to demonstrate the greatness of Britain, buoyed by 'aggressive patriotic emotion'. During the Falklands War there were three million people unemployed (a million had been added to the dole queue in twelve months); communities, especially those built around manufacturing industries, had collapsed.

Although 'Ghost Town' had expressed so much of the frustration and despair of 1981, in 2003 a bright spark in an advertising agency heard the word 'ghost' in the song and decided it would be the ideal record for a forthcoming campaign. Thus a song about urban despair came to soundtrack a TV commercial for Hallowe'en at Woolworths. This has become a feature of our current era: the past has been tamed, drained of its meaning. In the Seventies, afro hair was a revolutionary celebration of blackness; now afro wigs are sported by drunken revellers outside dodgy nightclubs. And Revolution is a chain of vodka bars.

Justin Timberlake and Nicole Appleton have both worn MC5 t-shirts in the recent past, and Jennifer Aniston's character Rachel wore one during the last series of *Friends*. Either this is an example of subtle, under-the-wire subversion, or these characters are blissfully unaware of the MC5's commitment to assaulting the culture by all means necessary, including, you recall, 'Rock & Roll, Dope, and Fucking in the Streets'. Fashion commentators have dubbed this phenomenon 'leftist chic' (another example is Kate Moss in a Che Guevara t-shirt), or, more delightfully, 'Prada Meinhof'. History happens the first time as tragedy, the second time as irony.

We've seen the deterioration of urban neighbourhoods in the 1970s, but we've also seen how the Seventies generation started making music, and a life, that reflected that struggle to survive. Characters from Crazy Legs to Roger Eagle, through various means, created communities, clubs and cells, often off the beaten track, in semi-derelict venues, around obscure record shops, secondhand clothes stalls, rehearsal rooms or reggae sound systems.

In the Seventies, as the politicians turned away from cities, young punks, DJs, arty types and freaks seized opportunities to live out their dreams; the alternative was silence, or violence. Kevin Rowland looks back at the strength of his desire when Dexy's formed like this: 'We were totally dedicated. We had nothing to lose.'

Today, the same dreams and desires drive rappers in Birmingham or Bradford, writers in Liverpool, and musicians in Manchester, but our cities have been annexed by property developers and big business, and the opportunities to establish the kinds of alternative communities that flourished in the late 1970s are fewer.

Writer Andrew O'Hagan was a child in the 1970s, if not a child of the 1970s. In his book *The Missing* he describes how cities, the places and spaces we live in, have been turned into a product. 'An age is upon us now that thinks of cities as having an image, a corporate face, that winks at investors, smiles at shoppers.'

In the 1970s, the walk through Birmingham to Barbarella's nightclub took you down wet underpasses, through unlit streets, past empty buildings and abandoned workshops. It was the same in Liverpool around Mathew Street; our cities were full of bomb sites, post-industrial debris, and wastelands waiting to be car parks. Now that walk to where Barbarella's was sited has changed beyond all recognition. Broad Street, repaved and redesigned, is lined by prestigious buildings, including an international convention centre and a concert hall. Cities are tidier now, better turned-out, though undoubtedly they're also blander and more homogenous.

Many of our cities also reveal how quickly regeneration can become corporatisation, and renewal nothing deeper than a PR exercise to maintain the blindingly shiny gloss; not dealing with the ugliness, but again, in another era, trying to convince us that everybody's happy nowadays. In the Seventies, the world was out on the street, in a cacophony of tribalism, football fans, gangs and threats from the NF. In comparison, it's now about image, not reality; the world, our desires, are now packaged and contained. Conflict and failure, inequality and violence haven't disappeared, but our cities have had a make-over, and perhaps it's now harder than ever to hold on to a belief that culture can be changed, not just consumed.

In earlier chapters we revealed some of the roots of the Seventies, and, by the same token, there's a debate to be had about when our real story of the Seventies ends. The most significant turning point in the last forty years is probably the miners' strike of 1984–85. The strike marked a moment of irreversible change; the ferocity of the industrial struggles of the Seventies was a symptom of the painful last gasps, the death rattles of heavy industry. For two hundred years, heavy industry – cotton, coal, steel and shipbuilding – had sustained the country's wealth and power, creating jobs and communities, especially in the North of England; the miners' strike was a desperate rearguard action at the end of an era.

In 1984 the unemployment rate in the North of England was 19 per cent; 10 per cent in the South. This was part of the background to the miners' strike (the Tory Government's de-regulation of the City of London was followed by sharp cuts in regional aid, which exacerbated a growing North/ South divide). In 1974 a 'Plan for Coal' had been devised, promising a major expansion of the coal industry before the end of the century, and more miners were recruited to deliver the plan. Ten years later this all changed. Chairman of the Coal Board, Ian MacGregor, announced in March 1984 that twenty uneconomic pits would close at the cost of 20,000 jobs.

In the lead-up to 1984 there was already talk of it being an iconic year, thanks to the George Orwell novel written thirty-six years earlier. His portrayal of a state-controlled society certainly had some echoes, especially given what we now know about secret service collusion in Northern Ireland during the Seventies and Eighties, the use of 'tricknology', and the extent of surveillance by Special Branch and military and civilian intelligence (which included the phone-tapping of leading CND members and trade unionists).

Orwell was also aware of how reality could be bent, not only by the rewriting of history, but also by newspeak and double-think, spreading disinformation and manipulating language. During the 1984–85 strike, for example, the Government branded miners 'the enemy within', and it's one of the most obvious features of where we are now; the Powerman has kidnapped important words – 'freedom', 'democracy' and 'the rule of law' – to justify his position, cut out any alternative world views, and control any debate about how a society should be organised, and its values.

Pressure to conform and cooperate is always being exerted. Back in 1976, Vaclav Havel supported the Plastic People of the Universe in their struggle for a right to pursue their brand of creativity because he felt they had a democratic right to challenge and ask questions. One of their songs ridiculed the rulers of Czechoslovakia for hiding the truth behind a heavily glossed surface, wishful thinking and double-speak, and extolled both the role of the young in bringing about change, and the power of collective memory: 'They are afraid of the young for their dreams / They are afraid of the old for their memory.'

The miners' strike lasted just one week short of a year, and began in March 1984 with a walk-out by miners at Cortonwood Colliery in Yorkshire, one of the first targeted for closure by the Coal Board. Within a week nearly 100,000 miners were on strike. During the dispute, the police restricted freedom of movement (to prevent a repeat of the flying pickets in 1972) and deployed anti-riot tactics learnt from the inner city riots of 1981.

The miners fought the law and the law won. Tory union legislation and the defeat of the miners broadcast a change. Throughout the 1970s the exercise of union power was visible and controversial; the 1980s would belong to employers and big business. Industrial chimneys were demolished and collieries decommissioned. One of the collieries that closed soon after the strike was at Wolstanton in Staffordshire, just north of Stoke-on-Trent.

At the outset of our story we visited Flares and found evidence of how the Seventies are represented. Wolstanton is an ideal place to explore where we are now, and what a difference three decades can make. Now, for example, supermarkets rather than factories are the focus for communities, or they're at least the biggest, most high-profile building, and often the major employer. They dominate the physical space and have squeezed out independent high street retailers. In Wolstanton a large Asda now stands on the site of the old colliery, next door to Homebase and Matalan.

The local pottery industry – including Royal Doulton, Spode and Wedgwood – benefited from the abundant clay and coal in this part of North Staffordshire, and pottery manufacturers funded an expansion of Wolstanton Colliery in 1916, intent on extracting as much coal as possible. Over the next decades, the pit thrived: in the 1950s it was connected by underground rail to the pits at Hanley and Sneyd; in 1961 a new shaft was dug at Wolstanton, at the time the deepest mining shaft in Western Europe; two years later, output peaked at one million tons.

Inside the front entrance to Asda there's a mini-mall of smaller shops – an opticians, a chemist, and branches of First Choice and Thorntons – and down one side of the building a full range of clothes by George (the Asda in-house brand). The aisles are packed, trolleys bumper to bumper. There is no muzak playing, but Debbie at the help desk explains that a computer system has failed and usually we'd be hearing Asda FM. 'It's just music and lots of adverts,' according to Debbie, who also explains that Asda FM is beamed by satellite to every branch of the supermarket in the country (later I discovered that with a Sky transponder you can even tune into Asda FM in the comfort of your own home).

With the music off and the technology in trouble, I considered offering to take in some turntables or audio files and fill in for Asda FM. I had plenty of ideas and it would have made a change, I'm sure. I'd find some music from the past to help illuminate the present: 'At Home He's a Tourist' by the Gang of Four, 'Career Opportunities' by The Clash, and 'Fairy Tale in the Supermarket' by The Raincoats.

There are some CDs available in the supermarket, and I ask Danielle, serving behind the counter, if she has anything by The Velvet Underground. 'What do you mean?' she says, then helpfully leaves her place and shows me the retro section spread over a few yards of CD racks. 'You have to look here,' she says. 'It's all meant to be in alphabetical order, but it's usually a bit jumbled up.'

Flicking through the CDs, most of the Vs are Various Artists. I ask Danielle what kind of music she likes. 'Lots,' she replies, 'but not the cheesy chart stuff.'

Outside I meet Mr Barlow, who has walked down the eighty steps of the embankment behind Asda to buy a sandwich. He's retired and seems happy to talk. We're underneath a sixty-foot tower carrying an Asda logo near the top (you can see it clearly from the railway, or the A500). The steel tower is built to look like a traditional colliery pit-head, complete with an imitation winding wheel. 'It's meant to be symbolic,' says Mr Barlow.

There's a cold wind blowing on this cloudless afternoon, and we stand there shivering as Mr Barlow slowly points out some landmarks to me, from left to right following the horizon. Extracting coal from deep underground produced tons of unusable dirt, and the spoil heaps from Sneyd and Hanley were once visible across the valley, but now they've been flattened, contoured and covered in trees and bushes. He tells me where the original pit-heads were, and where that shaft with the world-beating vertical drop was situated (in the flower beds outside Homebase).

Around and behind us, some of the town's houses cling to the sides of the hills, but down in the wide, flat, valley bottom, the industrial infrastructure has been dismantled. Mr

Barlow points out the remains of the steel works, and, away from the colliery, other parts of the coal-producing process, including the washery where the coal was prepared before being crushed, loaded and taken to power stations. He tells me how coal dust ignited underground at Sneyd on New Year's Day in 1942, and fifty-seven men were killed. Up over the embankment at the back of Asda there's a pub called the Swan; after another disaster, he tells me, they laid out the mutilated bodies in one of the rooms there (it's now a restaurant).

He tells me a lot, the stories come tumbling out, but we both know there's so much more history, a past, like the landmarks, contoured and controlled, fast disappearing. That's where we are now, in a supermarket; Danielle with her dreams, Mr Barlow with his memories.

ACKNOWLEDGEMENTS

I'm deeply indebted to my family and friends for their support during the writing of this book. Special thanks to my interviewees: Alex Patton, Paul Gilroy, Jayne Casey, Clover, Bob Dickinson, Mark Reeder, Eddy Amoo and Alan Jones. Thanks also to Catherine, Jack, Raili, my parents, Guy, KT and Marian; my editor Matthew Hamilton; Michelle Kane and Nicholas Pearson at Fourth Estate; Jane Bradish Ellames and Jonny Geller; Nick Davies and Andy Miller; Ty and Guy at 44media; Keith, Lucie, Lemn Sissay, Justine Alderman, John Locke, Susan, Kevin, Tracey Thorn, Mike Pickering, Ursula, Phil, Michael Herbert, Brenda Kelly, Sue Fletcher, Kristina Mottershaw, Steve Redhead, Marc Rowlands, Paul Lambert, Sarah Haughey, Andrea Csanyi, Tosh Ryan, David Dunne, Adrian Thrills, Rachel George, Andy McQueen, Mark Ealand, Louise Clarke, Andy O'Hagan, Jean McNicol, Ciaran Ryder, Izzy Grey, Deepa Parekh, Wayne Garvie and Ryan Minchin; the staff at Fuel café bar in Withington; the Rossetti in Manchester; and all at Alias Hotels.

Extended transcriptions of some of the interviews, and other relevant and random information, can be found at www.davehaslam.com

KEY TEXTS

Victor Bockris, *Patti Smith* (Fourth Estate, 1998)

Lloyd Bradley, *Bass Culture: When Jamaica Was King* (Viking, 2000)

David Childs, *Britain Since 1945: A Political History* (Routledge, 1997)

Ralph Darlington and Dave Lyddon, *Glorious Summer: Class Struggle in Britain 1972* (Bookmarks, 2001)

Ray Davies, *X-Ray* (Viking, 1994)

Angela Davis, *An Autobiography* (The Women's Press, 1990)

Bob Dickinson, *Imprinting the Sticks: the Alternative Press Beyond London* (Arena, 1997)

Mick Farren, *Give the Anarchist a Cigarette* (Jonathan Cape, 2001)

Nigel Fountain, *Underground: the London Alternative Press 1966–74* (Comedia, 1988)

Nelson George, *Hip Hop America* (Penguin, 1999)

Holly George-Warren (ed.), *Rolling Stone: the Seventies* (Rolling Stone Press, 1998)

Paul Gilroy, *There Ain't No Black in the Union Jack* (Hutchinson, 1987)

Marcus Gray, *Last Gang in Town: the Story and Myth of The Clash* (Fourth Estate, 1995)

Stuart Hall, *The Hard Road to Renewal* (Verso, 1988)

Robert Hewison, *Too Much: Art and Society in the Sixties* (Methuen, 1986)

Robert Hewison, *Culture and Consensus: England, art and politics since 1940* (Methuen, 1995)

Eric Hobsbawm, *Age of Extremes* (Michael Joseph, 1994)

Stuart Home, *Cranked Up Really High* (Codex, 1995)

Barney Hoskyns, *Glam!* (Faber & Faber, 1998)

Roger Hutchinson, *High Sixties: The Summers of Riot and Love* (Mainstream, 1992)

Michael de Koningh and Marc Griffiths, *Tighten Up: the History of Reggae in the UK* (Sanctuary, 2003)

Ian MacDonald, *The People's Music* (Pimlico, 2003)

Tony McGartland, *Buzzcocks: the Complete History* (IMP, 1995)

Arthur Marwick, *The Sixties* (Oxford University Press, 1998)

Martin Millar, *Suzy, Led Zeppelin and Me* (Codex, 2002)

Juliet Mitchell, *Woman's Estate* (Penguin, 1971)

Rick Moody, *The Ice Storm* (Abacus, 1994)

Charles Shaar Murray, *Shots From the Hip* (Penguin, 1991)

Mark Anthony Neal, *What the Music Said: Black Popular Music and Black Public Culture* (Routledge, 1999)

David Peace, *Nineteen Seventy Seven* (Serpent's Tail, 2000)

Ian Penman, *Vital Signs* (Serpent's Tail, 1998)

Jonathan Raban, *Soft City* (Hamish Hamilton, 1974)

Adrienne Rich, *On Lies, Secrets and Silence* (Virago, 1980)

Sheila Rowbotham, *A Century of Women* (Penguin, 1999)

Anthony Sampson, *The Changing Anatomy of Britain* (Hodder & Stoughton, 1982)

Jim Sangster, *Scorsese* (Virgin Books, 2002)

Jon Savage, *England's Dreaming* (Faber & Faber, 1991)

Harry Shapiro, *Waiting for the Man: the Story of Drugs and Popular Music* (Mandarin, 1988)

Alan Sked and Chris Cook, *Post-War Britain: a Political History* (Penguin, 1979)

Elizabeth Thomson and David Gutman (eds), *The Bowie Companion* (Da Capo Press, 1996)

Craig Werner, *A Change is Gonna Come: Music, Race and the Soul of America* (Plume, 1998)

David Widgery, *Beating Time* (Chatto & Windus, 1986)

NOTES

1970

p. 12 'The Seventies began...' Jon Savage, *England's Dreaming*, p. 557 (Faber & Faber, 1991).

p. 17 'A weakening of the ties binding the traditional family...' Evident, for example, in the creation in 1970 of 'Gingerbread', an organisation for single parents.

p. 17 'There are signs that some girls...' quoted in Arthur Marwick, *The Sixties*, p. 79 (Oxford University Press, 1998).

p. 18 'Clothes were our weapons...' Angela Carter in *New Society*, 1967; reprinted in Hanif Kureishi and Jon Savage (eds), *The Faber Book of Pop*, p. 316 (Faber & Faber, 1995).

p. 20 'Teds and skinheads...' Skinheads were among the most enthusiastic fans of ska and early reggae, and were regulars at many blues clubs in black areas, but racism became more prevalent as the skinhead movement grew. In 1978 *NME* felt it necessary to underline a distinction between skinheads who were 'quasi-mods' and the 'arsehole skinheads of Sham 78' (*NME Book of Rock*, 1978).

p. 21 'Skilful landscaping...' Lewis Wormersley quoted in Rod Hackney, *The Good, the Bad and the Ugly*, p. 21 (Frederick Muller, 1988).

p. 22 'Catastrophic...' Rod Hackney, p. 131.

p. 23 'The party was over...' Ray Davies, *X-Ray*, p. 79 (Viking, 1994).

p. 32 'The family appears as a natural object, but is actually a cultural creation . . .' Juliet Mitchell, *Woman's Estate*, p. 99 (Penguin, 1971).

p. 34 'Sex, by the early 1970s . . .' Sheila Rowbotham, *A Century of Women*, p. 426 (Penguin, 1999).

p. 34 'The expression of female erotic desire . . .' Sheila Rowbotham, p. 427.

p. 34 'Female singer songwriters . . .' Examples: Joni Mitchell, *Blue* (1971); Carole King, *Tapestry* (1971); Carly Simon, *No Secrets* (1972).

p. 34 'Twenty years ago . . .' Sheila Rowbotham, p. 418.

p. 37 'Beware the psychedelic businessman . . .' Jerry Rubin in 1970, quoted in *The Guardian*, 30.1.1994.

p. 38 'For women, as to a lesser extent for men . . .' Juliet Mitchell, p. 142.

p. 40 'As the life ebbed away from Meredith Hunter . . .' Harry Shapiro, *Waiting for the Man: the Story of Drugs and Popular Music*, p. 148 (Mandarin, 1988).

p. 41 'We got tired of all the bullshit . . .' Ozzy Osbourne quoted in Steven Rosen, *Black Sabbath*, p. 38 (Sanctuary, 2002).

1971

p. 42 'Nothing happened . . .' John Lennon quoted in *Rolling Stone*, January 1971; reprinted in Jann S. Wenner (ed.), *20 Years of Rolling Stone* (Ebury, 1987).

p. 45 'A new note of viciousness . . .' Elizabeth Nelson, *The British Counter Culture 1966–73*, p. 101 (Macmillan, 1989).

p. 50 'Starting to make a lot of sense . . .' Mick Farren, *Give the Anarchist a Cigarette*, p. 289 (Jonathan Cape, 2001).

p. 51 'Those who used psychedelic drugs . . .' Harry Shapiro, p. 142. As Shapiro documents so ably, drugs and music have had a long association – back to the jazz age and before – well before The Velvet Underground released 'Heroin' and The Beatles sang about 'Lucy in the Sky with Diamonds'.

p. 52 'Genuinely inspirational . . .' Jeff Nuttall quoted in Roger Hutchinson, *High Sixties: The Summers of Riot and Love*, p. 195 (Mainstream, 1992).

p. 52 'Horny guy in leather pants . . .' Mick Farren, p. 190.

p. 56 'The National Viewers and Listeners Association . . .' Mary Whitehouse was always happy to accept that her campaigns were designed to counter the 'red menace'. She claimed that the 'moral selfishness' of the pornographers was a breeding ground for Communism.

p. 58 'Mirrors the absurdity . . .' Lester Bangs in *Creem*, November 1970; reprinted in Lester Bangs, *Psychotic Reactions and the Carburetor Dung*, p. 32 (Minerva, 1987).

p. 59 'A preference for the "wrong" intoxicants . . .' Mick Farren, p. 204.

p. 70 'Strangled to death . . .' Howard Brenton quoted in Robert Hewison, *Too Much: Art and Society in the Sixties*, p. 212 (Methuen, 1986).

1972

p. 75 'Bulletin boards . . .' Nelson George quoted in Craig Werner, *A Change is Gonna Come: Music, Race and the Soul of America*, p. 76 (Plume, 1998).

p. 75 'He played what they felt inside . . .' Miles Davis quoted in Frank Kofsky, *Black Nationalism and the Revolution in Music*, p. 64 (Pathfinder Press, 1970).

p. 76 'Music is an instrument . . .' John Coltrane quoted in Frank Kofsky, p. 227.

p. 78 'It was a Southern sound . . .' Steve Cropper quoted in Craig Werner, p. 72.

p. 80 'I went blank . . .' Isaac Hayes quoted in Craig Werner, p. 170.

p. 81 'The Panthers articulated the rage . . .' Mark Anthony Neal, *What the Music Said: Black Popular Music and Black Public Culture*, p. 58 (Routledge, 1999).

p. 82 'We needed to broaden our sound . . .' Marshall Thompson quoted in *Black Music*, May 1974.

p. 84 'It was crucial to Travis Bickle's character . . .' Martin Scorsese quoted in David Thompson and Ian Christie (eds), *Scorsese on Scorsese*, p. 62 (Faber & Faber, 1989).

p. 85 'The ghetto too often means . . .' National Advisory Commission on Civil Disorders quoted in Robert A. Beauregard, *Voices of Decline: the Post-War Fate of US Cities*, p. 173 (Blackwell, 1993).

p. 88 'It's a class struggle . . .' Bernadette Devlin quoted in *The Times*, 23.2.1971.

p. 89 'Aretha's music of the early Seventies . . .' Craig Werner, p. 123.

p. 91 'In keeping with the candy-colored aesthetic of the period . . .' Nelson George, *Hip Hop America*, p. 104 (Penguin, 1999).

p. 93 'The growth of the urban drug culture . . .' Nelson George, p. 38.

p. 95 'Our basic finding is that the shameful conditions . . .' Commission of the Cities report quoted in Robert A. Beauregard, p. 189.

p. 97 'Britain's My Lai . . .' *The Guardian*, 29.2.1972.

p. 101 'The trauma of neighbourhood breakdown . . .' Black music during the 1980s and 1990s continued to narrow from a world stage to a smaller stage: neighbourhoods, street corners, the housing projects, Compton and the Bronx.

p. 101 As the buzz word 'ghetto' was replaced by 'disco', some in the black community made the transition (Nile Rodgers is a particularly interesting case; with a background in the Black Panthers, he went on to play a key role in Chic), while others were less comfortable with the shift. At the height of the disco era, Jesse Jackson campaigned against 'songs with suggestive lyrics and rhythms', expressing particular concern about KC & the Sunshine Band's '(Shake Shake Shake) Shake Your Booty'.

p. 102 'The funk and soul era still holds considerable value . . .' Not least in the rich source of samples – drum breaks, intros and horn riffs – provided for hip hop artists by the funk and soul acts discussed in this chapter (an extensive list of such samples can be found at www.davehaslam.com).

1973

p. 104 'Watershed . . .' Eric Hobsbawm, *Age of Extremes*, p. 416 (Michael Joseph, 1994).

p. 104 'Les trente glorieuses . . .' Eric Hobsbawm, p. 258.

p. 105 'Instability and crisis . . .' Eric Hobsbawm, p. 403.

p. 107 'The Shrewsbury pickets had committed the worst of all crimes . . .' Robert Mark quoted in Ralph Darlington and Dave Lyddon, *Glorious Summer: Class Struggle in Britain 1972*, p. 206 (Bookmarks, 2001).

p. 107 'I look forward to the day . . .' Ricky Tomlinson quoted in Ralph Darlington and Dave Lyddon, p. 260.

p. 111 'He smiles; you melt . . .' Tony Palmer in 1969 in the *Observer*; reprinted in Elizabeth Thomson and David Gutman (eds), *The Bowie Companion*, p. 35 (Da Capo Press, 1996).

p. 114 'Most erotic film ever . . .' Rick Moody, p.117.

p. 114 'The government is unfaithful . . .' Rick Moody, *The Ice Storm*, p. 71 (Abacus, 1994).

p. 118 'I'm gay and always have been . . .' David Bowie quoted in *Melody Maker*, 1.7.1972; reprinted in *The Bowie Companion*, p. 59.

p. 118 'New York was about drag queens . . .' Barney Hoskyns, *Glam!*, p. 25 (Faber & Faber, 1998).

p. 126 'I'm gonna be on Mars . . .' Ace Frehley quoted in Holly George-Warren (ed.), *Rolling Stone: the Seventies*, p. 201 (Rolling Stone Press, 1998).

p. 129 'Life on Mars . . .' In June 2003 scientists from Britain sent Beagle 2 to Mars. A dustbin-lid-sized contraption built in Milton Keynes, costing £35m, Beagle 2 was launched from Kazakhstan and was expected to reach Mars by the end of the year. It disappeared.

1974

p. 136 'Has Britain become ungovernable? . . .' *The Guardian*, 2.1.1974.

p. 144 'This Northern Soul scene is quite different . . .' Quoted in *Black Music*, June 1974.

p. 149 'The great radio victory for black music . . .' Dave McAleer in conversation with the author.

p. 159 'An authentic homegrown reggae scene . . .' See Michael de Koningh and Marc Griffiths, *Tighten Up: the History of Reggae in the UK* (Sanctuary, 2003).

1975

p. 167 'Terrace fashion experts . . .' In film and photographs of foot-ball grounds in the 1960s, the men in the crowd are all wearing jackets and ties, and, frequently, caps; the young men too, dress-ing like their dads. Cut to the early 1970s and the ultimate fashion role model for young men has gone from being Clement Attlee to Slade. On the terraces, ties and jackets were replaced by parkas, silk scarves, bomber jackets, Birmingham bags and Doc Martens.

p. 176 'The lumpen and aggressive music of Black Sabbath and Led Zeppelin . . .' It was an era in which men were becoming increasingly threatened and insecure about the women's move-ment – and the sexual revolution that came after the Pill – and there was something defiant and chest-beating about heavy rock. Led Zeppelin, for example, were one of a number of bands described in this period as 'cock rock'. Simon Frith writes well on cock rock in Charlie Gillett and Simon Frith, *Rock File 5*, p. 18 (Granada Publishing, 1978).

p. 178 'The city is soft . . .' Jonathan Raban, *Soft City*, p. 15 (Hamish Hamilton, 1974).

p. 179 Based on his own memories of seeing Led Zeppelin play in Glasgow in 1972, Martin Millar's novel, *Suzy, Led Zeppelin and Me* (Codex, 2002), captures the experience brilliantly, taking us through the build-up to the gig, immersing himself in the ex-pectation, sewing a triangle of cloth into the bottom third of his flared denims while listening to the first Uriah Heep LP, all the time racked with confusion about girls. Then, with mounting excitement, he joins 3,000 people at the gig and communal delirium ensues; the seats collapse, and the band's powerful per-formance creates chaos in the audience, and an unforgettable experience.

p. 183 'Wilson and Heath, walking about and blustering . . .' Alex Harvey quoted in *New Musical Express*, 19.10.1974; reprinted in Charles Shaar Murray, *Shots From the Hip*, p. 70 (Penguin, 1991).

p. 183 'If there's one group that could take credit . . .' Debbie Harry in Debbie Harry, Chris Stein and Victor Bockris, *Making Tracks: the Rise of Blondie*, p. 31 (Da Capo Press, 1998).

p. 184 'The most fucked-up and interesting people . . .' Debbie Harry in *Making Tracks*, p.14.

p. 185 'The occupation of rock and roll . . .' Richard Hell quoted in Victor Bockris, *Patti Smith*, p. 76 (Fourth Estate, 1998).

p. 186 'It was the greatest atmosphere to perform in . . .' Patti Smith quoted in Victor Bockris, p. 18.

p. 187 'Undoubtedly the most gripping performance . . .' Charles Shaar Murray in *New Musical Express*, 7.6.1975; reprinted in *Shots From the Hip*, p. 95.

p. 190 'I was taking the nuances of Richard Hell . . .' Malcolm McLaren quoted in Legs McNeil and Gillian McCain, *Please Kill Me: the Uncensored Oral History of Punk*, p. 307 (Abacus, 1997).

p. 196 'The outcasts, the unwanted . . .' John Lydon quoted in Jon Savage, p. 127.

1976

p. 203 'By all means propagate your views . . .' Judge McKinnon quoted in David Widgery, *Beating Time*, p. 52 (Chatto & Windus, 1986).

p. 206 'So many people in 1976 saw an enormous change . . .' Peter Savile quoted in a programme printed on the occasion of a memorial concert for Rob Gretton, FAC511, May 2004.

p. 209 'I hated Bromley . . .' Siouxsie Sioux quoted in Jon Savage, p. 183.

p. 210 'I loved disco and I loved the lifestyle as well . . .' For more of Alan Jones on disco see Alan Jones and Jussi Kantonen, *Saturday Night Forever* (Mainstream, 1999).

p. 213 'Soul Patrol . . .' The URL for Soul Patrol is http://www.soul patrol.com

p. 215 'A landmark event in the history of hip hop . . .' For more background to the early days of hip hop (and the rise of DJ remixes and 12-inch singles), see Bill Brewster and Frank Broughton, *Last Night a DJ Saved My Life* (Headline, 1999).

p. 219 'I loved the stuff . . .' John Lydon quoted in Jon Savage, p. 191.

p. 220 'In the Hulme area of Manchester . . .' For more on Hulme, see Dave Haslam, *Manchester, England: the Story of the Pop Cult City* (Fourth Estate, 1999).

p. 221 'Manchester was a very boring place to be . . .' Paul Morley in *New Musical Express*, 30.7.1977.

p. 222 'Now he'd surfaced in Liverpool . . .' For more about Roger Eagle and Eric's, see Bill Drummond, *45* (Little, Brown, 2000).

1977

p. 227 'Walls were draped with woodchip . . .' Simon Armitage, *Little Green Man*, p. 153 (Penguin, 2002).

p. 228 'I knew we weren't that great at the beginning . . .' Patti Smith quoted in Victor Bockris, p. 95.

p. 229 'Commercial madness . . .' Rick Moody, p. 3.

p. 231 'It's when you pull back them bloody curtains . . .' David Peace, *Nineteen Seventy Seven*, p. 298 (Serpent's Tail, 2000).

p. 236 'The established "dinosaur" groups didn't seem unduly perturbed . . .' Having stretched the credulity of their fans with some daft ideas (Rick Wakeman's ice spectacular at Wembley, for example), prog rock bands also began to feel the pressure from punk attitudes to musicmaking, and from the big appeal of the FM rock sound. After 1977, Yes and ELP moved away from thirty-minute epics, and by 1980 both bands had split up. The 1978 Genesis LP *And Then There Were Three* was something of a post-prog reinvention. Led Zeppelin played a number of massive gigs, but their moment, too, was over (see *Suzy, Led Zeppelin and Me*, pp. 126 and 152).

p. 238 'Society seems to have come to a dead end . . .' Greil Marcus in *Rolling Stone*, 20.10.1977; reprinted in Greil Marcus, *In the Fascist Bathroom* (Viking, 1993).

1978

p. 258 'Dennis Bovell was a key character . . .' See Ian Penman, *Vital Signs* (Serpent's Tail, 1998); and Lloyd Bradley, *Bass Culture: When Jamaica Was King*, Chapter 16 (Viking, 2000).

p. 259 'The way these kids looked at reggae . . .' Lloyd Bradley, p. 373.

p. 261 'It's not like today . . .' Basil Gabbidon quote from http://andybrower.co.uk/steelpulse.html; some brilliant Steel Pulse pages which provide many of the direct quotes in this chapter.

p. 262 'The white working class kids in bovver boots . . .' Carl Gayle in *Black Music*, July 1974.

p. 277 'A group of talented black players . . .' For more on how race played a part in the story of West Bromwich Albion during this period, see Dave Bowler and Jas Bains, *Samba in the Smethwick End* (Mainstream, 2000).

p. 278 'What part of Africa are you from? . . .' Margaret Thatcher quoted in David Widgery, p. 38.

p. 280 'The police were off the leash . . .' *Temporary Hoarding* quote in David Widgery, p. 107.

1979

p. 290 'Exposed the depths of our culture's misogyny . . .' Blake Morrison in *The Guardian*, 18.12.2003.

p. 298 'Nobody is in favour . . .' Clive Jenkins quoted in Anthony Sampson, *The Changing Anatomy of Britain*, p. 74 (Hodder & Stoughton, 1982).

p. 301 'Self-interest is a prime motive in human behaviour . . .' Keith Joseph quoted in Stuart Hall, *The Hard Road to Renewal*, p. 26 (Verso, 1988). Anti-trade union feeling was extreme among many of Thatcher's closest allies, among them Lord Chalfont, who had defected from Labour to the Tories in 1974. He'd written in the *New Statesman* (1.2.1974) attacking Communist activists in trade unions, calling them 'maggots and termites'.

p. 307 'I owe nothing to women's lib . . .' According to Madelaine Bunting, 'Expectations of the "sisterhood" was a daft naivety of 70s feminism killed off by Thatcherism' (*The Guardian*, 16.1.04). A number of works explore the relationship between Thatcher and feminism, some drawing very different conclusions; see, for example, Beatrix Campbell, *The Iron Ladies* (Virago, 1987), and Natasha Walter, *The New Feminism* (Little, Brown, 1998).

p. 310 'Eye witnesses who came of age during the Seventies . . .' Alex Patton has a Doors website at http://homepage-ntlworld.com/doors4scorpywag/

p. 312 'Aggressive patriotic emotion . . .' Anthony Sampson, p. 291.

p. 314 'An age is upon us . . .' Andrew O'Hagan, *The Missing*, p. 39 (Picador, 1995).

INDEX

Manzarek, Ray 52, 73
Marcus, Greil 237–238
Mark, Robert 107
Marley, Bob 1, 4, 8, 13, 102, 159,
    258, 265, 266, 268–269,
    271, 279, 284, 286
Marley, Rita 266
Martin, Phonso 275
Martyn, John 188
Massive Attack 282
Matlock, Glen 126, 237
Matumbi 159, 235, 258, 279,
    280
Maudling, Reginald 69, 97
Mayfield, Curtis 5, 74, 79–80,
    91–92, 94, 155
MC5 26, 46, 52, 57, 184, 241,
    297, 313
Mean Streets 1
Meinhof, Ulrike 40, 44, 96, 257
Mekons, the 253
Melle Mel 215
Melly, George 66
Melody Maker 63, 118, 217, 234,
    279
Mercer Arts Center 126–127
Merger 258
Metal Urbain 240
MFSB 142, 145
Middle Earth 59
Middle of the Road 50, 57
Middles, Mick 293
Mighty Two 272
Miller, Chris 225
Miller, Daniel 240
Miller, Jacob 265
Millett, Kate 33, 290
Miss World contest 12, 33, 40
Missing (O'Hagan) 314

Misty in Roots 159, 254, 258,
    276, 279, 286
Misuse of Drugs Act 54
Mitchell, Joni 34
Mitchell, Juliet 32, 38
Mohammad Ali 35, 84
Monterey pop festival 51, 90
Moody, Rick 114, 229
Moore, Bobby 24
Morgan, Robert W. 124
Morley, Paul 221, 293–294
Moroder, Giorgio 214
Morpheus 160
Morrison, Blake 290
Morrison, Jim 44, 48, 51–53,
    57, 63–64, 70–73, 120,
    187
Morrison, Toni 86
Mortimer, John 59, 66
Most, Mickie 147
Motorhead 188, 297
Motown 77, 82, 142, 156
Mott the Hoople 121–122, 125,
    180
Mottram, Buster 281
Moul (Mole) Express 67
Moulton, Tom 211
Mowatt, Judy 266
Mud 5, 125
Muggeridge, Malcolm 56
Muller, Gerhard 96
Murcia, Billy 64, 126
Murray, Charles Shaar 183, 186
Murray, Pauline 245
Mute 240
Muzik City 160
My Lai massacre 47–48
Myra Breckinridge 31
Mystery Girls, the 246